The Blessing of Life

The Blessing of Life

An Introduction to Catholic Bioethics

Brian M. Kane

LEXINGTON BOOKS
Lanham • Boulder • New York • Toronto • Plymouth, UK

Dedication

This book is dedicated to my mother, Marlene Carole Branley Kane, RN, and to my late father, Michael Dennis Kane. From an early age, I learned from them the meaning of caring and the blessing of life. Our home was always a welcoming and loving place for those in need. I will always be thankful for their example.

Published by Lexington Books
A wholly owned subsidary of The Rowman & Littlefield Publishing Group, Inc.
4501 Forbes Boulevard, Suite 200, Lanham, Maryland 20706
http://www.lexingtonbooks.com

Estover Road, Plymouth PL6 7PY, United Kingdom

British Library Cataloguing in Publication Information Available

Library of Congress Cataloging-in-Publication Data
Kane, Brian M., 1962-
  The blessing of life : an introduction to Catholic bioethics / Brian M. Kane.
     p. cm.
  Includes bibliographical references and index.
  ISBN 978-0-7391-2200-6 (cloth : alk. paper)
  1. Medical ethics—Religious aspects—Catholic Church. 2. Catholic Church—Doctrines. I. Title.
  R725.56.K36 2011
  174.2—dc22   2011009454

Printed in the United States of America

Table of Contents

Preface

In many ways, we have become numb to the influence of medical advances on our lives. Several hundred years ago, most persons struggled to survive. The efforts to produce enough food, to endure natural disasters, and to keep physically healthy occupied much of our lives.

Science has profoundly changed that circumstance. For those of us who have had the benefits of these marvelous discoveries, when the former world that we inhabited rudely intrudes into this safe bubble, we are left with the sneaking suspicion that if only we had more control, we could avoid these unpleasantries of disease and natural disaster. Of course, for the majority of people in those distant corners of the world who still exist in those circumstances (and this is not as far away as it seems to us), such experiences still define their lives.

There is a tendency when one is surrounded by the same environment to assume that the world is always as we perceive it to be. The modern person, existing in a world that has received much from science, breathes the scientific worldview like so much air. We accept it; in fact, we expect it.

It is difficult to separate one's experience of the practical benefits of science from the acceptance of science as a belief system. Like all forms of knowledge, science begins with some presuppositions. We who live in the world of investigation and invention simply accept the scientific system as true. Essentially, science addresses our physical needs. Even there, of course, it is true that of the many physical needs that we have, science may only solve a small percentage of them, and we often create new problems as a result of our solutions. New pharmaceutical products are rarely a "magic bullet" that solves a physical ailment without a corresponding side effect. Simply watch the television ads for new drugs and note that a good percentage of the commercial is devoted to explaining such occurrences.

Yet, we are left with a difficulty. In its origins, science emerged from a very particular belief system: Christianity. Since other, more brilliant authors have provided the historical details of this development in an uncontestable way, it will simply be noted here that part of the difficulty that the modern person faces is that we have now begun to accept a science that is disconnected from these roots and that if we ignore such a legacy, the modern-day quest to alleviate the human condition through the application of science will, in the end, be unsuccessful.

Science, to paraphrase Jacques Ellul, is a way of being in the world. How we live in practice depends upon a perception of how we *ought* to live. The doing is the result of an "ought," a belief about how we should act. That ethical perception is further dependent upon the truths that we hold to be absolute. A science disconnected from its historical roots in faith is very different from a science that thinks that salvation can come only from the control of the physical world.

Bioethics as an academic discipline is still rather new. Within the second half of the twentieth century, it has emerged as an academic field that is dominated by philosophers, most of whom subscribe to a form of utilitarianism, or a weighing of the effects of one's choices. The literature of bioethics is now decidedly the work of these thinkers.

Before there was bioethics, however, the morality of medical decision-making was largely performed by physicians and by theologians. Today, many writers have urged that those who discuss the moral implications of medicine be, first and foremost, clinical practitioners. Those who are at the bedside are best able to understand the complexities involved in such dilemmas. Yet, there is also a corresponding need for those professionals to be adequately trained in those systems of thought that will help them to clarify the issues at stake and to think logically and consistently. This book is a theological attempt to assist in that process.

Over the past two decades, I have had the privilege of teaching ethics in healthcare to countless nurses, physician assistants, and physicians, and I have been profoundly shaped by their experiences and their insights. They have challenged me to explain how Catholic theology helps them to make sense out of the dilemmas that they encounter in their work. At the same time, my undergraduate students, both those of traditional college age and adults, have also looked for a way to make sense out of Catholic teaching in their own lives. This book is the result of those many discussions.

The goal of this book is to offer an introduction to Catholic moral theological thinking on bioethics. As such, it does not attempt to give an exhaustive analysis of every bioethical dilemma that we currently face. Instead, it explores some general themes in contemporary bioethics from the viewpoint of Catholic thinking in order to explain the foundations of Catholic doctrine.

In the contemporary media, all too often the conclusions to Catholic doctrine on bioethical issues are reported with an undertone of incredulity. How can the Church still believe that contraception is wrong? Why is the Church against using science to help infertile couples conceive? Why shouldn't we kill the old and the terminally ill to alleviate their suffering?

In order to make sense of why the Church teaches that contraception in most cases is wrong, or the limits of assisting in reproduction, or the kind of care that should be offered to the weak and vulnerable, it is essential to first discuss the method and the foundations of moral thinking. Only then are we able to understand the conclusions in their proper context. So, each of the following chapters follows that path. We shall first discuss the theological foundations and the historical origins of different areas of bioethics. Only after doing so will we then move to the consideration of particular teachings. In following this approach, it is hoped that the reader will be able to apply this information not only to contemporary dilemmas, but also future ones.

Eventually, the reader will have to make his or her own ethical decisions. Those who are health-care practitioners will often have to assist their patients in choosing what is right, while the rest of us will be faced with making those decisions for ourselves, or for someone we love.

This book is offered as an introduction to a way of thinking that is often obscured by the promises of a world where science can do only good. While I am not against scientific advances, because I appreciate the many practical effects of modern health care, I am also not comfortable with the new frontiers of healthcare science that equate every practical success with a moral good. Often, the question of whether something *can* be done is not preceded by a consideration of whether it *should* be done. I hope that this book will assist those who will be faced with such dilemmas in the future to make the best choices possible.

Acknowledgements

The writing and preparation of this book would not have been possible without the assistance of numerous persons.

First and foremost, I thank my wife, Heidi. In our life together, I have been fortunate to be shaped by her wisdom, and her kindness. She has been generous and patient as I have labored over this project for so many years.

I would also like to thank my children, Caitilin and Andrew. In the beginning of both of their lives, they have faced the adversity of chronic illness with courage. Walking beside them as they have struggled to understand their diseases and their relationship with God in the midst of their suffering, I've admired how they have dealt with their challenges and become so thoughtful and compassionate. They see what others often don't. I wish for them both that their struggles lead them to a deeper sense of the connections that we all have to each other and to the God who made us.

DeSales University, as my scholarly community, has provided an environment in which I have been able to mature as a scholar. My colleagues, who are also my friends, in the Department of Philosophy and Theology have been sounding boards about so many things, allowing me, in the words of St. Francis de Sales, to "be who you are and to be that well." I am grateful that this project was started with a sabbatical leave from the university that allowed me to get the framework and the initial draft underway. DeSales University, and in particular Fr. Bernard O'Connor, OSFS, has also connected me with scholars around the world, in Bangalore, Kolkata, Delhi, Rome, and London. To be Catholic is to be universal, and I am thankful to have been given the opportunity to know so many faithful and courageous people around the world.

I would like to acknowledge my students at DeSales University who read earlier drafts of the book and who were the inspiration for writing it.

Lastly, thanks are also given to the deacons, the priests, the bishops, and the employees of the Dioceses of Tulsa, Evansville, Lexington, Wilmington, and Indianapolis, with whom I discussed the topics of this book. They have invited me into their homes and communities. It has been a privilege to be a part of their conversations and to share in their ministry.

Chapter One:
Foundational Issues in Moral Theology

Every day, it seems, there is a new and seemingly impossible bioethical dilemma on the front page of the newspaper. Cloning, stem cells, withdrawing life support—these have become the issues that absorb our attention. As soon as a new topic comes to our attention, however, it seems almost hopeless to read on. Our culture is morally paralyzed. We are unable to reach a consensus on how these topics should be addressed. How can we come to some sense of what the most ethical approach is?

In spite of the prevailing pessimism, there are ways out of this ethical quagmire. While it is true that good people will often disagree on how to finally decide some issues, the fact that we do not reach a common answer does not mean that every answer that someone proposes is just as good as another. There are better and worse ways of understanding the conversation.

The place we will begin is through questions that at first seem quite abstract: How do we know what we know? How can we be sure of anything, or making any kind of claim about what is true and what is false?[1] We must begin our study of bioethics with some basic considerations. Each will be a small building block that will allow us to understand the more complex issues. At first, our tendency might be to look at the various bioethical issues like technological reproduction or decisions that we must make at the end of life. But if we do that, we will become stuck in a kind of shouting match, where no one listens to anyone else.

So we will not begin with the explanation of various controversial topics, although we will certainly explore these later in the book. For now, it is important to establish some common ground so that we can engage in a conversation together. That way, when we do reach a point at which there might be disagreement, we have some tools to use to see if there might be some resolution.

So, on what can we agree? Most people are aware that there is a great deal of disagreement among people concerning which actions are moral and which are immoral. Yet, at the same time, we recognize that many people come to the same conclusions on many topics. Even though, for example, there are some people who steal, it might generally be concluded that most people think that this is wrong. We might even say further that even those who do steal recognize this as a wrong act at least some of the time. After all, even thieves don't like thieves stealing from them! So, while there are some highly controversial topics, we also recognize that we hold some ideas in common. We order our lives, make decisions, and live with the effects of those choices. How do we do this?

All of us live our lives, to a greater or lesser degree, being certain of some truths. We believe we have a residence in such-and-such town or city, that we have a name, and that there are some people who we do know. Yet, most of us never consider how we know anything.

When beginning a study of morality, this question about how we know is essential to address at the very beginning. In disputes about what we think is right or wrong, we often throw up our hands in exasperation at those who would disagree with us. Our culture reinforces this attitude through the mass media, which makes irreconcilable positions entertainment. There, disputes are often resolved with the use of furniture or words that are yelled at the opposing party. Hopefully, we can find a better way here to examine various conflicts and find some ways of making sense of the different positions that arise in ethical discussions.

So, at the start, we need to deal with an idea that some in our society hold to be true: relativism. This is the belief that two contrary positions can both be right at the same time. That is, we look at disagreements and conclude that since there is no easy way of resolving the conflict, both people are "right." Everyone has his or her own truth, and no one should tell anyone else what to think or to do. Upon closer examination, however, this cannot be true.

Let us suppose, for example, that one person believes $2+2=4$ while another believes that $2+2=22$. Are both right? What if both truly believe that they are right? Is there a way of knowing which person is right? Can it be proven? Most of us would side with the conclusion that the correct answer is four. We know this is the correct answer. How do we know? More importantly, what makes this the correct answer? Is it only because we believe it?

Relativism holds that both the person who thinks the correct answer is four and the person who believes the correct answer is twenty-two are both right. They are right because they believe it. We can perhaps see the difficulty in this position even more clearly if we take the following situation. Suppose that there is a person who is a relativist who is speaking to another person. The relativist firmly believes that what is true is true because he believes it. Now the person who he is speaking to does not believe in relativism. She thinks that it is false. The relativist would have to say that the person who thinks that relativism is wrong is just as right as he thinks that he is. But to accept this is to accept that he is both right and wrong. Logically, this doesn't work.

So, we must begin our investigation with an initial step. We have to accept that there are some truths that can be proven and can therefore be known to rational human persons. This is called absolutism. Without this assumption, there would be no knowledge of anything. If we are unable to begin by believing that there is knowledge to be understood, then we cannot learn anything. All of what we believe and know will be entirely made up and we will have no way of communicating between ourselves. If, for example, we had no common experiences, the mathematics examples, which were given above, would mean nothing. We would be attempting to describe a reality that is different for every single person.

Absolute truth, or the belief that there is a structured meaning to creation that is not dependent on our acknowledgement of it, is therefore a basic prerequisite for making any kind of statement of fact, or to any supposition that this or that is true. In response to the question, "If a tree falls in the forest and no one is there to hear it, does it make a sound?" the absolutist will reply affirmatively that it does. Now, absolutism does not say that just because the truth *can be* known, but because it *is* known. In other words, the sound occurs, but it is not experienced. In short, a person who accepts absolutism simply understands that truth is attainable. We can know truth.

If we accept that truth is not something that we create but is something that is encountered, does that mean that we will agree on what is truth and what is not truth? Obviously, this is not the case because we still have disagreements. Partly, one of the reasons that people of good conscience disagree is that as individuals, we experience the world, and therefore the truth, through our own experiences.

When and where we live, how we begin our lives, the people that we meet, the books that we read, and the accomplishments and the failures that we have all contribute to our understanding of the world and ourselves. Another word for this is subjectivity. Subjectivity means that all of the truths that we know are understood through our experience of them. Our knowledge is shaped by how we come to know.

Yet, even though we learn through individual experiences, there is a common thread that runs throughout all knowledge. Regardless of whether I come to know the principles of physics through this professor or that professor, the truth of it remains the same. It might be taught in a better or worse way, but the essential truth of science remains what it is. In the same way, even though we all experience love through this other person or that other person, the essential characteristics of love remain the same. A mother's love for her child is something that transcends this particular person. It is not just the way that a particular child experiences his mother's love. It is also present when your mother or my mother loves you or me.

This is called objectivity, meaning truth remains what it is regardless of who experiences it. We aim for objectivity in all knowledge. We want to understand truth as it really is, and not simply as we would like it to be. Yet, because of subjectivity, our objectivity is always an interpretation. We recognize that we are always attempting to move toward a more perfectly described objectivity.

So, morality, then, claims that it does possess objectivity. Otherwise, there would be no point in trying to understand how it is that we make decisions. It aims for the truth of the matter. It formulates principles, or objective standards for assessing the rightness or wrongness of different human actions. How we come to state these different principles, how they should be applied, and even what they are will sometimes be different.

Philosophy, Theology, Anthropology, and Moral Theology

Catholic theology has a particular point of view about what is objectively true and how we ought to formulate the principles that guide our decision-making. We come to morality with certain assumptions about how we know what is true, and how that is then applied to particular human acts, just like all moral theories do. In fact, one of the greatest differences in moral systems is not so much in their conclusions, but rather in their assumptions about where we might discern truth, and how it ought to then be used. Whether we speak of Catholic, Jewish, or Islamic morality, or even a philosophical ethics like utilitarianism, all have a certain assumption about how we know truth and how it ought to be applied. Often, we tend to concentrate upon the end point, the conclusions, without taking adequate regard for the starting point.

One of the first distinctions that we must make about ethical systems lies in the differences between philosophy and theology. As distinct fields of study, philosophy and theology differ in their approach to considering how we can know what is true. Philosophy may be literally defined as the love of wisdom. It studies the truth of human existence from the perspective of how a human person might be able to make sense of his or her world with only the experiences that are available to all human persons. That is, the philosopher uses human reason and human experience to make sense of our existence. Within philosophy, there are many different ways to use human experience and human reason to arrive at philosophical claims. Yet, they all have in common the insistence that human existence should be studied only with those tools that are available to all persons.

Theology, on the other hand, accepts two sources as possessing objective truth: revelation and reason. Philosophy, as we have defined it above, limits itself to reason as its principal source. Revelation, or supernatural knowledge, lies at the core of theology. It is knowledge that comes to us by means of some special event or channel. This knowledge is not accessible simply on the basis of common human experience. Rather, it is understood by faith.

According to the eleventh century English bishop Anselm of Canterbury, theology is "fides quarens intellectum," or "faith seeking understanding." The theological presupposition is that revelation is true and that the task of the theologian is not to prove this truth but rather to understand it. We encounter this truth and then try to fashion explanations that are consistent with it as we express that truth today.

To the modern scientific mind, this might seem an effervescent kind of knowing. If theology is based upon a belief that cannot be proven to be true, than how reliable is it as a kind of knowledge? Yet, let us look briefly at science as a kind of knowledge as well. Ultimately, science too relies upon some unprovable assumptions. The scientist believes certain ideas that are simply accepted as true but not provable. For example, one of the basic beliefs of science is that the world works in consistent and predictable ways. This belief is so much a part of science that we don't even realize it is a belief. While past events provide some measure of expectation, the fact is that we believe the world will continue to operate in this way and that if we wish to propose some scientific truth, other scientists will be able to reproduce whatever experiment that we design to prove this or that idea. Science believes in the predictability of the world. It cannot *prove* that the world will continue to be this way, although there is certainly some good evidence that might lead us to believe it.

In the same way, theology operates under some presuppositions. Christian theology, in particular, has a basic set of beliefs that it holds as true on the basis of revelation. It recognizes two primary forms of revelation: Scripture and tradition. Scripture, or the Bible, is a written revelation. It serves as a source of belief for Christian reflection.

In particular terms of our discussion of bioethics, it may be helpful to note here that as a revelatory source, Scripture tends not to contain very particular explanations for contemporary ethical problems. That is, one is more apt to find general principles in the Bible than a specific answer to this or that ethical dilemma. Certainly, on some basic issues, as we shall see, the Bible is very clear about the morality of certain kinds of acts. But one will not find a particular text there, for example, that spells out the approach one should take in evaluating the morality of cosmetic surgery. Dilemmas like this require a more careful study of the Bible in order to understand the overall beliefs within which we make ethical decisions.[2]

The other revelatory source, tradition, may be understood as truth that is expressed through the lived experiences of those who are Christians. It includes written documents, liturgical expressions, moral choices that are expressed consistently by believers in their daily lives, and other objectives forms. In the early Christian Church, it was often called the Regula fidei, or the "Rule of Faith."[3] It is the claim that the truth is something that is lived by those who are Christians. It is expressed through the believers in many different forms. As the early Christians tried to make decisions about complex issues, they often turned to this concept for guidance. By examining the experiences of believers and the consensus that naturally arises over time, they thought the truth would emerge. So, consistent ethical choices on some issues by the faithful will establish an objective truth. It also finds written expression in official and unofficial Church documents.

Together, Scripture and tradition serve as important sources for Christian bioethics. It might be helpful to note, in passing, that different Christian churches will weigh these two sources differently. Some will tend to favor Scripture and others tradition. Ultimately, however, they ought to be understood in relation to one another.

Theology, then, begins with a set of beliefs that it holds to be true on the basis of human reason and revelation. Broadly considered, there are two basic kinds of theological systems: polytheism and monotheism. Polytheism is the belief in many gods, while monotheism is the belief in one God. Hinduism is an example of polytheism, while Christianity, Judaism, and Islam are all monotheistic.

While it is not possible here to completely explain the similarities and differences between polytheism and monotheism, it is important to gain at least a basic sense of how they differ because these beliefs profoundly affect the moral systems that arise from their respective theologies. The connection that is important for us to understand is that the source of ultimate value that lies at the center of any ethical system has important consequences for how one makes conclusions. That is, the choices that we make are based upon basic beliefs about how we know what is right. From those beliefs, we then will reach specific decisions. In a theological ethical system, whether it is polytheistic or monotheistic, what one believes about the nature of God will ultimately affect one's decision to perform a specific act.

Polytheistic theologies have several characteristics that make them different from monotheistic theologies. Although there are many gods within polytheistic religions, these gods can be divided into two types: good and evil. One of the dynamic elements about polytheistic religions lies in the relationship of these various gods to one another.

The ancient Greek and Roman stories often center upon the conflicts between the various gods. In these systems, the gods possess characteristics that are at odds with one another. The stories focus upon how the gods work out the conflicts among themselves. In these stories, it is also significant that human beings are peripheral to the central conflict. Human actions are insignificant compared to the feats of the gods. This is important when one considers how to understand whether an action is ethical or not.

In the ancient world, the concept of fate took center stage. Humans are often portrayed as puppets in a divine play. The central focus of the ancient city-state was the religious worship that was oriented to fulfilling some ceremony that would appease the gods. In fact, if one were to examine the architecture of the ancient cities, one would see that they were built in the shape of the circle, with the temple in middle of the city. The temple was the source of order for the ancient city. Religious worship was one way that order was maintained. This characteristic of orderliness was associated with spirituality. Opposing this order was chaos, which attacked the city from the outside.[4]

In polytheistic systems, the gods were identified by their relationship to one of two extremes. We might say that they were either good, or evil. Although in some cases the gods presented complex motivations that were a mixture of both, for our purposes, let's look at the contrast in order to clarify the values that related to moral beliefs. Those gods who were evil tended to have several characteristics. They were connected to the material world, they were changeable, they were emotional, and they were chaotic. On the other hand, those gods who were fundamentally good were spiritual, static, rational, and orderly.

One can see this dynamic at work in the famous epic poem "The Odyssey." This two-part poem tells about the Trojan War and the difficulties of the hero

Odysseus. In the first part of the poem, the fight game of the Trojan War is described. While the human characters are important in the poem, the gods are as significant. The war is both a human and a divine conflict. In the second part of the poem, Odysseus must find his way back to his homeland because he has been banished for disobeying the gods. His journey takes him about ten years to complete. Along the way, he encounters many famous adversaries, such as the Cyclops, the Sirens, and the Lotus Eaters. The modern reader may be puzzled by Odysseus' actions. There are many places in his journey where he might have chosen to stay rather than encounter further trials. Yet, for the ancient listener, his actions are quite understandable. This person would understand that Odysseus would only be happy returning to his proper place in society. Since the primary value in the ancient city-state lies in maintaining the social order (which is also the religious one), one's worth as a person is intrinsically related to one's place in society.

The predominant theme in ancient stories is related to this emphasis. There are many stories that use confusion about social status as a theme, as in the story of Oedipus. The place of the stranger in this tightly controlled order is another

The concept of morality was that the person existed for the benefit of the society. From the polytheistic theological foundation, a morality developed that saw individual persons as less important than the society. What mattered was not individual happiness, but societal happiness. It is therefore not surprising that there was a rigid social hierarchy in the ancient society. One was born into a social class, and one was expected to fulfill the obligations of that status. There was no such thing as social mobility. If one were born a slave, then generally one would be a slave forever.

Looking at a Hindu society, until relatively recently, the caste system was rigidly enforced. Hinduism, a polytheistic religion, possesses characteristics that are similar to the ancient religious practices of Greece and Rome. In Hinduism, social status is thought to be a direct reflection of one's spiritual state in life. Reincarnation is the path by which one advances from one social class to another.

The theological foundation of polytheism results in a moral emphasis upon this society as a primary source of value. Individual morality focuses upon fulfilling social duties. So, ultimately, what really counts is whatever is good for society rather than the individual. It is the social good that has a priority, not the individual good.

A much different theological presupposition is monotheism. As opposed to polytheism, monotheism believes in only one God. The major monotheism religions of the world are Christianity, Judaism, and Islam. These three religions together believe that there is only one God, who is a good Creator. Where polytheism sees a division between the spiritual and the physical, monotheism sees a unity.

Let us look more carefully at this process. For the ancients, the most basic categories of existence were the spiritual and the material worlds. As mentioned in passing above, polytheism uses these categories as primary characteristics of the various kinds of gods. Once this dichotomy is accepted, then one's encounter with the world will tend to reinforce this belief.

Applying this idea to the nature of the human body, ancient theorists "discovered" the medical theory of the four humors. According to this theory, everything that exists in the world is composed of a combination of the four basic substances: earth, air, fire, and water. In the human body, these four elements correspond to four bodily substances, or humors. They are blood, phlegm, black bile, and yellow bile. When these four elements were in balance, then a person was said to be in "good humor," or have a proper "complexion." The goal of medical practice was then to keep these elements in their proper proportions. Practices such as bloodletting were direct applications of the theory.

So the process went something like this: We believe that there are two kinds of gods. The nature of these gods determines the nature of the world, which is a mixture of each. This balance results in the formation of opposing forces in the human body. These must be in balance in order for health to result. The patient is unhealthy and irritable. We should bloodlet.

Let us turn now back to monotheism. As opposed to polytheism, for most of ancient history, monotheism was a decidedly minority position. Although there are monotheistic aspects to some of the ancient Egyptian cults, like that of Aten and Ra, monotheism as an established, exclusive belief that changed one's moral behavior did not come to Western culture until Judaism. Some authors have termed the establishment of Judaism as the origin of "ethical monotheism."[5] What is meant by this term is that the relationship with God demands a personal response, or morality for the individual. Actions are not just oriented to the community but also to a development of the individual.

Judaism, and later Christianity, believed that it was the intimacy of a relationship with the Creator of the world that characterized morality. In other words, good choices are those that establish and perfect the full development of the relationship between God and his creation, particularly human persons. We will continue to develop this idea about the personal character of moral choice in a monotheistic system through the discussion of what we will term natural law. The contrast between polytheism and monotheism is that the first emphasizes the good of the community while the second concentrates on the good of the individual.[6]

The Development of Natural Law

From our brief exploration of some of the basic presuppositions of ethical theory, it is easy to see that there is often a great deal of disagreement concerning what is ethical. Often, these differences of opinion are the result of differences in epistemology. Persons begin their explanations of what is moral or immoral with some unstated assumptions. We have ideas about the nature of God and ourselves that are simply accepted as being true. It is easy to see that two persons who begin a discussion about ethics when one is a polytheist and the other is a monotheist may have difficulty in agreeing upon how one makes an ethical choice. We begin with different concepts about the nature of gods, which then results in diverse ideas about what it means to be human.

One of the key factors in the development of any ethical theory is therefore the presupposition that one has with regard to how one makes decisions. Beliefs about the nature of God eventually result in a working hypothesis about the nature being human. Morality, whether it is polytheistic or monotheistic, means choosing an action that best represents our conception of human nature. We act out our concept of what we think will make us happy.[7]

So how do we know what it means to be human? This is, of course, a very abstract question. It should not be surprising that that this question has been answered in many different ways throughout history. From ancient until modern times, philosophers and theologians have proposed many different theories about human nature, or as it is sometimes referred to, natural law.

Depending upon who uses the term, natural law can have many different meanings. It is necessary, therefore, to understand the context in which the term is used. To say something is natural or unnatural implies a set of assumptions with regard to how one knows what is natural and what source of ultimate value determines what is natural. As a general definition of the term, natural law is the objective demand of creation. That is, it is the claim that there exists within the created world a knowable purpose. All creation participates in a divine plan of intentionality. For human persons, the understanding of morality is that there exists both a purpose for our choices and the free will to choose them.[8]

To begin our explanation of different ethical systems, we will first, then, examine three of the most significant historical developments in the understanding of natural law. By seeing how the concept of natural law has changed throughout history, it will be easier to understand different ethical theories that work from these ideas.

The first concept of natural law we will call traditional natural law. This interpretation of natural law has its roots in the ancient world. Both polytheists and monotheists have used this theory to support their moral systems. In fact, this theory has been the predominant one for most of history. The basic methodology of a traditional natural law theory holds that faith provides the primary source for understanding human nature. The person uses religious beliefs as a source for what is true. That is, one begins by accepting a set of beliefs and then trying to understand how they are true. In weighing the two elements of faith and reason, faith is predominant. This methodology applies to both polytheistic and monotheistic thinkers. The key difference is in the content of what each believes, which leads them in very different directions on the point of determining what is moral or immoral.

To the modern reader, traditional natural law may be difficult to understand. This is because of our assumptions about epistemology. We have a different worldview than that of the ancient world. For them, theological beliefs were the source for all other knowledge. Beginning with their belief about the nature of the gods, or God, they then related the other knowledge to this basic belief. They did not question the truth of what they believed about God; they simply accepted it as true. From this foundational belief, they analyzed the nature of the world to see *how* their faith was true. From our perspective, this might seem naive. It is easy to caricature this position and make it seem as though it is ignorant. One can easily imagine any number of books and movies in which the person who is religious is thought of as someone who is really not all that bright. Yet, this viewpoint has a depth if one is willing to examine it more carefully. Religious zeal without an intellectual foundation is, of course, ignorant. However, if one begins to examine the nature of the world, one must choose some kind of absolute value. As we shall see when we look at other interpretations of natural law, all theories of human nature require some sort of a belief as a first step toward making any kind of conclusions. Both polytheists and monotheists have used the traditional natural law approach in developing their ethics. They differ, of course, in their theological beliefs, which results in some very different conclusions. The method is the same, however. Yet, because one system believes in many gods and the other in only one God, their definitions of what makes us human are quite divergent. The key characteristic of a traditional natural law ethic is that the nature of what is absolute is known through religious faith first. One believes in a revelation that then informs one's understanding of the world. Reason works with faith to form principles of ethical action. It is neither one reflective faith nor unfaithful reason. Together, faith and reason develop an ethical system. In the polytheistic system, the content of the faith leads one to a dualistic appreciation of the person. The person is seen as an accidental combination of matter and spirit, and the essential human characteristic is the spirit. Those who are more closely connected it to the material world are considered to be less human than others. Women, because of their connection to childbirth, were among those who were thought to be less human. Reason supported these theological beliefs. For example, in one very famous passage, Aristotle noted that that the "female is as it were a deformed male and the menstrual discharge is semen, though in an impure condition; i.e. it lacks one constituent, and one only: the principle of Soul."[9]

With a dualistic theological system, the anthropology leads to ethical actions that we would consider to be immoral. Since some humans are worth less than other humans, it is acceptable to treat them differently. The Romans, for example, saw no difficulty in allowing slaves and prisoners of war to be used as entertainment in the Coliseum. The spectacles that thrilled the crowds often involved the deaths of thousands of people on a given day. This was not thought of as an immoral act. Using a monotheistic belief in God in conjunction with a traditional natural law methodology, however, leads to very different conclusions. In the very beginning of the book of Genesis, we are introduced to this concept of God. This God is a "good creator." There is not a tension between the physical and spiritual. What is created is itself good. Creation is not accidental but deliberate. Human persons, both male and female, are valuable intrinsically because God created them. So, we begin with a theological belief, which then translates into anthropology, and then results in an ethical system. The early Christians were vehemently opposed to many Roman practices. In addition to their abhorrence of the spectacles in the Coliseum, they also opposed practices such as infanticide. When a child was born, it was traditional for the child to be placed upon the ground. If the father, who was the head of his household, picked up the baby, then he acknowledged it as his own. In effect, it became his property. If he did not pick up the child, then it could be abandoned. Remembering our previous discussion as to who was important, it should not be surprising that the babies who were most likely to be abandoned were female. This practice still continues today in cultures that are polytheistic.[10]

In contrast, the Christians believed that male and female were fundamentally equal. Of course, the larger culture around them influenced how they applied this information. In looking at the writings in the early Church, one sees tension between this ideal and the cultural practices that surrounded the Church. In fact, even today we struggle with the effects of dualism. In principle, however, Christianity had the ability to affirm the dignity of women. This concept of natural law, which placed faith first and reason second, was the predominant method of understanding human nature until the sixteenth century. It was then that the Renaissance began to affect Western culture. The word "Renaissance" is French for rebirth. It points to an increasing emphasis on the goodness of humanity. In the historical period immediately preceding the Renaissance, the Middle Ages, humans were considered mostly in terms of their sinful nature. The Renaissance shifted our focus toward the creative characteristics of human nature. Michelangelo, Da Vinci, Galileo, and Newton were all significant figures of this era. In their work, they exalted human accomplishment. From this outpouring of human creativity came the birth of modern science. Isaac Newton, who is sometimes referred to as the father of modern science, proposed the scientific method, perhaps one of the most significant developments in Western culture. Instead of accepting truths simply on the basis of faith, Newton believed that we should follow a method in which truth is considered from a hypothetically "objective" viewpoint. Scientists proposed a hypothesis, or a conditional idea, which was then analyzed to see whether it was true. The key element was whether the analysis would stand up to a verifiable proof, and whether it could be reproduced.

The introduction of the scientific method had a profound effect on the understanding of natural law. What was thought to be natural was no longer simply accepted. Now it had to be proven. In the seventeenth and eighteenth centuries, two new interpretations of natural law emerged: the "Law of Nature" theories and the "Rejection of Natural Law" theories.

The first is a collection of theories that worked from the premises of Newton's scientific method. Just as he proposed that truth should be objectively verified, these theorists argued that human nature could be known through reasonable criteria. Once we could prove what human nature is, then we should believe it. So, rather than approaching the question of human nature from the perspective of faith initially with reason supporting this revelation, they suggested that reason provides the content of what is to be believed. For them, it was reason first and faith second. There are many theorists who belonged to this "strand" of natural law. Thomas Hobbes, for example, believed it was possible to prove that human nature was "nasty, mean, and brutish and short."[11] John Locke is another. He thought that religious faith was rational and that we could prove that belief in God was justified. The effects of this new interpretation of natural law on Western culture were profound. Science grew rapidly and developed as a significant source of knowledge. In politics, democratic claims challenged the prevailing model of the monarchy. The founding of the United States, for example, was justified on the basis of rationally known "inalienable rights." The first Americans believed that this nation belonged to them by natural right. The claims of the British monarchy to ownership of this country were rejected because of this methodology in natural law. Within Christianity itself, Protestantism emerged in the sixteenth century as an effect of this changing perspective of natural law. Martin Luther, John Calvin, and other significant Protestants criticized practices and beliefs that they believed were rooted in reason. In general, these emerging churches emphasized human experience over traditional doctrines. Everything from the nature of the Church to the practice of marriage became open for analysis and possible revision.

In the eighteenth century, a further development of natural law arose. Thinkers such as Karl Marx, Friedrich Nietzsche, Ludwig Feuerbach, and Auguste Comte took the position that reason finally results in rejecting the idea of a natural law. These thinkers, who are part of the strand that we will term the "Rejection of Natural Law" theorists, believed that, ultimately, what cannot be proven to be true is not true. Where the Protestants and other "Law of Nature" thinkers left some place for reasonable beliefs that could not be definitively proven, these thinkers came to the conclusion that unproven beliefs are simply superstition and ought to be rejected. Religious faith is, to them, an irrational belief. In Marx's words, religion is the "opium of the people." Only ignorant people believe in God. It seduces them with false promises of an afterlife in heaven. Nietzsche's disdain for Christians was famous. With their rejection of the belief in God, these thinkers had to substitute some other absolute value in its place. Not surprisingly, perhaps, they chose humanity, either individually or collectively. For Nietzsche, the ultimate purpose of life was to become "ubermensch," which is normally translated into English as "superman." By this, he meant an emancipated human, one who makes his or her morality. Since intrinsic natural goods do not bind us, we can decide for ourselves what is good. We must thus "murder God, and become god."

Ludwig Feuerbach had a similar solution as Nietzsche. He, too, thought that God did not exist. Instead, God was a collective human desire. Feuerbach observed that our depictions of God around the world resemble the people who believe in him. He concluded that the attributes that we give to God are actually our own human desires projected into this superior being. He thought that we should strive to attain those qualities that we give to God.

Together, these three strands of natural law form the basis for most ethical theories. We have assimilated the ideas of traditional natural law, law of nature, and rejection of natural law thinkers into the cultural discussions of morality without really understanding the differences. The choice of one epistemological foundation over another has consequences for the kinds of conclusions one is likely to reach. All too often we become too focused on the differing conclusions without understanding that there are real differences in assumptions. If we take any ethical issue and examine it carefully, we can see the effects of these epistemologies.

Natural Law and Catholic Morality

Catholic reflection on morality is thoroughly grounded in the traditional natural law strand. We believe that we can know, through both revelation and through reason, what is ethical. We believe in the content of revelation, that is, knowledge that has been given to us directly by God. The Bible and tradition are sources of this revelation. In Scripture, there are many truths that are revealed by God. Tradition, which we defined earlier as the lived truth of the community of believers, is another source. For Catholics, this tradition includes formal statements of the Church, such as papal encyclicals, pronouncements by ecumenical councils, and the writings of the faithful. Tradition also includes truth as it is expressed in the lives and choices of believers. Together, revelation and reason help us to discern how we should make moral choices. The first key idea that we need to understand is that Christian anthropology forms the foundation for Catholic ethical reflection. The person, who was created in the image and likeness of God, has a natural purpose that has been given to us by God. We are meant by God to know him and to love him. We have within our very nature the ability to know we are, and to act in a way that will bring that relationship about. God has given us the capacity to be able to be in a relationship with him and with each other. Since God has already determined our nature, human actions have a meaning that already exists prior to our choosing them. For Catholics, morality is not about determining the nature of the acts that we choose, but of choosing the correct acts. The kinds of actions that we choose will enact predetermined natural goods or evils. We do not create what good and evil are. What we do is to choose those actions that will help us to be in communion with the reality that already has a meaning that has been determined by God.

One of the primary sources for helping us to understand our relationships with God and with each other is Scripture. As a Christian source for reflection, its significance for moral theology tends to lie more in its articulation of a way of understanding our covenantal relationship with God than in specifying the absolute rightness or wrongness of specific human acts. I am not suggesting that the Bible does not speak to moral issues, nor that there are some acts that are clearly thought of as wrong in Scripture. Rather, I am simply saying that we will usually not find a specific list of answers on moral questions. For example, one will not find a definitive answer to the contemporary quandary over the ethics of stem cell research. There are clearly "signposts" that will point us in a particular direction, but a specific passage will not be found that conclusively settles the issue for us. Scripture is helpful for moral theology because it sets the foundations of the discussions. We find there the doctrines that are then applied to specific situations. Its morality needs to be drawn out through prayer and reflection rather than prooftexting. Catholic morality then focuses upon how we can best understand the nature of what it is that we choose. We are created by a loving God who desires that we exist in relation to what he has made. This is a key feature of how we live our lives. Our faith calls us to choose the actions that aim at what is objectively good. Notice here that while the motivation is to seek what is already good, to perform a moral act, it is not necessary that the act always realize that good, or that evil is nonexistent. In other words, we do not decide whether an act is good or not purely on the basis of what it accomplishes. It is not a pure consequentialist evaluation. Nor do we have to only act when evil is not present. What is required is that we do not deliberately choose evil and that we choose in order to accomplish an objectively good object. The act of making a moral choice can be broken down into three parts: the object, the intention, and the circumstances. In order for an act to be moral, all three parts must act as a consistent whole. If any one of the three is deficient, then the act is immoral. By immoral we mean that the act itself does not achieve the natural good to which it is oriented. In other words, the person who chooses the act separates himself or herself from the natural good that ought to be achieved in performing the action. This occurs regardless of whether or not the person understands what it is that he or she has done. There's a difference between saying something is "immoral" and saying that the person is culpable or responsible for that act. We can make the determination that objectively the act does not achieve the good to which it is oriented. However, this is not to say that we can know with certainty whether the person who performed the act that was wrong had a sufficient knowledge to be responsible for the bad choice. Let us look a little bit more carefully at these three elements. The object is often the most difficult to understand. One way of thinking about the object is that it is the "what" of the act. It is the natural good that the act aims at. Let's use an example to more clearly illustrate what the object is. Suppose two people are having a conversation. Why do they talk to one another? One could say that they enjoy talking to one another. As friends they share experiences and memories. This particular conversation might be about things that happen to them during the day. Or, they might be discussing something more abstract. If we look more deeply into this conversation, we might say that regardless of what they say, these two friends are sharing something about themselves. The object of this conversation is not simply to convey information. Really, it is to communicate something that is true; it is to connect to another person. If it were not true, the conversation would most probably end. Most people will not waste their time on a conversation with someone who is false or who constantly lies. Speaking, then, has a natural object to it: to communicate the truth. Whatever we say is already bound to this natural good. The key characteristic of the moral object is that it aims at a natural good, regardless of either our understanding or our acceptance of it. Although we can choose to act against the object of the act as it exists, it doesn't change the fact that it does exist. In the example given above, if we choose to lie, it doesn't therefore mean that speaking doesn't have a purpose that is already there. As Catholics, we choose these goods in order to exist as the creatures God intended us to be.

At this point, before we continue with a discussion of the other elements of the act, we must address one significant criticism of this view. Within Catholic theology, there has been a debate among theologians concerning the method by which we know our obligations and apply them to specific moral situations. One group of theologians has argued for the existence of absolute moral norms that always bind us, while another has argued that good choices need to be made within a specific set of circumstances. This second group, who are known as proportionalists, would disagree that the object of a moral act has an intrinsic meaning apart from a consideration of the intention and the circumstance. According to proportionalism, a person ought to understand the object within a context. There is no such thing, they argue, as an object that exists apart from other elements of a moral act. Therefore, it is wrong to suggest that there are such acts that are always and everywhere evil. John Paul II has condemned this position in his encyclical, *Veritatis Splendor*.[12] The intention is the "why" of the act. It is the personal reason that we choose this kind of act as opposed to another. To continue with our examples above, we may choose to speak to this person because we like them. Or, we may choose to speak because we are angry. The intention, then, is more subjective. We make an individual choice to engage in a particular kind of act whose object is already determined. We, ourselves, do not determine the nature of speaking. We choose whether and why we will speak.

So our intention alone does not determine the morality of the act. It is one element among three. There is an old saying about intention that captures this belief that we can make an act right just by our desire that it be so: "The road to hell is paved with good intentions."

The last element in a moral act that we need to examine is the circumstances. This may be thought of as the "how" of an act. Circumstances describe all of those qualities of an act that enable a person to achieve the object and intention. They are the means by which the act is performed, including specifically how the act is carried out and the results, or the consequences of performing the act.

If there is a deficiency in the object, the intention, or the circumstances, then the act is immoral. All three elements must work together in order for the person to perform a moral act. In other words, the person must choose a kind of act that is consistent with human nature, he or she must intend a good purpose by the act, and the act must be carried out in a way that is consistent with the object and intention.

This analysis of the nature of a moral act means that moral decision-making is not about deciding what is ultimately good but rather discovering it and conforming our decisions to it. What is good remains good regardless of whether we recognize it as good. God has already determined for us what we are. Our purpose in life is to understand what God has given to us and to choose to seek it for ourselves.

Being able to discover the truth and to choose out of love is the challenge of a moral life. For Catholics, we come to know the truth not only individually, but also as a community. The Church helps us to form our conscience because as a community, we believe that it teaches the truth throughout history. It is one way that God reveals himself to us. We are challenged to constantly seek the truth and to form our conscience correctly.[13]

Another way of trying to understand truth consists of choosing the proper kinds of habits for one's life. As humans, we live our lives through repetitive actions. We often do not think about these choices on a daily basis. Instead, we tend to simply do things. We act, but do not think about how we act.

Virtues and vices are habits that we incorporate into our lives. A virtue is a habit that seeks a good object, while a vice seeks a bad object. The key characteristic about virtues is that they make seeking what is good an intrinsic part of daily life.

When we look at many Americans, we can see that physically, they are in poor health. A key reason for this is that they choose habits that are opposed to being healthy. We eat fast food, we don't exercise, and we fail to get enough rest. So, our daily habits push us toward a goal that we really don't want. An entire industry has grown around our desire to look and feel good. Yet, invariably, we look for the quick fix. We know that a proper diet and exercise will keep us healthy, yet we refuse to do this. Why?

The reason for this is that until you adopt good habits, they seem to be painful and joyless changes. If one is not in somewhat reasonable physical shape, the experience is very discouraging. It is hard to see the incremental steps. Yet, if people who exercise regularly can't work out, they often feel bad. Their bodies feel tired from not exercising. For someone who eats healthy foods (fruits, vegetables, and lean meats), a trip to the fast food burger joint is not all that fulfilling. The food really doesn't taste good enough to make it a habit.

This is a characteristic of virtues and vices. Often, virtuous habits don't feel very good in the beginning, but long term, they achieve a good object that makes us happy. Vices, on the other hand, usually feel very good in the beginning, but long term they become self-destructive.

The seven traditional virtues are separated into two categories: the theological virtues of faith, hope, and charity, and the moral virtues of prudence, temperance, fortitude, and justice. The seven "deadly sins" or vices are pride, gluttony, lust, anger, greed, envy, and despair. Virtues and vices are opposite habits. For every virtue, there is a corresponding vice.

The Principle of Double Effect

If we follow a traditional natural law ethic and accept the three-part structure of the moral act as object, intention, and circumstance, then we are sometimes left with a problem. Human actions are not always simple ones. At times, there are many different elements to a human act, and we might find ourselves with a number of consequences and even some confusion about what the object of the act that we perform really is. The principle of double effect is a tool that helps us to clarify what it is that we do in a complex action. It takes each of the three elements of a moral act and examines them in relation to the action that is being performed. The principle of double effect has developed over many centuries. Its earliest formulation is found in the work of Thomas Aquinas.[14] Today, it is used not only in Catholic moral reflection but also in the law. The principle itself may be stated as follows: One may perform an action, which is good in itself, which had a greater proportion of good over evil.

This principle may be broken down into five criteria that must be met in order for the act to meet the requirements of the principle.

First, in relation to the object of the act:

1. The act, in itself, seeks an object that is good, or at least morally indifferent

Then, in relation to the intention of the act:

2. The good effect must be directly intended, while the bad effect must be unintended, but foreseen.

With regard to the circumstances of the act:

3. The good effect is not achieved by means of the bad effect.

4. The good effect and the bad effect are proportionate to one another.

5. The good effect must be achieved concomitant with the bad effect.

Each of these criteria is meant to clarify the three essential elements of object, intention, and circumstances. Thus, the principle of double effect flows from that basic framework.

It is not enough, however, to simply apply the principle in a mechanical way. Although the criteria need to be met, they are applied in light of virtue. Due prudence must be used in order to make a determination as to whether the conditions are applied lovingly. One aspect of the traditional natural law analysis of moral acts that has been criticized by many authors is what is called casuistry. Casuistry refers to the application of these principles to moral acts in a way that focuses on the strict mechanical requirements of an act. Unfortunately, sometimes the use of the method led to an objectification of the act in such a way that the judgment seemed to have no place for individual conscience or circumstances. It seemed to some that the principles were supplied as a kind of strict legalism without consideration for the individual person who needed to decide. Even today, casuistry still has an effect on the way that Catholic ethics is sometimes understood. Many people equate a Catholic natural law morality with a set of rules to which one must rigidly adhere. Morality simply becomes the process by which one knows the rules and follows them. Sin is violating the rules and bringing about some bad effect in the process. This unfortunate use of the principles is, of course, not in keeping with their fundamental purpose.[15]

Obviously, this analysis is dependent upon a clear and objective analysis of the act. One may not use the principle to justify what would otherwise be an immoral and repulsive act. Such acts that are intrinsically evil by reason of their object would always and everywhere be wrong. In *Veritatis Splendor*, John Paul II writes about these kinds of acts and categorizes them as follows:

> Whatever is hostile to life itself, such as any kind of homicide, genocide, abortion, euthanasia and voluntary suicide; whatever violates the dignity of the human person, such as mutilation, physical and mental torture, and attempts to coerce spirit; whatever is offensive to human dignity, such as subhuman living conditions, arbitrary imprisonment, deportation, slavery, prostitution, and trafficking in women and children; degrading conditions of work which treat laborers as mere instruments of profit, and not as free responsible Persons.[16]

Therefore, we must be clear about the nature of the object. A good effect is not equivalent to a good object. Murdering an innocent person so that many others would not be killed is such an example. Simply because there is a good result does not mean that the object of the act is good. Murder remains evil even if it achieves good. The intention of the act must also be good. The agent must desire to achieve some good object. In terms of bioethics, the intention would ordinarily be related to restoring or preserving the health of the individual patient. As noted above, the intention is the personal choice of the agent to achieve some objective good. As such, it is related to the object. The agent seeks the object through the kind of act that is chosen, but the particular conditions of the choice are the subject of intention. A helpful rule of thumb is to say that the object refers to a kind of act, while the intention refers to *this* particular act. The third condition is that the effect must be achieved concomitant with the act itself, and not as a result of an evil object. Thus, the effect occurs because of the direct and immediate consequence of the act. It is not necessary that the effect occur immediately in terms of time, but that it occurs immediately in terms of causality.

Let us then apply the principle of double effect to a particular case to illustrate how it works. In this particular case, the patient has been diagnosed with cancer. In fact, the disease has now progressed to a stage where the patient has been declared terminal. As part of the treatment plan, the patient has been prescribed morphine to control the pain. Unfortunately, the dose is insufficient to completely eradicate the pain. The moral dilemma is this: may the morphine be increased for this patient, even though there is the risk of bringing about this person's death sooner? One of the side effects of morphine is a depression of respiration, although this can often be mitigated when it is increased in stages.

How would we apply the criteria? Using the first principle, that the act, in itself, seeks an object that is good, or at least morally indifferent, we must carefully determine what it is that we aim for in this act. What is it that we are actually doing? In this case, the moral act is to give an injection. This act embodies the object of caring for this person's physical body. Next, the act has two effects: an intended good effect and an allowable evil effect. The good effect cannot be obtained in any other way, and the evil effect is inextricably tied to the good effect. In this case, morphine is irreplaceable. There is no other drug that is as effective. It alleviates the pain, but it inevitably has the side effect of reduced respiration. Thus, the second criterion has been met. Third, the evil effect cannot be directly willed; it is only permitted. Here, the evil effect is the possible early death of the patient. If the person who administers the injection were using the injection in order to kill the patient, then the criterion would not be met. If, however, the effect of alleviating pain were aimed for, then it would meet the criterion. We may never choose to bring about the death of an innocent person. Next, the principle of double effect requires that the evil effect is not a means to producing the good effect. In this case, the question is whether the alleviation of pain is brought about by the death of the patient. Obviously, it is not, so the fourth criterion is met. Finally, there must be a due proportion between the moral object and the evil that occurs. Here, the good of injecting morphine in order to alleviate pain and suffering must be balanced against the possible early death of the patient. This is not something that can be measured exactly. Rather, we must determine this with some prudence. The key is that the good not be something that is insignificant but that it be of sufficient importance that we can agree that the possible evil be allowed.

The principle of double effect is a useful one in bioethics because it permits us to carefully analyze the complex parts of a moral act. It is used to determine the morality of an act not only in specific medical procedures like surgery or the giving of injections, but also in social ethical situations like determining the degree of cooperation between a Catholic and a non-Catholic health partner in providing certain kinds of medical services.

Conscience

Another topic that needs to be discussed in ethical method is conscience. Conscience may be defined as the awareness of moral truth. It is the ability to know what is right from what is wrong. Our individual conscience binds us to a vision of truth, and it gives us the motivation to act correctly. It is a natural ability that both religious believers and nonbelievers recognize. All persons recognize an obligation to do good and to avoid evil.

Yet even though we recognize this duty, this does not always mean that we are objectively correct in our judgment. As individuals, we have the tendency to assume that our understanding of truth is correct. Yet, we often discover later that we have made errors in empirical facts, or that we choose to abide by principles that are not as well thought out as others. Or, we may not completely understand the obligations that certain principles place upon us. Our subjectivity sometimes gets in the way of our objectivity. We have a duty, then, to constantly evaluate our conscience in light of reliable sources of truth. In other words, we need to develop an informed conscience, one that is educated about the truth and not ignorant of it. As we said earlier, the truth is something that exists independently of us; it is something that we encounter rather than create. So, in order to assist ourselves in acting rightly, we will tend to abide by some fundamental principles of action. We create a code of conduct for ourselves that we seek to put into practice. Conscience is an awareness of these principles and the motivation to practice them. In the words of the Vatican Council II, "Deep within his conscience man discovers a law which he has not laid upon himself but which he must obey. Its voice, ever calling him to love and to do what is good and to avoid evil, tells him inwardly at the right moment: do this, shun that. For man has in his heart a law inscribed by God. His dignity lies in observing this law and by it he will be judged."[17]

By our nature, we are aware of moral truth. Conscience is a law, or obligation, that was created as part of who we are. For Catholics, this natural obligation is enhanced by faith through the Church. We believe that the Christian community itself is an objective form of truth and that it communicates that truth throughout history. We can know the principles of conscience through human reason enlightened by faith. So, Scripture and formal pronouncements of the Church in pastoral letters, encyclicals, addresses, and other forms help us to form our view on ethical questions.

It is important to understand that Catholics follow Church teaching because they themselves are internally motivated to form their conscience by it. It is not an external imposition of "do this and don't do that." The person must choose to give a "ready submission of will and intellect."[18] Put another way, Catholics follow Church teaching because we believe that the teachings possess an objectivity guaranteed through the Church by God. For some kinds of questions, the Church has a long history of commenting, and its doctrine is quite clear. For other topics, there may be less of a tradition. Depending upon the clarity and consistency of the teaching, there is a greater or lesser obligation to abide by that teaching. The key point for Catholics is that since as a community we believe that the Church is an objective source of moral truth, we are obligated to form our conscience with a careful consideration of Church teaching. To dissent from Church teaching is a legitimate choice, but only after one fully understands the teaching, and even then it is done reluctantly and with a sense of humility and an obligation to continue to understand the Church's position. One also forms his or her conscience through other objective sources. In bioethics, one must understand not only ethical theory, but also biology, medicine, psychology, sociology, and many other discrete sources of knowledge. It is essential to use the information from these areas in order to truly understand the choices that one can make. All too often, we make decisions based upon incomplete knowledge. Physicians, nurses, and other health care professionals are often ignorant of ethical theory, while conversely many ethicists lack a sufficient knowledge of science.

Philosophical Ethical Theories

As we said above, Catholic morality is based upon the first strand of natural law, a traditional natural law that begins with faith and then uses reason to understand the faith. Beginning in the sixteenth century, other interpretations of natural law arose that are collectively called the Law of Nature School. These interpretations of natural law began with reason and then concluded with a set of beliefs based upon that reason. From this strand of natural law arose several different ethical theories. The focus in these theories was to provide an objective and non-religious foundation for ethics. The development of these systems began with a "reasonable" conjecture about human nature that then filtered down into a rational process by which choices were to be made. Ultimately, two kinds of ethical theories were developed, with nuances in each. Those that focused upon a set of natural duties are called deontological theories. The other type is known as utilitarianism or teleology. Deontological theories focus upon acting ethically out of a duty to some principle. The Greek word "deon" actually means duty. The German philosopher Immanuel Kant developed the most prominent deontological theory. Kant suggested that the rational basis for ethical action would be a universal principle that all people could know and could easily follow. Kant called this principle the "Categorical Imperative." He wrote that we should only act on that absolute maxim that we could will to be a universal law.[19]

According to this principle, we are obligated to only act in such a way that we would require every other person to act in the same way toward us. The key aspect of this theory is that one does not act because of what will happen in the particular situation but because there is an obligation to a natural duty. Kant gives many examples of acts that are absolutely prohibited by the categorical imperative. One may never lie, for example, because we would not want someone lying to us.

There are two major difficulties with Kantian ethics. First, his basis for forming universal principles can easily be used to create nonsensical universal principles. "Whistle when you are in the dark," is innocuous enough, but should we obligate everyone to do so? A second difficulty is that Kant does not give us a way to resolve conflicts between universal principles. We may say that we should not lie, nor should we kill an innocent person. But what do we do when an attacker who is intent on killing the innocent person who has hidden in our house asks us if that person is inside? Within Kant's system, we cannot resolve the conflict. Another approach to ethics is utilitarianism. These theories are sometimes call teleological theories because the Greek word "telos" means end or goal. Utilitarian ethics focuses upon the results that are achieved in choosing an act. In the eighteenth century, Jeremy Bentham and John Stuart Mill developed basic utilitarian ethics. Mill formulated the principle of utility in this way:

"Actions are right in proportion as they tend to promote happiness, wrong as they tend to promote the reverse of happiness."[20]

The main object of utilitarianism is to maximize the attainment of happiness. Mill does not identify the idea of happiness as simply selfishness. Instead, it is the seeking of a good that extends beyond oneself to others. Elsewhere he writes that it is "not the agent's own happiness, but that of all concerned." The agent should choose in a disinterested way, "as a benevolent spectator" of a situation.[21] Within utilitarianism, there are many divergent opinions about what, exactly, is meant by the good to be achieved. Mill and Bentham originally defined the good in terms of physical pleasure and pain. More broadly, the good could be understood as a benefit that is not strictly physical but is more intangible.

Today, utilitarianism has developed into two specific interpretations: act utilitarianism and rule utilitarianism. Act utilitarianism examines each individual act to weigh what good will be maximized here and now. The key aspect is that the good that is achieved in a particular set of circumstances is not considered to be an absolute good but a relative one. In a similar set of circumstances, it is possible that the good that is chosen now might not be the same one that is chosen in the future. The assessment is applicable only to this situation. One could liken it to a clinical examination of a patient's symptoms. One is guided by the presentation of a problem, and the solution will vary, perhaps only slightly, from situation to situation. The determination of a solution is weighed in every particular circumstance. Rule utilitarianism also looks at the good goal that is sought in a particular act, but it does so on the basis of a rational rule. It asks what kinds of acts maximize happiness over time in many different situations. For example, although it is possible that lying might result in the maximization of good in a particular set of circumstances, as a rule, it does not. So, the rule utilitarian would argue that lying should never be chosen because overall it does not bring about more good. Even if lying brings a good effect in a situation, one should nevertheless not lie. If we return to our analogy of a clinical examination, rule utilitarianism is like formulating clinical pathways for the treatment of certain conditions. Upon testing, we choose those treatment modalities that are shown to be effective. By adhering to the proven principles, we become better at treating similar conditions, or moral situations.

It is easy to see how good people can disagree about ethics. With all of these ethical processes present, we often disagree not only about the correct choices that we should make, but also the very methods by which we should make them. In fact, it is most often the disagreement about methods that drives ethical debate. We tend to focus on the conclusions, but in fact the differences of methodology are deeply imbedded in our culture. All of the theories that we have outlined above are used by different ethicists to justify diverse conclusions. It is essential in any discussion of ethics to identify the method that the person uses to argue his or her case. Otherwise, we can easily become enmeshed in an argument that is insolvable.

Although it is true that disagreements will continue in ethical discussions, we should realize that all is not as confused as many think. On many issues, there is considerable agreement about foundational ideas, and not every solution is widely accepted.

For our primary purpose with regard to understanding Catholic approaches to bioethics, it is important to understand the fundamental beliefs upon which theologians think about these issues. Catholicism offers a unique way of understanding the human person, and when we begin to study bioethics, it is essential to have familiarity with these basic beliefs. Otherwise, we will look at the conclusions and will see little reason to accept the teaching. In fact, it is this unfamiliarity with the whole of Catholic belief that often makes Catholic teaching so foreign to modern ears. As we begin our task of understanding the major issues in modern bioethics, therefore, we will return to these beliefs so that the Catholic perspective on bioethics becomes clearer.

Notes

1.   This is the focus of what is called epistemology, which is the study of how we come to know truth.

2.   Ultimately, scripture is interpreted through a community. Its objectivity is always mediated through their historical experience. So, its interpretation requires an understanding of the relative balance between the objectivity of what it is, and the subjective interpretation of what it means. Within Biblical scholarship there are many different theories of interpretation, and it would be beyond the scope of this book to engage in an extended discussion of these. Simply put, interpretation should strike a balance between treating the text simply as some sort of literal document and understanding its meaning as determined solely by the experiences of the reader.

3.   References to the rule of faith can be found in the writings of Irenaeus, Tertullian, and Athanasius, among others.

4.   For an interesting analysis of these interconnections, see Richard Sennett, *Flesh and Stone: the Body and the City in Western Civilization* (New York: WW Norton, 1994).

5.   The term was first used by the Reform Jewish Rabbi Leo Baeck and has been more recently championed by Dennis Praeger, in his book, *Think a Second Time* (New York: Regan Books, 1996).

6.   I would like to emphasize that these categories are not mutually opposed. With ancient cultures, for example, there are theological and philosophical systems that do discuss the perfection of the individual. Certainly, one need only look to the work of Plato or Aristotle to see this. Conversely, Jewish and Christian thought is not radically individualistic. The community plays a very significant role in the formation and the support of the human person. The point here is one of emphasis.

7.   In my use of the term here, "happiness" is not euphoria, or a feeling. Rather happiness is choosing what is good. This choice often results in a pleasant emotional response, but it does not necessarily have to. I am happy, for example, when I work to get the best grade that I can, even though it is not pleasurable to read abstract ethics books.

8.   See, for example, Thomas Aquinas, *Summa Theologiae*, I-II, Q. 91, Article 2, "Therefore since all things subject to divine providence are ruled and measured by the eternal law...it is evident that all things partake in some way in the eternal law, in so far as, namely, form its being imprinted on them, they derive their respective inclinations to their proper acts and ends."

9.   Aristotle, *Generation of Animals,* (II.iii), ed. T.E. Page (Cambridge, MA: Harvard University Press, 1953), 175.

10. See John Boswell, *The Kindness of Strangers: The Abandonment of Children in Western Europe from Late Antiquity to the Renaissance* (Chicago: University of Chicago Press, 1988) and Darrell Amundsen, "Medicine and the Birth of Defective Children: Approaches of the Ancient World" in *Medicine,*

Society and Faith in the Ancient and Medieval Worlds (Baltimore: Johns Hopkins University Press, 1996) 50-69.

11. Thomas Hobbes, *Leviathan* (Cambridge: Cambridge Univ. Press, 1991), 89.

12. Even after the condemnation, however, proportionalists continued to insist that the characterization made by John Paul II was incorrect. Fr. Richard McCormick, S.J., wrote in *The Tablet* (11/30/93) that "No proportionalist that I know would recognize himself or herself in that description."

13. This is an application of the doctrine of infallibility. Catholics believe that the Church, when speaking about matters of faith or morals, cannot be wrong. This is not to say that every single document that is issued by the Church is correct, but that the truth will be expressed over time.

14. Thomas Aquinas, *Summa Theologiae* II, II, Q 64, A. 6.

15. See Servais Pinkaers, O.P., *The Sources of Christian Ethics*, trans. by Sr. Mary Thomas Noble, O.P., (Washington, DC: The Catholic University of America Press, 1995), for a fuller discussion of the sources and effects of casuistry.

16. John Paul II, *Veritatis Splendor*, Encyclical. (Boston, MA: Daughters of St. Paul, 1993), n. 80.

17. Vatican Council II, "Gaudium et Spes," in *Vatican Council II: The Conciliar and Post-Conciliar Documents*, Vol. I, trans. by Austin Flannery, O.P., (Boston: Daughters of St. Paul, 1975), 916.

18. Vatican II, "Lumen Gentium, in *Vatican Council II: The Conciliar and Post-Conciliar Documents*, Vol. I, trans. By Austin Flannery, O.P., (Boston: Daughters of St. Paul, 1975), 379.

19. Immanuel Kant, *Groundwork of the Metaphysics of Morals*, trans. H.J. Paton (New York: Harper and Row, 1964), *Critique of Practical Reason*, trans. Lewis White Beck (Upper Saddle River, NJ: Prentice Hall, 1992).

20. John Stuart Mill, *Utilitarianism*, (Indianapolis: Bobbs Merrill, 1971), 18.

21. Mill, 24.

Chapter Two:
Professionalism in Health Care

So far, we have sketched out some of the basic ethical theories that we will need to explore in health care ethics. In the remaining chapters, the approach that we will take will be to look at some of the foundational values that underlie ethical conflicts. By looking at the abstract values, we will gain a better understanding of the places where disagreements occur. As mentioned earlier, most controversies are rooted in differences with regard to these fundamental values. Our first topic centers upon the meaning and the application of professionalism. In the common use of the word, professionalism has come to mean any kind of activity in which someone invests his or her time and energy in order to produce something of quality. We speak of professional auto mechanics, professional hairdressers, and even professional dog groomers. Common to all of these uses is the characteristic of doing a job well, of providing something that is distinctive.

It is this thread that binds our contemporary use of the word to its historical meaning. The meaning of work has changed over time, fluctuating with our societal perspectives. As we noted in the previous chapter, our understanding of the ethics of an act is directly related to the absolute value that dominates the society. As our beliefs about what is ultimately of value have shifted, so has our appreciation of work and of professionalism in particular.

The Ancient Greeks and Work

The ancient world was polytheistic. All that existed was understood in relation to the dualism that pervaded the society. Spirit was good, and matter was evil. The emphasis, then, was to perfect the mind and the spirit, and to minimize one's attachment to the world. Everything that exists in the ancient civilization is given meaning through this lens. Social standing, architecture, marriage, religious practice, and the meaning of work are all applications of this basic belief.

It is not surprising, then, that for the Greeks, manual labor was considered to be, as one author states it, "a curse and nothing else."[1] It was the work of slaves and women, who were thought to be less than perfect persons. Work was necessary for the preservation of the society, but it was to be done by those who were not suited for the life of the mind. It was to be avoided whenever possible.

For Aristotle, to not have to work at a trade was a positive social good.[2] One should not seek to do manual labor, or to engage in business: "The citizens must not lead the life of mechanics or tradesmen, for such a life is ignoble and inimical to virtue. Neither must they be herdsmen, since leisure is necessary for the development of virtue and the performance of political duties."[3]

In Aristotle's culture, manual labor was the work of those who were inferior. True, a certain amount of labor was necessary to the functioning of society, but those who did such work were thought to be less human than those who did not. Manual labor was often the work of slaves, who were denied citizenship. To Aristotle, one of the main objections to manual labor was that it denied the people the leisure to develop themselves. Leisure is necessary to develop the life of the mind, and to contemplate truth and beauty. To the ancient world, work was tied to the endless cycle of physical existence. To be locked into this cycle was to exist in the grip of evil itself. Therefore, one must try to break out of the endless repetition through advancing the spirit and the mind. To escape the cycle is to become immortal, to be remembered through the generations. Otherwise, one's very existence becomes enmeshed in the anonymity of biological existence. Only a worthy few are thus able to rise above the others. Hannah Arendt has written that "the distinction between man and animal runs right through the human species itself: only the best (aristoi) who constantly prove themselves to be the best . . . and who prefer immortal fame to mortal things, really are human; the others, content with whatever pleasures nature will yield them, live and die like animals."[4] Greek society reinforced this basic framework in their social structures, justifying the labor by slaves that made such a life possible for those who were inclined to the life of the mind. In Aristotle's opinion, "... the use made of slaves and of tame animals is not very different; for both with their bodies minister to the needs of life .... some men are by nature, free, and others, slaves, and for these latter slavery is both expedient and right."[5]

From this framework comes the Hippocratic ideal of medicine. In the famous oath, the physician is called to practice within a specific set of obligations. First, the physician is bound to the gods, next to his colleagues, then to the patients. Overall, the physician is obligated to use his knowledge of medicine to help the sick. It is significant that physicians are "not to use the knife, even upon sufferers from the stone." That is, they should not perform surgery. Although we will develop a more nuanced interpretation of the Hippocratic model of medicine later in this work, for now it suffices to point out that the physician is one who applies ideas to the treatment of disease. Hippocratic medicine pointed toward a theoretical approach to the practice of medicine that systematized the treatment of disease. The intellect imposes order upon the disorder of illness. They are to apply knowledge and to direct those who do the manual labor.[6] In this civilization, then, to be a professional was to be someone who dealt in ideas, who was virtuous, who was a certain kind of person.

Judeo-Christian Concepts of Work

The Jewish belief in one God brought a different perspective to the value of work. This God was not only good but was also a creator. This was a complete reversal of the polytheistic view of the nature of the world and of work. Creativity was an end in itself, a participation in the action of God. In Genesis, the Jews are commanded by God to cultivate and to care for the Garden of Eden.[7] Later, of course, this commandment takes on another dimension when the difficulty of labor was also identified with the consequences of sin, but the idea of creativity itself was understood to be a direct participation in the goodness of God. Everyone was expected to work. Within this understanding, work was a positive good that enabled the person to become more connected to God and his creation. Of course, this was based upon a different set of absolute beliefs and anthropology. The material world was not something to flee from. Rather, it was an expression of God's goodness.

The Jewish concept of work arose out of their sense of being a covenanted people. God established a permanent relationship with the Jews, and their work was an expression of who they were. Although Genesis does explain the burden of work in light of the sin of Adam and Eve—"By the sweat of your face shall you get bread to eat"—work itself is not identified with negativity.[8] Rather it is seen to be an expression of a covenanted people. In its ancient form, a covenant was initiated in a three-step process. First, the two parties to the covenant exchanged gifts. Then, they made mutual promises, and once this was complete, an ontological change occurred. The last step was understood to be a change in the nature of the two parties. They were irrevocably transformed by the covenant so that they were no longer who they were before but now had a new identity. There was now an intrinsic relationship between who they were and what they did. Once the parties entered into the covenant, they were bound to the process of living it out. If we look to marriage as an example, we can see the steps more fully. In a covenantal marriage, the couple marries each other. Everyone else—a priest, minister, rabbi, or judge—is simply a witness to what the couple does between themselves. First, they give themselves to their prospective spouse and they receive the gift of the other person in turn. Once this occurs, they exchange marriage vows. On the basis of these two acts, the couple is thus transformed from two individuals into one married couple. As married persons, all that they do ought to be an expression of this primary relationship. They act out of this identity so that whatever they do is an expression of their covenantal gift and promises. A covenant differs from another kind of relationship, a contract. Where a covenant is expected to be permanent, a contract is assumed to be a temporary agreement. The contract explicitly lists the conditions of the relationship. Each party agrees to certain obligations and, on the basis of that obligation, other rights become operative. For instance, a loan is a contract. When we sign loan papers, we enter into an agreement that binds us to fulfill certain conditions. As a borrower, we agree to pay on time and to keep whatever property we offer as collateral in good condition. The lender agrees to give the money and to treat us fairly during the life of the contract. Both parties expect the agreement to end at a particular point in time.

When we enter into a contract, we are not identified with the other party. We are not regularly known to other people as a "student loan borrower." The contract does not constitute a primary identity of who we are.

By contrast, in a covenant, the parties do not even know all that they bind themselves to. They do not agree on a specific list of obligations. Instead, they agree to a responsibility of caring for the other party to the covenant, not an exhaustive list of tasks that must be fulfilled. It is probably fair to say that most people who marry do not fully understand the implications of what they have vowed when they marry. There is a benefit, however. Covenants enable us to commit ourselves to a future goal of being a certain kind of person.

In marriage, for example, we choose a goal that will take years to accomplish. As newlyweds, most couples are unaware of the struggles of maintaining a loving marriage over time. They are caught up in the emotions of falling in love. While this provides an initial boost that will get the couple through hard times, it is not what creates the intimacy of later years. For many couples, they continue on through rough times simply because they have committed themselves to each other, not because here and now it feels good. The covenant provides a way of being married that balances our individual desires with a common goal.

Covenants, then, establish an identity. The person who enters into a covenant is committing himself or herself to being someone. They identify themselves with this relationship so that, over time, they realize a goal. All that they do is reflective of this relationship. In a tangible way, the wedding ring symbolizes this totality of self-giving. It is an outward sign of the promises. Practically, it identifies those who are married, and it attests to the socially lived part of the covenant. Our vows are not just something that we have done privately. They are a public part of us, an aspect that identifies who we are to others.

We enter into covenants in many different aspects of our lives. In our personal, religious, and working relationships, we have the possibility of being covenantal. Obviously, to maintain these relationships takes a great deal of effort. We become who we want to be by establishing these permanent identities. If we continually enter into only contractual relationships, we will, over time, live a superficial life.

Health care professionals have tended to understand themselves more in covenantal than contractual terms. In the Hippocratic Oath, for example, there is not an exhaustive list of "do this" and "don't do that." The oath points toward a way of practicing medicine. It establishes relationships.

As Christianity emerged from Judaism, it absorbed both Greek and Jewish concepts of work into its ethics. Christianity developed first among the urban poor in the Roman Empire. The apostles were fishermen and tent makers. Jesus was himself a carpenter. The earliest Christians, then, came precisely from those classes in the Roman Empire who were thought to be less important than those at the top. The Judeo-Christian message of the sanctity of all life, the blessedness of a creation that was intended by God, found its soil in these groups. As Christianity developed, this Jewish emphasis spread throughout Western civilization, gradually replacing the ancient dualism with its pessimistic view of material creation.

By the late fourth century, Christianity had become the dominant cultural force in Western civilization. The Roman Empire split into two parts, the Eastern and the Western Empires, and gradually diminished in importance. As a political and social force, it ceased to dominate. Slowly, other cultures seeped into the formerly conquered lands. The "Barbarian Invasions" signaled the rise of local cultures that eroded the influence of the Roman Empire. While the invasions did have some militaristic characteristics associated with them, their effects were more cultural in their influence.

As the Roman Empire faded, Christianity began its ascent. Slowly, over many centuries, Christianity gained in influence, transforming the political and social structures of the Roman Empire and integrating them with the local cultures, while modifying them toward its own purposes. The local cultures were assimilated through extensive missionary work, like that of St. Patrick in Ireland in the seventh century, and through the intellectual contributions of the Apostolic Fathers and the early theologians like Augustine. The new, emerging culture of Christendom was thus a blending of the Roman and local cultures with the theology of Christianity.

One of the effects of this shift was that the Jewish appreciation for work began to be the norm. Christians built upon this tradition and elevated work as a worthy activity, so long as one did not become too immersed in the pursuit of wealth. Work was to be done out of a sense of obligation to one's neighbor, so that work was not an activity that was either completely individual nor something that only found its meaning in social contribution.

Of course, this transition was slow. Early Christianity was profoundly affected by the culture that surrounded it. Many early theologians simply equated the materialist pessimism of the dualists with the doctrine of Original Sin. Salvation was seen for some as a separation from the world.[9] Over the Middle Ages, the appreciation of the value of work varied. One author has argued that it was not until the sixteenth and seventeenth centuries that the effects of dualism were effectively overthrown.[10]

This vision of the nexus of individual achievement and community life found both its fullest expression and its rejection in the development of monastic communities. During the Middle Ages, the archetype for all of these communities was the Benedictines. The Benedictines are typical of what is called cenobitic monasticism, where the members of the community form a community life together. Arising out of the ascetic spirituality of the Desert Fathers, particularly Antony of Egypt, these groups tried to develop a common spiritual life. Other types of communities were also formed at the time, where individual hermits pursued their own spiritual life in close proximity to others but without the communal element. One good example of this latter emphasis is Simon Stylites, who is noted for spending his life on top of a pillar, or style. During the Middle Ages, the Benedictines grew in terms of their numbers and influence. By the time of the Renaissance, the Benedictines were arguably one of the richest land-holders in Europe.

The Benedictines were founded by Benedict of Nursia, who organized community life by a set of conditions that were collectively known as the "Rule." In Benedictine life, work was seen as integral to the pursuit of spiritual goods. Part of this Rule focused upon the proper perspective on work. Manual labor was essential to the proper functioning of the monastic community. All were to integrate labor with their spiritual lives, in a strictly defined schedule of work and prayer.

The schedule remained the same in the thousands of Benedictine monasteries throughout Europe. All of the monks awoke at the same time each day. They prayed, ate, and worked together. Tasks were systematized. The monks varied the work that each did so that anyone could handle a task. Work was thus for the monks not something that was merely a necessity, but an integral part of their spiritual lives.

Throughout the Middle Ages, this integrated life became a powerful ideal that influenced the development of many new religious orders. Even though the vision of monastic life that Benedict proposed was not always followed, it points to the emphasis in Christian theology of work as a part of one's spiritual life. In fact, even within Benedictine monasteries, the practice of work fell short of Benedict's vision. By the high Middle Ages, many monasteries fell back into ancient divisions of work and spirituality, with "choir monks" adopting the spiritual activities of the order, while worker monks did the manual labor. Various reforms of monastic life, like the Cistercians, attempted to recall this synthesis of spirituality and work.

It was in this integration of work and spirituality that "professionalism" as we know it emerged. Although it is true that a concept of professionalism may be found in the emergence of certain ancient traditions like the Hippocratic ideal in medicine, it was in this joining of work and spirituality that the concept of professionalism truly took root. In fact, one might say that the first "professionals" were really the monks, who took vows to God and the community.

The four traditional professions, medicine, law, priesthood, and the military, were all related to this monastic synthesis of spirituality and work. Work was seen as a manifestation of one's spiritual life. The goal was an integrated prayer to God, a joining of labor and prayer so that what one did was a direct expression of whom one was. The monks made a profession of vows that bound them to the community. As an organized, unified whole, the community lived a life that gave glory to God. Within this community, then, one's individual work was given meaning and purpose. Although on one level work is always a solitary activity because it is the individual who does the labor, on another level, it is both because of and for the community that the work is performed.

Both the individual and the social dimensions of work come together in the monastic concept of professionalism. In the Middle Ages, the emphasis was mostly on the community aspect of professionalism. This is not surprising since, in general, the social obligations of the person were seen as more important than "individual fulfillment." Medieval society was dominated by this communal identity.

Unfortunately, there was a growing emphasis in monastic communities on a division between a life of work that was oriented around spiritual activities and one that oriented toward physical labor. The dualism of the Greek ideal gradually seeped into some communities, and they began to emphasize more intellectual pursuits as the purpose of the order.

Gradually, throughout the sixteenth and seventeenth centuries, a new emphasis on individualism began to emerge. Today, we speak in terms of a career, or an individual pursuit of happiness in our work. We try to fit our personalities to the labor that we choose. In many ways, this is good. We recognize that work should relate to the individual person. We want to express who and what we are in our labor.

Yet, there is also a danger here. Too often, we lose sight of the communal aspect of work. We see work only as an individual activity. As a society, we seem to need to acquire wealth, no matter the consequences. In *Laborem Excercens*, John Paul II addresses this concern, noting that we focus too often on the accumulation of material goods, without considering its effect on others.[11] Particularly within American society, our riches often blind us to the needs of others. We become too comfortable in our insulated communities and fail to see the needs of others around the world, or even our own little corner.

In the sixteenth and seventeenth centuries, the concept of work changed fundamentally both with the shift in ideas toward reason and the rise of the Protestant Churches. The Reformation brought a new emphasis to the appreciation of work. John Calvin and Martin Luther both emphasized the nature of work as being fundamentally good. They attempted to retrieve the concept of work that was found in the early monastic communities.

Work for Luther and for Calvin was seen as a way to live out one's spirituality. Like the early monks, the Protestant reformers felt that work was a simple way in which a person could find a motivation to do what was right—to support themselves and to contribute to the community. It is for this reason that we often refer to this emphasis of work as the "Protestant work ethic."

Key to understanding the Protestant approach to work was that they believed that the Church had lost the sense of what was proper to its mission. By the sixteenth century, it was impossible to ignore the many aspects of church life that were in need of renewal. In the hundred years prior to Martin Luther's "protest," the Church had struggled with the competing claims of up to four different "popes" at the same time! Power struggles between secular and papal authority were part of this environment, and Luther's solution to the problems that he saw were that the secular and religious authorities should return to their proper roles. He argued that there were two "Kingdoms," the Earthly, or political, and the Heavenly, or spiritual.[12] Each had a sphere of influence that was separate from the other.

The Earthly Kingdom is the realm of creation, where the natural order of the world is lived. Civic life, economics, and law are practiced there. The spiritual life is lived in the Heavenly Kingdom, through faith. According to Luther, Christians lived in both places at once. It was necessary, however, to realize the division so that each could properly reach its perfection. The accumulation of wealth and property was proper to the Earthly Kingdom. One of the principal criticisms that Luther made was that the Church had improperly acted in the political arena and that it should relinquish its role in the making of wealth.

Luther particularly emphasized that salvation was achieved through faith and not through good works. So, in emphasizing work as a secular activity, Luther sought to separate it from its insular role in the Church. Ultimately, this led to the development of modern capitalism. Calvin took the emphasis a bit further and said that everybody must work and that the work was considered to be reflective of one's state in life. Calvin proposed a unique paradox: one should deny the riches of the world because they could not guarantee salvation; yet, it was a duty to glorify God, and one of the best ways of doing this was to be a success at one's chosen work. So, work was not what got you into heaven, but it was certainly reflective of the spiritual life.

Although Catholicism still emphasized an integrated concept of work, Protestantism and the Enlightenment culture gradually eclipsed its influence. Eventually, Western culture shifted toward an individualism because of the transformation from a communally oriented society that was founded in the monasteries to one in which the individual was seeking his or her own salvation in relationship to a community, but not solely through it. There is much discussion about the cause of this shift. One may look to various latent trends in medieval thought. Or, we might credit the Guttenberg printing press as the catalyst that propelled Western culture toward this individualism.

As we move toward what we would recognize as modern society in the end of the sixteenth and the beginning of the seventeenth centuries, professionalism then begins to take on an individual quality that it did not have in the monastery life. It tended toward more of a contractual model than a covenantal one. In the former framework, professionals were those who sought what was good for its own sake, or at least the common good. While remnants of this language remained, more and more the pursuit of work became separated from any sort of social ideal.

Gradually in the eighteenth century, with the rise of industrialism, we got other kinds of philosophies that made explicit this emphasis upon work as an individual pursuit. For example, we can look to the influence of Social Darwinism in the late nineteenth century. Herbert Spencer proposed a harsh "survival of the fittest" philosophy to human society.[13] Where Charles Darwin had refused to apply his work in the *Origin of the Species* to human society, Spencer came in. Many of the industrialists of the age quickly incorporated Spencer's view of the world as an explanation for their accumulation of wealth.

Andrew Carnegie, for example, was very much a Social Darwinist, and he preached the continual improvement of the society in order that the species could survive.[14] Those who were economically well off were really the top of the evolutionary chain. Those at the bottom were meant, by nature, to die off.

One of the most vivid examples of the influence of this Spencerian view in the nineteenth century concerned the potato famine in Ireland from 1845 to 1850. When the potato crop, which was the main staple for the Irish people, failed, the English Government had been occupying Ireland for several hundred years. Many of the most fertile fields were used to grow grain, which was exported back to England. Debates ensued in Parliament as to whether or not the grain should be given to the starving Irish or should continue to be exported. Some members of Parliament argued that it was better for the Irish people if those who could not provide for themselves actually died off.[15] Many did.

In the twentieth century, we saw many aspects of this changing view of the nature of work. The Industrial Revolution transformed the common experience of work from an individual enterprise to corporate systems. In health care, this has resulted in the consolidation of hospitals and their reorganization into national health care systems. Nurses, who were once primarily identified by their membership in religious orders, are now seen more often simply as interchangeable employees of a health care business. Physicians are more dissatisfied than ever with their profession because they have less and less control over the practice of medicine. More and more, insurance dictates the scope of medical practice.

At the end of the nineteenth into the beginning of the twentieth century, American health care was composed of small community based or religiously sponsored hospitals. Within the past one hundred years, it has grown rapidly into the sophisticated modern facilities that we have today. The transition has been rapid, and the pace of development has often outpaced our ability to make sense of it. Individual hospitals have struggled financially, culturally, and practically to keep up with this transformation.

One of the best ways to understand this changing environment is to look more closely at nursing, which has had many different forms throughout its existence. What does it mean to be a professional nurse today? There are many ways to enter the profession: diploma schools, associate degree programs, and baccalaureate programs. In practice, there are a wide range of activities that are defined as "nursing." Licensed practical nurses, or LPNs, are proficient on a small range of clinical skills. Nurse practitioners and nurse anesthetists are at the other end of the range.

Defining professionalism is something that is very difficult in a world that is mostly motivated by economic efficiency. The traditional historical roots of professionalism lay waiting within the language of nursing. Yet, in practice, it is difficult to return to this sense of the cohesion between vocation, community, and individual work. There is a practical chasm between the ideals of nursing and the everyday settings in which nurses practice. As the economic demands of health care assume a privileged position, it is not a coincidence that there is a shifting of value systems in nursing.

Where once nurses were motivated by a code of abstract values, now many enter the profession not out of a sense of vocation but because they are attracted to the salary. Unfortunately, in a system that reinforces economic rather than vocational goals, it is becoming harder and harder to attract potential nursing students. The reality of the job does not compensate for the money that is to be made. There has been a change in nursing, which now tends to emphasize patient management instead of care and technological proficiency with machines rather than interpersonal skills. Obviously, this is not an either-or distinction. Both are needed, but it is clear that less patient interaction is becoming the norm in clinical practice.

Physicians also struggle with this. With insurance reimbursements dropping and costs rising, they are forced to find ways to trim costs and raise revenues. One of the only ways in which this can be accomplished is to increase the number of patient visits. Obviously, the only way to do this is to decrease the amount of time for each visit, limit time, or use auxiliary staff to routinize some of the care. The physicians' vocation of healing the sick is made more difficult by the modern economically driven context of medical practice. In short, professionalism is now lived as a contract, while it continues to use the language of covenant.

Issues in Professionalism

Several issues arise in the discussion of professional ethics for health care. We will approach these issues in terms of particular types of relationships. Health care professionals have primary relationships with patients, fellow professionals (both within and outside their own particular profession), and institutions. We will take each of these in turn.

The relationship between professional and patient is dependent. Especially in critical care settings, the patient is a person who is incapacitated and is often unable to fully articulate his or her own decisions. He or she may require added support in order to make choices about medical care or to be committed to the healing process. This means that the relationship is not fully equal in terms of the power.

Professionals, because of their education and experience, are often placed in a superior position by patients and their families. While one should rightly argue that patients are equal partners in health care decision-making, the actuality of day-to-day clinical practice is that patients are often not able to fully understand or to enact their choices.

So, while ideally patients should participate in their own treatment decisions, it is clear that often times they are unable to do so without additional assistance. The goal of the professional-patient relationship ought to be to restore the patients to health and to make them equal partners in their own health care.

When imbalances of power exist, they require additional diligence to ensure that the ultimate goal of equal participation is achieved.

It is precisely in the situation where an imbalance of power exists that ethical dilemmas arise. One of the most significant is truth-telling. How should one resolve the conflict of interest when a critically ill patient demands to know information that can adversely affect his or her care? The classic example is of the mother who has been transported to the emergency department of the local hospital after an automobile accident in which her child has died. How should the professional respond to her pleas to know the status of her child's condition? Is it moral to withhold information? Should she be told? When?

If the patient's autonomy were the most important value, then it would seem that whatever information the mother asks should be given. Her right to know should be absolute. How do we resolve this dilemma?

To begin, we have to recognize once again that the mother's request is a good one. Yet, just because it is asked of us does not mean that we must follow through on it. The nurse also has an obligation to care for the patient, and because communication involves both the nurse and the mother, we must consider the nurse's obligation to the patient as much as the mother's asking of the information.

Truth-telling, or communication, is not simply a one-way act. It is reciprocal. Here we come to a fine distinction, the difference between being obligated to tell the truth and the means by which one does it. Again, we go back to the nature of the moral act. Even though there is a good object here, we must also consider the intention and the circumstances. How something is said is as important as what is done and why it is done. So we might distinguish between two different kinds of acts: a lie, which seeks an object that is not true, and an act in which all information is not given because to do so would distort the truth of the situation.

One must be careful about expressing the truth in ways that are not understood by the person to whom one is talking. For example, when we speak to children, we do not do so in ways that are overly complicated or complex. We use words and expressions that relate to their experience so that they can understand reality. Some people make the mistake that children do not want the truth, or they will make up a truth that seems to fit the child's imagination. This is distortion and a kind of lie. Although done with the best of intentions, it is not a moral act. Instead, we should try to communicate to children on a level they can understand. It is the same thing with the mother in this regrettable situation.

She asks for the truth, and the professional is obligated to give it to her, yet it must be given in ways that are both caring and accurate. Truth-telling is not truth-telling if it is destructive to the person. Telling the truth does not mean that the information should cause harm to the person. There is a special obligation to try to communicate what is true in a way that will be understood best. In the situation that we outlined, there is a dependent relationship between the mother and the professional. One must be careful not to take advantage of this situation, but we also recognize that there is a special care that must be given to the patient in this special set of circumstances.

So, while we recognize the right of the mother to knowledge and to truth about what has happened to her child, we must make certain that whatever information is conveyed is not harmful to her health. Ideally, the nurse should give enough information to satisfy the mother without causing her harm. The goal ought to be to prepare her for the reality of what has occurred at the appropriate time and place.

On a practical level, this means that information, or "the facts," are not, by themselves, the truth. Knowledge is contextual as well as objective. We must also look at the one who does the communicating. Here it is essential that the nurse be aware of the reality of the information and its effects on the mother. Only one who truly knows the truth can therefore communicate it. The choice of words and the information selected are a matter of prudence. It is not simply the words that are used but the total act of the person who gives that truth to the other person.

In that sense, truth-telling is a personal act. It is an act that witnesses to the living presence of truth in the person who tells it. It also involves a reception of the truth in the person who hears it. Both giver and receiver are conveying who they are in the act.

Even factual information can become a lie if the wrong person speaks it. That is, one can say something that is objectively true yet it can be a lie if the intention is to miscommunicate. We must be careful that, in allowing a withholding of the truth in a specific set of circumstances, we do not at the same time promote a continued dependency in other situations where no such need exists. The aim of such a situation should be to try to regain an equal footing between the patient and the health care provider.

Truth-telling provides a structure by which we can understand the professional-patient relationship. While we ought to aim at encouraging the full participation of patients in caring for themselves, it is also true that an imbalance in knowledge and ability will often create a situation where the professional must assume a greater part in the relationship. The professional will often possess more power than the patient in understanding and being able to enact a decision about care. With this power comes increased responsibility. Although it is true that this has sometimes resulted in abuses in patient decision-making, that does not invalidate the responsibility. The fact that some abuse their responsibility is not a reason to abdicate it completely.

A further subject, which is related to the general obligation to tell the truth, is the different cultural practices surrounding truth-telling. In many non-Western cultures, information is often withheld from patients, especially if they have a chronic or life-threatening condition. In Japan, for example, patients are routinely not told all of the facts surrounding their condition.[16]

However, this does not mean that the physicians do not tell the truth. Rather, it is the cultural practice that they communicate with the family members who are given the responsibility of caring for their spouse or parents. The families and the physicians serve as the medical gatekeepers for the sick. Partly, this practice may be attributed to a common belief that full disclosure will sap the patient of his or her energy to fight the disease or condition. If the patient does not know the prognosis, or the extent of the disease, he or she will not be distracted from getting better because of worry about his or her condition.

To those of us who are accustomed to making our own choices, this sounds very strange. We want to be in control of our own decisions and to know the options for treatment. While remaining aware that our cultural tendency is to emphasize our individuality and that there is a good sense of social care that is implicit in the practice, it seems that it would be better to give to each person the ability to make his or her own choices. While it is important that we support one another, this does not allow either family members or health care professionals to usurp individual decision-making without a clearly compelling reason. While we are sometimes extreme with regard to individual decision-making, this practice reflects the opposite tendency.

Until relatively recently, there has been a tendency for physicians to "close ranks" and to not divulge details to those outside of the profession. In the original Hippocratic corpus of work, physicians were cautioned to not let patients know all about the medical procedures that were to be performed. Information was to be given sparingly so that the physician could do what was best for the patient. Just as in the case of far Eastern cultures, the withholding of information was justified on the basis of seeking what was best for the patient.

At other times, withholding information has been done in the name of a greater social good. In the twentieth century, the U.S. Public Health Service at the Tuskegee Institute in Alabama conducted controversial experiments from 1932 to 1972 to analyze the progression of syphilis. Patients were told that they were being treated for "bad blood," and they received minimal treatments to keep the appearance that they were being helped. Eventually, twenty-eight men died of the disease, another one hundred died of complications from the disease, forty of their wives became infected, and forty of their children were born with syphilis.[17] Other clinical trials of oral contraceptives, in which patients were given placebos instead of effective contraceptives, were also performed without fully informing patients of the risks that they faced in participating.[18]

Another issue that is related to truth-telling in the professional-patient relationship is the treatment of children. Ordinarily, the professional obligation would be that the patient, even if he or she were a child, should be involved in the decision about his or her care. Obviously, given the complex nature of treatment decisions, it is not possible to give complete autonomy to children. However, there should be an effort to not simply explain what is being done but also to allow some choice within the process, when that can be done. As the child gets older, the decisions should defer toward his or her desires, so long as the professional is able to assess the ability of the child to make rational decisions.

For chronically ill children, this sense of control is very important. Medicine, while it aims at the ultimate benefit of enabling each person to achieve his or her own highest degree of health, can sometimes be dehumanizing. A simple example might be found in childhood immunizations. While as adults we recognize the benefits of giving the immunization, we must also recognize that the lack of control in the situation can be traumatic for the child. At times, of course, it might be necessary to subject a child to a treatment or a test for his or her greater good. However, the more that this is done, the more the child becomes someone who is acted upon, rather than someone who will assist the professional in the common goal of bringing the child to the greatest degree of health possible. As the child develops, it is important to shift the responsibility for decision-making to him or her so that he or she will ultimately be empowered to understand and to enact the kind of decisions that will keep him/her healthy.

In acting for the benefit of the child, health care professionals will have to have a strong sense of their own role in assisting patients in achieving their own health. They are obligated to care for their patients and to act for them, in conjunction with parents or guardians. In certain limited circumstances, this advocacy role may sometimes be in conflict with a parent or guardian. In exceptional circumstances, where the failure to act will result in serious adverse health conditions or even death, the professional may have to override the choices of the parent. In the few circumstances in which courts have ordered a decision that is in conflict with the parent or guardian, the burden of proof has been on the professional to establish extreme circumstances. Even then, the rulings have been somewhat inconsistent.

For example, in cases where the choices of Christian Scientist or Jehovah Witness parents are challenged, the courts have not always sided with the professional. In general, however, the more that a life is in danger, the more likely the court will be to compel cooperation with the treatment.

The health care professional also has a responsibility to one's fellow professionals. In the past, this relationship has been so important that it has sometimes been seen as the professional's primary responsibility, even ahead of patient care. In the Hippocratic Oath, for example, the obligations to one's teachers and fellow physicians come before the duties to patients.

As a profession, medicine is supposed to be self-regulating. Ideally, this means that physicians have an obligation to help one another to develop both the art and the science of medicine. Medicine is practiced both as a personal and as a technical act. The tekne, or technique of medicine, is to become as proficient as possible in the clinical skills of medicine. Obviously, a physician who has not mastered these skills is unable to affect any change in the physical well-being of the patient. At the same time, medicine is also *arete*—an art. The physicians live what they aim to share with their patients. The profession is the community in which these two aspects of medicine are practiced.

Professionalism has often devolved into the practice of simply minimizing the harm done rather than enabling the professional to achieve the highest degree of their own personal practice. Obviously, there are always everyday demands that will distract us from always being reflective about professional practice. While acknowledging that the pace of our contemporary life diverts us from being fully conscious about the purpose of our work, one must also realize that today we tend to emphasize the individuality of the physician rather than the obligations that one has toward the profession.

Professional obligations are often framed in terms of technical competence, rather than personal holiness. Traditionally, the two were inextricably linked. The mastery of the skill was accompanied by a mastery of self. Even today, although we certainly prize the ability to know the content of medicine, patients express a preference for physicians who will listen to them and will respond to them as persons and not just as subjects who are acted upon.

To reflect upon professionalism, then, means that we explore the myriad relationships that impact practice. Health care professionals act out of a covenantal relation with God, their fellow professionals, and their patients. This understanding rejects a pure contractualism of practice. The professional never acts only as an individual.

Another ethical dilemma arises when we consider this added dimension of practice. Just as we act in relation to others, so also the effects of our actions move beyond a simple professional-patient relationship. It may be that in caring for patients, the professional is sometimes involved in other kinds of actions that either enable or actively promote evil.

One must carefully consider the relationship between individual actions and how they promote social structures. This is especially true in modern health care where work in a complex organization can contribute to other actions that are immoral. For example, Catholic health care systems have had to carefully consider the kinds of relationships that they will have with other health care providers who are not Catholic. Obviously, there are times in which an organization will need to work with others who might not agree with Catholic moral teaching on certain medical issues. One obvious area concerns various applications of reproductive and beginning-of-life issues like assisted reproduction and abortion.

In these instances, both the individual professional as well as more complex health care organizations need to give careful thought about the effects of their work so that their participation with other professionals or organizations who would disagree with Catholic moral teaching does not enable the kinds of actions that are objectively immoral. In general, the more direct the participation, the greater likelihood there is that the action should not be performed.

Let us consider two different situations. First, let us think about a nurse who works on a medical/surgical floor at a secular hospital that performs abortions. She refuses to assist with the procedure and has made this known to her employer. In the course of her shift, however, she is sometimes asked to provide post-operative care for patients who have had abortions. On average, she has two to three patients a month for whom she is responsible. Is this moral? Does she act immorally by treating these patients? Is any cooperation in caring for these patients a violation of her ethics?

In order to answer these questions, we must look at how directly the nurse's caring for a patient, an act that in and of itself is certainly within the moral scope of her practice, contributes to the act of procuring an abortion. One immediately sees that there is some distance between the act of performing the abortion and the one aspect of this nurse's responsibility to care for patients who have had surgery. Not every patient that she cares for is a patient who has had an abortion. In fact, most have had surgeries other than the one to which the nurse morally objects.

Catholic moral theology has distinguished between different levels of cooperation. These distinctions are helpful for analyzing the degree to which one participates in an immoral act. The first category of cooperation is called formal cooperation. This describes the case where the moral agent chooses the same act as another person who commits a wrong act. The person agrees with the object, or the purpose of the act. In this case, the person is indistinguishable from another person who actually performs the act. That person wills it with the other person. Morally, it is equivalent to that person doing the act himself. If, for example, one would wish some harm to come to another person and urges someone else to do it, he formally cooperates with the act. Even though the person does not perform the act himself, he desires the same purpose as the person who actually performs it.

Material cooperation, or assistance with attaining some good that coincides with the performance of an evil act, requires that the act not be a direct cause of the evil act. The more directly one wills the object or intention of an act, or one provides the resources necessary for another person to accomplish an evil act, the more one is actually moving toward formal cooperation. A distinction is made between immediate and mediate material cooperation.

Immediate material cooperation means that the person directly cooperates in the performance of an evil act. This term describes the person who may say that he objects to the evil act but who also provides the way in which the act is performed. If, for example, one person says that he disapproves of someone's desire to kill another person, but then he offers his gun, he would be guilty of immediate material cooperation.

Mediate material cooperation involves a person who indirectly provides the opportunity for another person to commit an evil action. That person does not will the evil and would avoid it if he could. If a man, for example, works for a large company that employs many people, it is possible that another division of that business might be engaged in evil actions with which he might disapprove. An employee of a company that manufactures a drug that is used for abortions might fall into this category. Although he does not agree with the production of the drug, he is employed by the same company who makes it. He is not involved in the direct manufacture or distribution of the drug, but he is employed by the company who does. One can see that at some level, his work is contributing to the success of this company. Yet, since his work is not directly related to the immoral act, he may act morally by performing a different job that is separated from the evil.

One must be careful, however, in assessing the degree to which one's work makes possible the immoral act. One may, and sometimes must, mediately co-operate when one's cooperation prevents a greater evil from occurring. There is a fine line here between the person who claims to disagree with the immorality of the act but who nevertheless provides the means by which another person is able to perform the act and one who disagrees with the evil and would prevent it if he could but who provides a service that may tangentially create the conditions under which the evil is accomplished. The latter is only permissible if there is no alternative way of acting, and if the person, in acting, helps to mitigate some additional harm.

Another facet to be taken into account is what is called scandal. One should not give the impression to others that one is allowing an immoral act to occur, or that one is performing the act. This would serve to legitimize the immoral action, especially if others perceive that the person in question is someone who ordinarily acts in an exemplary way.

In the case that we began with above, the medical/surgical nurse would have to judge how her care of patients after an abortion contributes to the ability of others to perform the act in the first place. In the situation described, the nurse would not be immediately related to the act, since the care of these patients is not a significant part of her job. As the frequency of such care continues, there would have to be a judgment on the part of the nurse as to how much of her work does allow such an act to occur.

The nurse would also have to assess how much her cooperation contributes to the perception that she agrees with abortions. She should be wary of giving the impression to others that she condones such acts.

If we extend this case just slightly, we can see that our assessment would be very different for a nurse who assists in the operating room. Even if the abortions were only sporadic, her assistance would be directly necessary for the act to be performed. She provides immediate material cooperation, if not formal cooperation.

These distinctions help us to discern more carefully the covenantal obligations of the health care professional. The distinctions are precise, yet they are reflections of a basic attitude about the relationship between the professional and the patient. Ultimately, the professional acts in such a way that his or her practice is reflective of a way of life. He or she cares for patients and helps them to understand the reality that both the professional and the patient share. It is not knowledge that seeks to place either party in a position of advantage. Obviously, with a disparity of knowledge, the professional is likely to have a greater influence in the outcome of the decision, but this ability must be tempered with a sense of humility and care.

The recent emphasis on autonomy in health care was a reasonable response to the tendency of some professionals to abuse their position. As a correction, it accomplished its purpose. The difficulty lies in the assumption that just because patients also must exercise choice, their choice becomes moral simply by their choice. Health care, ultimately, reflects a relationship between the professional and the patient. There is an implicit obligation of care that takes place. While it does not condone an absolute paternalism where patients have no power to make their own choices, it does mean that the professionals are in a position of more authority.

In and of itself, a disparity of power is not wrong. The question is how this is used. Ultimately, the professional and the patient are bound in a kind of mutual subjection. Patients place themselves under the care of physicians, nurses, or other health care professionals in order to become healthy or to maintain their health. Alternatively, the professionals choose to accept a life of service that often limits their time and ability to seek their own good. The professionals must also give way in medical decision-making to the ultimate will of the patients, which is difficult when one can see the consequences of some heath care decisions.

By virtue of his or her position, the professional is also able to experience the sanctity of life in a way that is sometimes difficult to express for those who do not have the same experience. Caring for the bruised, damaged, and weakened body of another human person opens the door to a greater understanding of God's gift of life. Death and birth are not an abstract idea but are a reality that takes place with this person or that person. Addiction and accidents all have a face and a place. In caring for a patient, there is a unique opportunity to experience the sanctity of life that encompasses every human person.

Notes

1. Adriano Tilgher, *Work: What It Has Meant to Men through the Ages* (New York: Arno Press, 1977), 3.

2. Aristotle, *Politics*, I, viii, 9. Ed. By Ernst Barker, (Oxford: Oxford Univ. Press, 1958) 20-21.

3. Aristotle, *Politics*, in *Basic Works of Aristotle*, ed. Richard McKeon (New York: Random House, 1941), 1141.

4. Hannah Arendt, *The Human Condition* (Chicago: Univ. of Chicago Press, 1958), 19.

5. Aristotle, Politics in *The Works of Aristotle*, ed. By W.D. Ross (Oxford: Clarendon, 1952) 1254 a-b.

6. Hippocrates, "Selections from the Hippocratic Corpus," trans. W.H.S. Jones, The Loeb Classical Library (Cambridge: Harvard University Press, 1923) Vol. 1, in Stanley Joel Reiser et al., *Ethics in Medicine: Historical Perspectives and Contemporary Concerns* (Cambridge, MA: MIT Press, 1977), 5–9. Until relatively recently, physicians did not perform surgery, or many other treatments. Their expertise was in the knowledge of medicine, which others then used. The traditional red, blue, and white barber pole was an advertisement for bloodletting and poultice applications.

7. Genesis 2:15.

8. Genesis 3:19.

9. See Augustine, for example. In *De Trinitate* (I, 8), he defines the goal of our lives to be the contemplation of God. Also, Thomas Aquinas, *Summa Theologiae*, II, 2, Q. 180, art. 4.

10. Lee Hardy, *The Fabric of the World* (Grand Rapids, MI: 1990), 16. Hardy's book is an excellent analysis of the historical transitions in our concepts of work. He analyzes these changes from the perspective of Reformed Christian theology to show how the developments of this tradition are essential for developing a contemporary Christian ethic of vocation.

11. John Paul II, *Laborem Exercens* (14 September 1981) 13-14 (Boston: St. Paul, 1993).

12. As many scholars have pointed out, Luther's Two Kingdoms is reflective of Augustine in *The City of God*.

13. See Herbert Spencer, *Social Statics* (London: Chapman, 1851) and *A System of Synthetic Philosophy*, 9 vols. (London: Williams and Norgate, 1870–1884).

14. Andrew Carnegie, "The Gospel of Wealth," *North American Review* 148, no. 391 (June 1889): 653–662.

15. R. Dudley Edwards and Desmond Williams, *The Great Famine* (Dublin: Browne and Nolan, 1956), 177.

16. See R. Kimura, "Death, Dying and Advanced Directives in Japan: Sociocultural and Legal Points of View," in *Advance Directives and Surrogate Decisionmaking in Health Care: United States, Germany and Japan*, ed. H.M. Sass,

R.M. Veatch, and R. Kimura (Baltimore, MD: Johns Hopkins University Press, 1998) 187–208.

17. James Jones, *Bad Blood: The Tuskegee Syphilis Experiments* (New York: Free Press, 1993).

18. The first birth control pill in the United States, Enovid, was first tested in clinical trials in Puerto Rico, Haiti and Mexico. In the study in Puerto Rico, two women died of heart attacks, which was probably related to the high levels of hormones in the study drug. With the widespread acceptance of the Pill, blood clots were identified as one of the most significant side effects.

Chapter Three:
The Sanctity of Life

One of the distinguishing characteristics of Christianity has been its understanding of the created world. As has been developed in earlier chapters, the monotheistic beliefs of Judaism and Christianity were marked departures from the epistemology of the ancient world. The ancient civilizations of the Western world thought of the physical world as something from which to flee.

Early on, Christians adopted a radical position in relation to Roman culture. In one early Christian letter, they were contrasted with the Romans in this way:

> . . . there is something extraordinary about their lives. They live in their own countries as though they were only passing through. They play their full role as citizens, but labor under all the disabilities of aliens. Any country can be their homeland, but for them their homeland, wherever it may be, is a foreign country. Like others, they marry and have children, but they do not expose them. They share their meals, but not their wives. They live in the flesh, but are not governed by the desires of the flesh. They pass their days on earth, but they are citizens of heaven.[1]

The Romans delighted in gladiatorial games in which slaves and prisoners were used as playthings for the amusement of the crowds. In the phrasing of the Roman poet Juvenal, the Roman emperors used "bread and circuses" to keep the population amused. They were also accepting of practices in which unwanted infants, usually girls, were abandoned. In contrast, the Christians proposed an ethic that valued the worth of every person. In interpretations of the book of Genesis, they emphasized a freely created world that was good by its very nature and that came into existence out of nothing. This biblical account of creation raised fundamental questions of a theological, political, anthropological, and, finally, ethical kind. In this, they explicitly rejected both the foundational polytheistic epistemologies of the Roman world and also its ethical application.

Very early on, Christians lost the "exemption" of religious practice that the Jews of the Roman Empire enjoyed. Over the first three centuries of Christianity, persecutions arose, first locally and then throughout the entire Empire. Many of the early Church leaders died in the persecutions, and much of the early Christian literature that we have points to their effect on the development of the Church. The usual charge was "atheism." The integral relationship between religious beliefs and civic duties made this inevitable. The early Christians, by refusing to accept the Roman emperors as deities, threatened the fabric of Roman culture. By refusing to worship the emperor, they set themselves on a collision course with the government. To reject the religious claims of polytheism inevitably meant that they would be a threat to the Empire, even if they insisted that all that they desired to be were loyal citizens.

The monotheistic anthropology emphasized the equal creation of all persons. Not surprisingly, Christianity grew rapidly among the urban poor, who heard a Gospel that spoke to their condition. While it was not meant to be directly political, the result was. Over the first four centuries of Christianity, the Roman Empire changed remarkably. Eventually, Christianity became its sole legal religion. One of the key characteristics of Christian belief was that human life was sacred. It was not to be valued because of the social status of the person, or because of his or her contribution to the society. Instead, there was an insistence upon the idea of human life as reflective of the creative power of God.

The Nature of Personhood

In the contemporary discussion of personhood, we have the benefit of science to help us make sense of our experiences. Science validates our beliefs, although it can never provide us with the proofs for it. One cannot argue someone into believing this or that because, ultimately, a "leap of faith" is still required. Nevertheless, science is a valuable tool for determining the actual concrete reality that we are trying to understand. In order for faith to be true, it must inevitably make sense of the concrete world; otherwise, our ideas are nothing other than fantasy. So, in our attempt to outline an appropriate Christian answer to the question "Who are we?" we will need to make use of science in order to adequately address the concreteness of our experiences. It is essential at the beginning to understand who and what we are. Otherwise, we will find ourselves in the position of sacrificing one another in the name of some greater good, only to realize later what it is that we have actually done. At many points in human history, society has done this. Whether we speak of our acceptance of slavery, the denial of the rights of women, or our imperialistic attitudes to other non-Western cultures, there are many times that we have failed to fully appreciate who we have excluded, and harmed, by our incomplete definitions. What exactly is a person, anyway? A good working definition is that a person is the bearer of rights. People have a moral status that places them above mere objects, which can be used by moral agents. Traditionally, for example, human society has recognized restrictions on our right to kill other persons that is different from limitations on killing animals that are not persons. While we may kill a deer or a cow to eat it, we may not simply kill another person unless that person has chosen a kind of act by which they threaten the existence or exercise of free will. Prohibitions against murder do not apply to animals, but they do apply to persons. That is, if you are a person, then you have the right to life, which can only be usurped by another person who acts in defense of other innocent persons. Your existence is ordinarily protected by your status. Defining a person in this way, however, doesn't solve our problem of identifying who is or is not a person. While we might agree that persons have certain rights (and responsibilities), this does not tell us who is or is not a person. Some theologians and philosophers have gone so far as to claim that small mammals are persons, while at the same time denying that a newborn infant is a person. Others have set the line at some point in human development. For example, they might claim that only when the fetus has a brain is it a human person.

The fundamental question is how we determine who is identified in this way. What are the criteria? Is a person a being who has the capability to do something, or is status accorded because the being is already something? This is a principal point of disagreement in contemporary ethics. Many thinkers argue that personhood is a status that is gained (and therefore lost) by ability. That is, personhood is a description of something that we do, such as thinking. If a being is never capable of this activity, or if he is no longer able to do it, then he loses his personhood. Personhood is a description of what one is able to do. Others contend that personhood is the description of what a particular being already is, even if he never does anything other than exist. For this position, personhood is a description of the kind of being one is, even if that being is unable to act in some particularly distinctive way. Personhood is not about an ability but about existing as a kind of being.

Which direction one takes will determine the ethics of many different kinds of situations, especially at the beginning and at the end of life. For example, in deciding the moral course of action for abortion, or for euthanasia, one must determine what kind of being we are speaking about. Our society, for example, permits the killing of aged pets through "putting them to sleep" but does not generally accept doing this to human persons. Of course, there are places that permit assisted suicide, such as the Netherlands, Switzerland, and the State of Oregon in the United States. They are, however, the exception rather than the rule. It is not coincidental that the movement to legalize euthanasia and physician-assisted suicide often couches its arguments in quality of life language. In effect, they argue that a certain type of existence so violates the nature of the human person that the person loses his or her humanity. Some proponents even go so far as to argue that when a person is comatose, only a body remains. The person no longer exists.

So, personhood may either be an attribute that arises out of what one is capable of doing, or it is a quality of what a being already is. At first, resolving the differences between these two positions may seem to be a question somewhat like, "Which came first, the chicken or the egg?" We recognize that there are certain characteristic abilities that humans have. We also know that our abilities are somewhat related to the kind of beings that we are. To use an example from the animal world, we know that horses gallop, so is it a horse because it can gallop, or can it gallop because it is a horse? The shift in contemporary bioethics is decidedly in favor of the position that a person is defined by his or her ability rather than by his or her being. This transition is of relatively recent origin in bioethics. It would be difficult to identify either one crystallizing event or person who is responsible. The movement has been gradual, beginning in medical theories and political and judicial decisions that have set the stage for recent theorists to emphasize the need to be able to perform at a certain standard in order to fall under the label of "personhood."

Some authors correctly note that the Nazi genocide of the early twentieth century was motivated by a broader biomedical vision.[2] The Nazis applied earlier eugenic and Social Darwinist ideas that were outlined by the German physicians Karl Binding and Alfred Hoche in their essay "Permission to Destroy Life Unworthy of Life."[3] According to Rudolf Hess, deputy führer of the Nazi Party, "National Socialism is nothing other than applied biology."[4] In choosing to kill certain groups of people, the Nazis sought to implement a biomedical theory in which the Volk, the people, are cured of the social parasites who infect them. The mentally and physically handicapped, alcoholics, those with congenital malformations, political dissidents, and, of course, the Jews were all categorized in this way. It was the duty of the physician to heal the Volk, and therefore to kill these people, just as one would use medicine to kill germs. It is not coincidental that the Nazis began their killing within medical institutions, or that the "selections" on the ramps of the concentration camps were made by physicians.

It is important to stress that the influence of these ideas was not merely a Nazi aberration. Within the United States, the famous case of *Buck v. Bell* was decided by the U.S. Supreme Court in 1927, or in the time period just prior to the ascendancy of Adolf Hitler as chancellor of Germany in 1933. At issue in the case was the application of a Virginia statute that permitted "mental defectives" to be involuntarily sterilized. Carrie Buck, a twenty-one–year-old daughter of a prostitute, was committed to a state institution by her foster family after she became pregnant at age seventeen, after a probable rape by a relative of her foster father. Based upon evidence that her mother was also institutionalized and that her seven-month-old child did not appear to be "quite normal," Carrie Buck was ordered to undergo sterilization.[5] In the opinion of the chief justice of the U.S. Supreme Court, Oliver Wendell Holmes, the action was justified on the grounds that "three generations of idiots is enough."[6] Although it is easy to vilify those who advocate for euthanasia and physician-assisted suicide as "Nazis," that is not my intent here. Kevorkian, as we shall discuss later, does come close to a Nazi model in his advocacy of an active role for the physician in bringing about death. Yet, the modern American movement for a "right to death" is more highly motivated by a perceived individual right than the application of a social good. In effect, although it ends up at the same place, an evaluation of the "worth" of an individual life, it does so from the perspective of individual autonomy.

Within the twentieth century, we moved the justification to treat people as valuable because of what they are able to do from an advocacy of social goods to the supremacy of individual rights. Now, it is not the society that appears to benefit from our categorization of persons by ability, it is the individual, who can assert his or her "right" to a "death with dignity." Yet, just as we have trampled individual rights by the assertion of an overarching social good, we now turn the tables. The social good becomes discarded in favor of the individual. In practice, what this means is that those who are able to assert their "rights" most forcefully are able to get what they want, while those who cannot do so must rely upon the benevolence of the rest. Care for others, though, often seems to slip through the cracks when the protection of a right for the powerless requires giving up something that one wants.

Within bioethics, this trend emerged in the 1970s. In one telling editorial in *California Medicine*, the choice was described in this way: The traditional Western ethic has always placed great emphasis on the intrinsic worth and equal value of every human life regardless of its stage or condition. This ethic has had the blessing of the Judeo-Christian heritage and has been the basis for most of our laws and much of our social policy. The reverence for each and every human life has also been a keystone of Western medicine and is the ethic that has caused physicians to try to preserve, protect, repair, prolong, and enhance every human life that comes under their surveillance. This traditional ethic is still clearly dominant, but there is much to suggest that it is being eroded at its core and may eventually even be abandoned.[7]

The editors suggested several reasons for this trend, including a growth in population, a diminishing supply of natural resources, and "a quite new social emphasis on something which is beginning to be called the quality of life." This new point of view, they wrote, "will of necessity violate and ultimately destroy the traditional Western ethic" and "it will become necessary and acceptable to place relative rather than absolute values on such things as human lives, the use of scarce resources, and the various elements which are to make up the quality of life or of living which is to be sought. This is quite distinctly at variance with the Judeo-Christian ethic and carries serious philosophical, social, economic, and political implications for Western society and perhaps for world society."[8]

One of the leading advocates of this "new morality" was Joseph Fletcher, an Episcopal priest. Fletcher is most identified with his book *Situation Ethics*, which argued that the basis for any morality is "reasoned choice" within individual situations.[9] He believed that ethics should eliminate the use of rules in favor of a situational calculus of maximizing happiness. Fletcher's ethics was created in response to what he perceived to be two unworkable approaches to morality: the rigidity of legalism, and the erraticness of antinomianism (which means literally "against law"). Legalism was an outdated approach to morality that still clutched the Catholics in "its coils." Here, he thought that absolutes were so stringently applied that the variation of individual circumstances could not be rightly considered. Great efforts had to be made, he argued, to use love to evade the "laws' cold abstractions."

Antinomianism, on the other side, takes a completely opposite view. Decisions are made randomly within the individual situation. This is described as "the approach with which one enters into the decision-making situation armed with no principles or maxims whatsoever, to say nothing of rules." This eventually leads to decisions that are "random, unpredictable, erratic, quite anomalous.

.. [and] literally unprincipled."[10]

The answer to these two extremes was "situation ethics." Fletcher believed that his morality bridged the gap between these two polar opposites. Instead of an adherence to objective rules, or a completely variable acceptance of circumstances, what were required were guidelines for action in individual circumstances.

The essential element of this morality was to act with love. According to Fletcher, it was "principled relativism."[11] Principles would help to guide a person in a situation, but "even the most revered principles may be thrown aside if they conflict in any concrete case with love." They are only "maxims of general or frequent validity; their validity always depends upon the situation."[11]

Fletcher's system quickly attracted both advocates and critics. Supporters tended to agree with his flexibility and most particularly with the exceptions to traditional norms that he advocated. In invoking love as the primary purpose of ethics, he accepted the use of birth control, premarital sex, and adultery in particular instances.

Critics generally charged him with ambiguity. Fletcher, they argued, changed the meaning of the word "love" to mean whatever he wished it to mean. One reviewer noted that the word "'love' like 'situation' is a word that runs through Fletcher's book like a greased pig. . . . Nowhere does Fletcher indicate in a systematic way his various uses of it."[12] Another wrote that this approach is highly dualistic. Love is defined more through an activity of the mind, which describes whatever action one desires; no human act has an intrinsic good or evil.[13]

Perhaps Fletcher's most vocal critic was the Protestant theologian Paul Ramsey, who developed in his work an ethics of covenant responsibilities. As he wrote, "We are born within covenants of life with life." Our existence is always in relation to one another. Therefore, Ramsey argued, the ethical question is "What is the meaning of *faithfulness* of one human being to another in every one of these relations?"[14]

The key element in the development of an ethics for medicine involved recognizing the place of the human person within creation. Creation was objective and was the "external basis and possibility of covenant."[15] In other words, although one could affirm creation as a religious act, one could also recognize one's covenant responsibilities on a natural level as well. We owe one another justice, fairness, righteousness, faithfulness, canons of loyalty, the sanctity of life, hesed, agape, and charity.[16]

In spite of these objections, Fletcher quickly gained notoriety, and eventually influence. Ramsey and other theorists fought against the Fletcherian theory, but eventually they became a minority position in contemporary bioethics. It is not an exaggeration to say that Fletcher is one of the founding members of modern bioethical thought. Many of his early ideas have become standard practice for modern medicine, including genetic engineering and allowing those with terminal illnesses to kill themselves. He foresaw many of the current ethical debates and through his writing influenced many contemporary bioethicists.

With his rejection of absolute principles, Fletcher attempted to redefine the meaning of human life. Quickly, he dismissed the claim that human life itself was sacred. Existence itself was not of any consequence. Instead, what counted was what one was able to do with that existence. In his words, "No one in his right mind regards life as sacrosanct."[17]

Fletcher made a distinction between human life and personal status. Working from contemporary arguments about abortion, Fletcher argued that an embryo or a fetus was definitely alive; it was a human life. But this did not mean that this human life had any rights. The essential question, he wrote, was "whether we may assign personal status to fetal life." What counted was not what was "natural," but what was "personal." One had to carefully define the differences between a human life and a personal life, in order to know how one should respond to this being:

> Defective fetuses, defective newborns, moribund patients—all of these are human lives. Some physicians would "sacrifice" such human lives, others would not. But do they understand the import of their policy? If there is any ground at all, ethically, as I would contend that there is, for allowing or hastening the end of such lives, it must be on the qualitative ground that such human lives are subpersonal.[18]

Biologically, then, one may possess human life, but one is not a subject of rights until one also meets some other criteria. Fletcher proposed fifteen characteristics as an initial inventory of personhood. They were minimal intelligence, self-awareness, self-control, a sense of time, a sense of futurity, a sense of the past, the capability to relate to others, concern for others, communication, control of existence, curiosity, changeability, a balance of rationality and feeling, idiosyncrasy, and neocortical function.[19]

This last criterion, neocortical function, was, in Fletcher's words, the "cardinal indicator," or the sine qua non—the indispensable trait. Essentially, a person must possess the biological structure to be able to think. "The essential, minimal quality of any truly human individual (person) is the ability to be reflective, to carry out those synthesizing and voluntary functions of the cerebral cortex that we call thinking. Other things besides cerebration, yes; but without that one trait all the others would at most add up to subhuman," he wrote. Thus, if one is unable to minimally think, one is not really human.[20] They may be biologically human, but they are not in any real sense a human person.

In explaining the implications of his argument, Fletcher wrote that "both law and morality assume that without sufficient mind to reason the effects of what we do, we are not to blame. Such is the case with children and morons, and imbeciles. [Idiots] are not, never were, and never will be in any way responsible. Idiots, that is to say, are not human."[21] Essentially, personhood requires a minimal brain size and the ability to use it. According to Fletcher, "Humanoid status calls for at least a thousand grams of brains, but human status calls for several billion neurons properly hooked up for storage, retrieval and synthesis."[22]

Fletcher was the first person in contemporary bioethics to take the distinction between being a "human being" and a "human person" and to argue for its application. His influence has significantly formed many, if not most, contemporary bioethicists.

One particularly outspoken opponent of this trend in bioethics has been Dianne Irving. She represents an alternative interpretation of personhood that focuses more on the being of a person and not his or her ability. In her work, she uses her expertise as both a molecular biologist and as a philosopher to examine the foundations upon which we make our claims for personhood.[23]

Why should we accept Fletcher's determination of the beginning of personhood at the point of the operation of the neocortex? Irving argues that Fletcher places too much emphasis upon a step in human development that is already determined by earlier, more significant events. The focus on thinking is misplaced because of reliance upon the distinction between a human body and a human mind, which were proposed by the seventeenth century philosopher René Descartes.

Irving thinks that Fletcher falls into a kind of dualism that sees the body and the mind as separable. In fact, biologically, it is impossible to speak of one without the other. Cartesian philosophy's greatest difficulty is in explaining how a mind can suddenly come into existence without some kind of causative factor. Where does the mind come from? It cannot just "appear" out of nothingness.

In response to Fletcher's determination that a functioning neocortex is necessary for personhood, Irving contends that it is not a significant enough event. Here, we must make some quick distinctions about the importance of certain kinds of changes.

Irving uses the distinction between what are called substantial changes as opposed to accidental changes. A substantial change means that the development changes the kind of thing that exists. In other words, its "substance," or nature, changes because of some event or another. A good example here is the change from a caterpillar to a butterfly. In transforming from one to another, the nature of the thing is changed. Accidental change involves only a minor alteration. The characteristics, or "accidents," of the object are affected, but none of these change what the thing is. If I gain weight, I do not become someone other than who I am, but my body will appear different than what it was.

Fletcher's criterion of neocortical function is an accidental change and not a substantial change, Irving argues. One doesn't switch from a non-human into a human because the neocortex becomes operational. Biologically, this change arises out of the process of human development that begins at syngamy, or the transfer of chromosomes between the ovum and the sperm. Only then is a substantial change present. The two gametes cease to be simply an ovum and a sperm; they lose that nature in favor of a new nature as a human being.

Irving contends that only syngamy represents a substantial biological marker event, one that signals the change in form from one kind of being to another. In support of her position, she uses biological information. For example, syngamy is the beginning of the process of human development. All changes in the zygote relate back to this one point. Once chromosomal transfer is complete, the zygote continues on a path that is already determined by this information.

Some authors have contended that the zygote as it exists right after syngamy is undifferentiated, a formless blob of tissue. Irving responds with evidence that shows that any change is related to this first transfer of information. In embryology, these changes are known as the cascading effect. Each development is caused by each preceding step.

For example, during the process of embryological development, cells become more specialized. Where the zygote at the three-cell stage has cells that can become any kind of cell, eventually they become able to only be a kidney or heart cell. It is important to understand the process by which this happens. Part of what occurs is the process of methylation. In cell development, what occurs is that genetic information is turned on and turned off so that the developing cell may use only certain parts of it. The cell loses the ability to use certain kinds of information. No information is added to the cell. This is why investigators are able to do "DNA profiling" from any kind of human cell. The DNA information remains, only its use by a particular cell is lost. This is a key fact for determining whether or not personhood develops. Biologically, the original zygote is actually the source of all that follows. The absorption of molecules and the selective reduction of the use of genetic information are determined by the blueprint that first comes into existence at syngamy. A zygote does not change from an undifferentiated blob of tissue into something that is then specialized. In fact, as we can tell from methylation, this has the process reversed. The zygote develops from a powerful cell into a collection of cells that are limited in their abilities by the information that is used by the original single cell zygote. The difficulty for those who would argue for the transformation of a human being into a human person is identifying the point at which something creates a substantial change. Fletcher's definition of neocortical functioning as that point ignores the fact that the neocortex arises out of a process that is already begun at the point of syngamy. It doesn't appear out of nothingness in some transformative event. It is intrinsically a part of the process of development that has already begun.

Fletcher argues that the ability to think is the "sine qua non," the essential characteristic of human status. We think, therefore we are a person of moral status. Our biology means nothing without thinking. Irving offers a contrary position that moral status is contingent upon a change in the nature of something. It is not what we do but what we are that matters.

More recent discussion in bioethics has challenged the assumptions that human persons have rights over other creatures. Peter Singer, in particular, has argued that if neocortical function is the requirement for personhood, then it is conceivable that there are some animals whose rights would have to be preferred to humans. Singer has written that personhood is a quality of any being who has the ability to perform certain tasks:

> To avoid speciesism we must allow that all beings who are similar in all rele-
> vant respects have a similar right to life – and mere membership in our own bi-
> ological species cannot be a morally relevant criterion for this right. There will
> surely be some nonhuman animals whose lives, by any standard, are more val-
> uable than the lives of some humans. A chimpanzee, dog, or pig, for instance,
> will have a higher degree of self-awareness and a greater capacity for meaning-
> ful relations with others than a severely retarded infant or someone in a state of
> advanced senility. So if we base the right to life on these characteristics, we
> must grant these animals a right to life as good as, or better than, such retarded
> or senile humans.[24]

The discussion about the nature of human rights that we have just outlined
is extremely significant for the morality of issues related to the sanctity of life.
Essentially, the dividing line on many of these issues is predicated upon the
point at which there is a human person present. If we follow the Fletcherian
view, then only when a human being has the ability to think can we have a moral person present. If a person were not present, then the rights of a person would
be preferred over that of a non-person. If we accept the position offered by Irving, then the point at which a person is present will be moved back to the point
of syngamy. Both theorists would agree that a person would have more rights
than a non-person; they just disagree about what that point is.

In Vitro Fertilization

In looking at the morality of in vitro fertilization, it is important that we return to our earlier discussion of moral theory. As we mentioned, Catholics use a
natural law morality. The moral act is comprised of three elements: the object,
intention, and circumstances.

In this case, let us first examine the intention of those who would wish to
conceive a child through technological means. In a heterosexual marriage, the
desire for children is natural. The couple desires to love one another and to have
that love be expressed through the creation of a family. In fact, procreation is
considered to be one of the three vows of marriage. Couples who enter into a
sacramental marriage promise to procreate.[25] Children are the tangible result of
the love that the couple expresses between themselves. It makes what could be a
purely private act into something that grows beyond the two people. Through
sexual intercourse, the couple gives themselves to each other completely. If a
couple is infertile, a natural desire to express love is thwarted. It is easy to understand how that woman and that man would wish to find a solution to allow
them to have a family. So, looking at the intention of the act, one could argue

that their intention is to express their love to one another through the gift of children. That, in and of itself, is good.

The difficulty is in the kind of act that they are doing in order to accomplish this good intention. Sexual intercourse is the natural way in which this intention is carried out. The couple mutually gives and accepts each other both physically and spiritually. Is in vitro fertilization the same kind of act?

According to Catholic magisterial teaching, it is not. One of the main reasons is that although it does result in procreation, it does not do so as a result of the couple's love made concrete through a personal act, but through the impersonal means of laboratory manipulation. Although the act uses the sperm and the ovum of the couple, the act of procreation is not the direct personal act of the couple.[26] Instead, it is the direct act of the person who combines the gametes.

Intercourse has two natural objects: it expresses the love of the couple and it is procreative. In vitro fertilization retains the second, but it eliminates the first. So, even though procreation results from the act, it does not do so as an act of personal love. The couple's intention of creating a family is not the same as this object of love. Some people might object to this description of in vitro fertilization, arguing that it is an act by which the couple expresses their love for one another. But, even though their intention is to express their love, in fact, they themselves do not perform the act of in vitro fertilization. Since the act of procreation is separated from the couple, they end up distorting the very goal of love in the process of creating a child through technological means.[27] Instead, what they do is to give their gametes, the sperm and the ovum, to someone else who, in turn, combines them and then inserts the embryo into the woman's uterus for gestation. The couple is only the donor of the gametes, not the persons who procreate.

This understanding of in vitro fertilization might be clearer if we consider the use of another person to gestate the child. Many people who accept in vitro technologies might be apt to reject surrogacy arrangements. Yet, they are linked by this indirectness of activity. Our humanness is not simply mental; it is also a bodily experience. The act of giving birth is intrinsically tied to our sense of what it means to be a mother. A woman is not a mother simply because of the donation of her ovum, although this is certainly an important element in what we mean by a mother.[28] The bonding between mother and child begins during pregnancy and continues after birth. A mother is not just an egg donor.

This is why the Catholic Church insists that any attempt to overcome sterility should focus upon assisting the couple to perform an act of intercourse, between themselves, so that procreation remains the direct act of the couple. In vitro fertilization removes procreation from its context as an act that expresses personal love. Once we see procreation as simply a technology, it loses its personalism. In fact, even the harvesting of gametes from the couple has the tendency to objectify them.[29]

Thus, we can make a distinction between two kinds of reproductive technologies. Those that assist the couple in perfecting a conjugal act that they themselves perform would be morally acceptable. Those that attempt to replace the personal act of the couple with another kind of act would not be.

Another concern about the procedure is that the process itself creates more embryos than can be implanted successfully. When ova are extracted, many more are harvested than can be used in a single in vitro attempt, so additional embryos are created and then frozen for future use. As one can readily see from the earlier discussion of personhood, the moral status of these embryos is a key issue. If they are persons, then they ought not be frozen for some future "use," either by the couple themselves or by anyone else. They possess a dignity, which is not adaptable to someone else's needs, however noble they may be.

For example, recent calls for "embryonic stem cell" research argue in favor of using these frozen embryos in order to extract information to treat chronic genetic diseases. Since the early cells are not yet methylated so that they act only as a certain kind of cell, the idea is that they can be adapted to treat genetic disorders. Although the Catholic Church does not object to all stem cell research, it does object to embryonic research precisely because of the moral status of the embryo.

By separating the act of procreation from a personal act of the couple, these possibilities come into being. Fertility assistance itself is not the issue. What is in contention is what is done in relation to the sexual act. Any assistance that replaces the personal act of the couple is wrong because it distorts one of the objects of the act of intercourse, which is the expression of love between the couple. In essence, there is a substantial difference between an act of procreation that occurs between the couple and one that is performed by a third party in a laboratory. Although both may result in procreation, the first is not identical with the second in terms of its morality. Vatican II addressed this point in *Gaudium et Spes*:

> By their very nature, the institution of matrimony itself and conjugal love are ordained for the procreation and education of children and find in them their ultimate crown. Thus a man and a woman, who by their compact of conjugal love "are no longer two but one flesh," (Matt. 19) render mutual help and service to each other through an intimate union of their persons and of their actions. Through this union they experience the meaning of their oneness and attain to it with growing perfection day by day. As a mutual gift of two persons, this intimate union and the good of the children impose total fidelity on the spouses and argue for an unbreakable oneness between them.[30]

Conception that takes places outside the body and that is controlled by persons other than the married couple violates the nature of marital intercourse. In the words of *Donum vitae*, an instruction by the Congregation for the Doctrine of the Faith, this process "entrusts the life and the identity of the embryo into the power of doctors and biologists and establishes the domination of science and technology over the origin and destiny of the human person. Such a relationship of domination is itself contrary to the dignity and equality that must be common to parents and children."[31]

In vitro fertilization (hereafter referred to as IVF), then, violates this understanding of the meaning of intercourse in several ways. The procedure takes place in several steps. First, the woman's ovaries are stimulated in order to generate multiple eggs or oocytes. These are then collected by means of a "direct needle puncture of the follicle, usually transvaginally with ultrasound guidance or less commonly with laparoscopy."[32] Sperm is commonly obtained through masturbation, which is then "washed" to collect the most active gametes. The oocytes are then fertilized with the sperm and are cultured for about forty hours. A number of embryos are then transferred to the uterus for implantation.[33]

Beyond the intervention of persons other than the husband and wife in the act of procreation, there are several other moral difficulties that arise in IVF. With hyperovulation and the subsequent fertilization of numerous embryos, it is inevitable that some embryos will either be deliberately killed because they are not implanted, or they will be frozen for use at some later time. The destruction of any embryo in this way is morally equivalent to direct induced abortion because the embryo possesses a dignity as a human person from the moment of conception.

Although freezing the embryos does not involve a direct destruction, the suspension of its life is itself an imposition of the will of the parents on the existence of the embryo in a way that treats the embryo as a means to the end of parenthood. Embryos are taken to be inanimate objects that can be used for the will of the wife and the husband. This, of course, simply supposes that the embryo would be retained for the use of the couple. The moral evil is compounded in situations where the embryos are further objectified and are simply considered to be "research material" that may be donated to science for future discoveries, as in the calls to use embryos for stem cell research.

The use of third-party donors for gametes would further degrade the sanctity of the couple's act of procreation.[34] It becomes a mechanical act that is stripped of its human dignity. Here, procreation retains little, if any, of the personal expression that naturally defines the act of a married couple between themselves. There have also been several cases where the embryos are created and implanted in the uterus of a close relative like a sister or even the genetic grandmother of the embryo. *Donum vitae* stresses that it is a natural right of the child to have life as a result of the personal act between one's parents.[35] By including another person's gametes, or uterus, into the process of procreation, the natural link between parent and child becomes distorted. While certainly adoptive parents are mother and father to a child, they do not have the same kind of relation that is naturally found between biological parents and their offspring.[36]

Fertility assistance, then, may be acceptable provided that it does not fundamentally change the nature of the act of intercourse. If such assistance served to help the natural process of intercourse remain procreative, it would generally be considered moral. There are a number of different types of fertility assistance. Some would be permissible for Catholics, while others would not be.

Those that would be contrary to this analysis would include Pronuclear Stage Tubal Transfer (PROST)[37] and Intracytoplasmic Sperm Injection (ICSI). In the first procedure, the gametes are collected in the same way as for IVF. Then, either the single cell zygote or a fertilized pronuclear stage oocyte is transferred to the fallopian tube. For ICSI, sperm is inserted into the oocyte through a needle. Once fertilization occurs in vitro, the zygotes are then transferred to the uterus. The practical differences between the procedures are simply where the fertilized zygote is deposited in the body and that PROST requires a laparoscopy in order to access the fallopian tube.[38] Since fertilization takes place outside of the act of intercourse, these procedures are as unacceptable as IVF.

Other procedures that have some conditional acceptance among Catholic theologians include Intrauterine Insemination (IUI) and Gamete Intrafallopian Tubal Transfer (GIFT). In IUI, sperm is introduced into the uterus through a catheter inserted through the cervical canal.[39] GIFT involves the same collection of gametes as in IVF, but the crucial difference is that the gametes are then inserted into the distal point of the fallopian tube (at a site near the ovary), and then fertilization will take place in vivo, or within the body. There have been contrasting opinions by Catholic theologians concerning the morality of these procedures. Those who argue in favor of the procedures accept them only under certain conditions. First, only the gametes of the husband and the wife can be used. Next, the sperm cannot be collected through an act of masturbation. It must be collected by means of a perforated Silastic sheath that is used during an act of marital intercourse. In this way, although sperm is collected, the act retains the possibility that it is procreative in and of itself. Third, the ovum must be collected on the same day as the sperm. Both must be used within seventy-two hours of the sperm's collection, since that is the point of its natural viability. Finally, the gametes must be separated in the catheter by an air bubble so that fertilization takes places in vivo. IUI would also have to be performed under these circumstances. In both cases, minimal intervention is the goal. It is doubtful, for example, that procedures that "washed" the sperm would be morally acceptable.

These authors contend that with these conditions, GIFT is morally acceptable because it assists the couple in completing an act of procreative intercourse between themselves and it does not replace this act.[40] *Donum vitae* states that homologous artificial insemination may not be used unless it "is not a substitute for the conjugal act, but serves to facilitate and to help so that the act attains its natural purpose."[41] Homologous refers to the source of the gametes. They come from the same source, the married couple. Using a gamete from a third party would be labeled "heterologous." Theologians who argue in favor of these technologies think that they retain the essential qualities of marital conjugal relations while assisting the couple to reach the act's natural end of procreation.

Other Catholic authors have disagreed.[42] In their opinion, GIFT and IUI are too disassociated from the couple's act of intercourse. The medical procedure of placing the gametes in the body for fertilization are not performed by the couple and are not part of the conjugal act. What the couple does perform is an act so that sperm can be obtained. The use of a perforated Silastic sheath does not keep the act's natural goal intact. GIFT is then a substitute for the couple's conjugal act.

Both positions are strongly argued by respected theologians. At this time, there has been no specific Church teaching on GIFT and IUI, so individuals may choose to accept either reasoning. All of the authors listed agree with the reasoning of *Donum vitae* and the requirements that would make assisted reproduction morally acceptable. They disagree, however, with the application of those principles.

One final approach to fertility assistance should also be mentioned. Thomas Hilgers, M.D., of the Pope Paul VI Institute for the Study of Human Reproduction, has developed what he calls NaPro (natural procreative) technology. He defines it as "the use of one's medical, surgical and allied health energies in a way that is cooperative with the natural procreative systems."[43] The NaPro approach first diagnoses the specific infertility problem before treatment. Infertility is assumed to be the result of "some underlying organic and hormonal dysfunction or diseases." Couples are then treated for those medical conditions that are found in an extensive clinical examination, which begins with an observation of menstrual cycles. NaPro technology never directly interferes in the couple's conjugal act. Instead, it attempts to treat any conditions that would interfere with its natural goal of procreation.

In contrast to the Catholic position, other authors would define the nature of the act differently. Many Protestant authors would contend that the primary purpose of intercourse is the expression of love. Therefore, since sex without procreation could be considered moral, then procreation without sex would also be moral, provided adequate safeguards were enacted to mitigate the bad consequences of technological reproduction.

Contraception

In contrast to in vitro fertilization, where the couple will find technological means in order to procreate, contraception gives us the opposite situation. Here, the question is whether a couple may choose to limit the procreative purpose of sexual intercourse.

Christianity's prohibition of contraception has had a long history. It has inherited the Jewish emphasis upon the essential goodness of procreation. As stated earlier, both Judaism and Christianity insisted upon a vision of the world that believed that the physical world, because it was the good gift of God, was fundamentally good. It was a primary means by which God and humanity were able to relate to one another. Procreation was thus an act that was significant because it allowed human persons to cooperate with God the Creator in making a good world.

In the ancient world, this insistence upon the intrinsic goodness of procreation was denied. Procreation was a power, but it was not understood as an act that established a relationship with a personal God. Although sex was sometimes used as a religious act, as in the case of Bacchanalian orgies, it was not interpreted in the Judeo-Christian way. Procreation was a compulsion in order to maintain an impersonal order, rather than the free act of a person who was in an intimate relation with a personal God.[44] It was understood to be an act that could be used to establish and to maintain the state, or it was a required duty in the service of an intemperate god. Sex was a potent force, but its use was not a personal expression but a duty that was externally imposed.

Sexual expression, then, was understood in terms of the norms of the ancient societies. Since the most important values focused upon the preservation of a polytheistic culture, sex was understood in terms of how it affected the social order. Laws concerning sex dealt with those aspects of sex that could cause social problems.

So, adulterous sex with someone else's wife was wrong because it was seen to be a kind of theft. Since women were property, to have sex with someone else's wife (or even unmarried daughter) was to trespass. Of course, married men who had sex with concubines did not act wrongly because they did not violate any property rights. They retained ownership of themselves, and, therefore, so long as the woman did not belong to anyone else, as in, for example, a slave, there was no violation of rights.

Similarly, acts of male homosexual sodomy were accepted because they did not involve a direct threat to the order of the society. In fact, pederasty, or the "mentoring" relationship between a mature man and an adolescent boy, which involved the exchange of both intellectual matters and body fluids, was tolerated and, at times, exalted in ancient Western society.

In this culture, the use of contraceptives was acceptable so long as they did not violate the basic norms of the society. In general, ancient civilizations had an ambivalent attitude about procreation. With its emphasis on an ultimate good that was disconnected from the material world, at best procreation was good because it contributed to social stability. In this context, contraception could serve a social good in that it could control the effects of fertility. The broader theoretical foundation, though, was dualistic, and contraception was acceptable to many ancient pagan cults because it broke the cycle where the spirit becomes entrapped in the material world.

Christians had a very different vision of the world that led them to reject contraceptives. The early Christians were a community who defined themselves in light of three different foci: the revelatory experience of Jesus, the culture of the Romans, and the heritage of the Jews. In the beginning of the Christian community, it is clear that there were certain practices and beliefs that were strongly held. These were simply accepted and practiced. At the same time, the Christians were aware that they were at once the inheritors of the Jewish tradition and also now were different from it. The Roman culture also exerted its influence on the Church. The earliest Christians, then, were a people set apart from both the Jews and the Romans. Their adherence to a belief in the revelation of Jesus and the practices of baptism and Eucharist had a profound effect upon them. It was such an extraordinary transformation that the apostles ceased to be afraid of arrest and death, and they sought out the public places in order to preach the Gospel.[45]

In understanding themselves, the Christians also realized that the Jewish scriptures were to be interpreted in light of their experience of Jesus. They interpreted the texts allegorically, seeing in them a revelation that was fulfilled in Jesus. Their teaching on contraception reflects this interpretation.

In the Genesis account of creation, men and women were blessed by God and invited to "be fertile and multiply; fill the earth and subdue it."[46] Their mutual gift to God was a participation in the good creation. Since the created world was fundamentally good, any denial of its processes, especially those that resulted in the creation of new life, was wrong.

Jewish society was built upon the relationship between procreation and holiness. A family was a blessing from God, and the fertility of the family, especially the woman, was seen as being favored by God. In some rabbinic teachings, it is only after marriage and the union of man and woman that the image of God becomes present in the individual person.[47] The ideal was that man and woman would marry and procreate. Their children were a mark of the covenant, a sign of God's favor upon them. Only one Old Testament reference exists in which someone chooses celibacy. Otherwise, the absence of children is thought to be something negative.[48]

One must also note that although procreation was seen as a good, there is, at the same time, a negativity with regard to sex itself in the scriptural texts. It is often identified with lust, and sexual activity purely for pleasure is wrong. Women, especially, become identified with lust in intercourse. Eve is considered to be the tempter of Adam, and Bathsheba is the cause of David's evil act of killing her husband.[49]

In Jewish culture, contraception was generally condemned. It was acceptable only in limited circumstances, where it was thought to be consistent with the ideal of procreation. That is, a married woman could contracept if the woman's health was endangered or to preserve the religious or social status of the potential child.[50]

In forming their doctrine on contraception, the early Christians were influenced, then, by both the Roman and the Jewish cultures. The broader Roman culture was a standard against which they fought. They were consistent with the Jews in rejecting these attitudes. Procreation was thought to be a positive good and a reflection of the covenant between God and his people.

One of the distinctive aspects of early Christian doctrine was its development of a marital ethic. Marriage, in the New Testament, becomes one of the primary symbols to describe the Christian relationship to God. There are explicit passages in the Gospels and the epistles of Paul that deal with issues of divorce, remarriage, and celibacy. These are extensions of, and in some cases, rejections of, the Jewish ethic. The Christian development of its doctrine on contraception must thus been seen in relation to its understanding of marriage and celibacy.

The early Christians adopted a marital doctrine that not only limited divorce but also emphasized celibacy "for the sake of the kingdom." Common to both of these teachings was the Jewish understanding of sexuality as being a gift from God. Whatever one's ultimate choice of virginity, marriage, or even widowhood, one's sexuality was to be placed at the service of God. In fact, as one author has pointed out, the Church's interest in sexual ethics was only because of her concern for how one would live out the baptismal covenant.[51]

Baptism was the most important sacrament in the early Church. At baptism, the new convert received a gift from God—a new relationship. Baptism erased original sin and allowed the new Christian to be able to live the life that God intended at our creation. How one lived one's life after baptism was the response to that gift. Once baptized, Christians were called to live a life that was a reflection of this generosity. Although celibacy was considered to be the ideal vocation because it was such a complete gift of self, marriage, or even remaining a widow after the death of one's spouse, were also understood to be appropriate gifts.

Marriage is reflective of baptism. Those who are married are expected by the Christian community to live out a life with each other that is like a gift. In St. Paul's words in Ephesians, he emphasizes in one passage that wives are to be subordinate to their husbands. What is often neglected in the passage is the implicit emphasis that the obligation is reciprocal. Husbands are not to dominate, but to serve, just as wives do.[52] In this, they reflect Christ's love for the Church. In becoming human, dying, and resurrecting, he "delivered himself up." In the same way, husbands are commanded by Paul to "love their wives as their own bodies."

In this context, sexual expression is an extension of this gift of self. The couple is to act out of their obligation not only to one another, but also to God. In giving themselves to each other, they also give to God. By caring for their spouse, they practice the love that God has for them. In particular, sex within marriage is expressive of the creative power of God. When the couple lovingly accepts children as a result of their sexual acts, they cooperate with God's creative power.

Procreation is not, then, the primary obligation of the couple. That is, they do not marry simply to procreate. It is more nuanced than that. Procreation is, of course, an expected outcome of intercourse. But, the couple does not marry merely as a means to produce children. Rather, parenthood is an extension of their primary obligation to love one another. Children are accepted as the result of the sexual gift of self. The distinction is a precise but necessary one. Children are not simply products. Procreation is entirely proper, but it is not the primary emphasis in Christian marriage. Therefore, couples who cannot procreate are validly married because their sexual acts are expressions of love that are reflective of the love that God has for us. Procreation will be a natural result of this act, but sterility does not cease to be an expression of the baptismal covenant unless the couple does something that would distort its natural purpose.

The early Christians, then, understood marriage and sexual expression to be a response to baptism. As God bestowed upon them a gift of relationship, so they in turn were to give this same gift to one another and to the children who came from a sexual gift of self. Contraceptives were not in keeping with the spirit of baptism.

Partly, this was because of the identification of contraception to the Roman culture. Christian converts knew they were a people set apart from that way of life. For those who were Jews, that was already clear. With their monotheistic worship, the Jews were definitely different. They had been for centuries. Although some Jews did assimilate, by and large, most Jews remained separate from the conquering cultures of the Babylonians, Greeks, and Romans. For those who were Gentiles, the change was apparent in the way in which the early Christian communities acted in relation to the culture. They lived communally, cared for the poor, and made a point of distinguishing their sexual ethics.

The early Christian apologists noted these differences in their defense of Christianity. Tertullian, for example, wrote, "We who are united in mind and soul have no hesitation about sharing what we have. Everything is in common with us—except our wives." He continues by contrasting the Christian practices with those of the Greeks and the Romans: "They not only usurp the marriage rights of their friends, but they hand over their rights to their friends with the greatest equanimity. This results, I suppose from those who were older and wiser, the Greek Socrates and the Roman Cato, who shared with their friends the wives whom they had married, so that they could bear children in other families too."[53] Monogamy was an essential characteristic of Christian practice.

In *The Apostolic Tradition*, Hippolytus also makes mention of Christian belief about sexual conduct. This document describes, among other things, the baptismal practices of the early Church. Among the guidelines for those who wished to be admitted as "Hearers of the Word," the first step toward baptism, was that "the man be instructed to content himself with his wife and the woman to content herself with her husband." Additionally, panders, prostitutes, licentious men, and eunuchs were all to be rejected as candidates.[54]

To the modern ear, this seems to be a foreign way of understanding the nature of sexual expression. The modern world has adopted the ethic that orgasm leads to spiritual fulfillment rather than that sex becomes a form of worship of God. Sex becomes the means to fulfillment, rather than an act that grows out of conversion. Many authors have addressed this topic, so I will not devote much time to explaining its origin, nor its conflicts with Christian theology.[55] The end result is that the understanding of the intrinsic meaning of sexual expression has changed. Now, it is the individual who determines what will be signified by sex. In this view, there is no natural sense of what it already means. Instead, we fill the act with whatever emotional expression we desire.

As one can see, this is a very modern concept of the nature of human acts. In the ancient world, whether one was a polytheist or a monotheist, the nature of the world was not changeable. Rather, it was fixed. So, in a sense, the ancient question was always, "What is?" Today, we concentrate on another question: "What can be?"

The second inquiry has been, in many ways, good for humanity. We have eradicated some diseases, improved our lifespan, and been able to correct many disabilities. Yet, the question of what can be created presupposes an answer to the first question. Unless we have some sense of what is ultimately good, we lose sight of how to determine which creations we should pursue and those we should not. Modern medicine is driven, almost irrationally, by this second question. We clone, we fertilize, and we contracept with abandon because we presume to be able to determine not only what will be, but also what already is.

Medicine's clinical language reflects this emphasis. In discussions of embryonic and fetal development, for example, many authors speak of a "pre-embryo," or the "products of conception." This description avoids the entire discussion mentioned earlier about the nature of the embryo at very early stages of development. Language plays a very important role in the development of a moral viewpoint. Especially in the abortion debate, language dominates the understanding of the moral issues.[56]

There is also the tendency to simply subsume moral choice under the title of "testing." An example might be the expectation that prenatal tests for genetic abnormalities are standard clinical practice, without discussing with patients the implications of what choices they might have to make if the results are not normal. In many instances, clinicians simply presume that positive test results for abnormalities will result in the decision to abort the pregnancy.

An acceptance of contraception, then, is often accompanied by a corresponding moral sense that emphasizes the role of the individual decision-maker to determine the meaning of what is done. Thus, it is often framed in two distinct ways. First, we have the tendency to simply assert that whatever moral decision is made by an individual becomes right simply because it is chosen. We have previously discussed this position in the earlier chapter on moral method. The second is to make the decision into a kind of utilitarian calculus, where one attempts to wring as many good effects as possible out of the act. The thinking here tends to assert the following: people will always have sex; therefore they must protect themselves against pregnancy so that when pregnancy is chosen, it is a rational choice that benefits the future child.

There are, of course, numerous errors in the logic of this position. It assumes that sex is inevitable, but then in the same breath argues that it can be controlled. It also assumes that rational parenthood is preferable, or even possible. The relative independence of the person to choose what sex will mean is inferred as well. Finally, it suggests that the good of children is a relative good, one that is tied to the happiness of the parents. Let us examine each of these in turn.

Although clearly sexual acts are natural, that does not mean that we act out of instinct as animals do. I would suggest that we do not simply force sexual acts upon our partners but that we make a choice to engage in them. So, although there are natural inclinations, as human persons we choose particular acts to accomplish human goods. We also choose not to perform certain acts in order to reach a goal. To maintain an ideal weight, for example, we may choose to not eat that piece of cake or the cookie. Sex is the same way. We are not forced by nature into intercourse. We choose it, or refuse it, depending upon our sense of the good involved.

It is true that some people do not control themselves. Gluttony, whether of food or sex, is wrong. That does not mean, though, that we should change our sense of what occurs just because there are some persons who choose not to be in control of themselves. The logic of this position in relation to contraception is clear if we were to apply it to teenagers and food. The thinking would be something like this: teenagers will get fat from eating too much junk food, so we should place something in their body that will prevent it from absorbing the calories. Instead, a preferable approach would be to simply not eat the wrong things.

This leads to another point. Although we clearly have control over the kinds of acts that we engage in, we should not assume that we have complete control over parenthood. This is not to suggest that parenthood is irrational (although some might debate this!). A couple chooses to become parents not by having a complete control of the process, but by participating with God in what he decides. As many couples will attest, while there may be an agreement among themselves that they would like children and a plan for when that may occur, families do not usually stick to such a plan. Couples may find themselves being surprised at the gift of a child, or alternatively they may find that they cannot simply become pregnant on their own timetable. Parenthood is more about the acceptance of a gift that comes from God than a plan that can be determined at the start by the couple.[57]

There is an unspoken assumption in contraceptive language that individuals need to be "protected" from pregnancy. Sex, it is implied, is really about getting what you want from the act without being harmed. Pleasure, or perhaps some intimacy, might be what the individual desires, without the possible natural consequence of procreation. So, the individual seems to have the ability to decide what the act will mean for him or her.

Yet, it is precisely because sex is a naturally intimate and procreative act that we choose to engage in it. We choose *this* kind of act rather than another because it does express this meaning. We know what it means and then we set out to change it. We have free will, but we choose to use our individual power to change what is already present.

Finally, there is a tendency in American society to believe that children will only be happy when the parents are happy. This will only happen, it is thought, when the ideal elements of a middle-class lifestyle are present. While it is true that parents need to care for the physical and emotional needs of their children, we often confuse the ability to provide all of the consumer goods of our culture with happiness. All too often, we refuse the gift of children because we idealize what is required for a family. Advertising pitches this car, that house, and the latest age-defying cream and tells us that these will make us happy. Too many people buy into this romanticized life. In the process, they end up chasing an elusive vision of happiness that doesn't really exist.

Partly, this is due to a false sense of freedom—a subject that we have discussed earlier. Many people today see happiness as being connected to disattachment. Freedom is thus to be rid of any obligation. Yet, this is exactly the opposite of reality. What we need is a rootedness to the right obligations. In fulfilling our duty for certain good goals, we then become the kind of person who reaps the happiness of a life ordered correctly.

The discussion about the morality of contraception within the Church has been contentious for decades. On the one hand, we have those theologians who have focused on this issue in order to argue against the casuistic emphasis of pre-Vatican II magisterial teaching. Without necessarily agreeing with this analysis of morality, one could say that there is sometimes a tendency in the Church to present many moral positions as a fait accompli. To be clear, a criticism of communication is not a rejection of the substance of the teaching.

On the other hand, there has been a strong shift in American Catholicism from an insular toward a secular culture. As income levels have risen for American Catholics, they have become more like other Americans in their beliefs. The furor over *Humanae vitae* in 1968 was the spark that ignited both of these trends. Polls have indicated that there is a gap between the magisterial teaching on contraception and the practice of many American Catholics. American society as a whole has moved toward an individualized sexual ethic, and Catholics are following.

Especially on issues of reproductive ethics, there is a growing divide both within the Catholic Church and also between the Church and the world. What is at stake is a fundamental way of viewing the world. Already, the practical predictions that were made by Paul VI in *Humanae vitae* are coming true. With the widespread use of contraception, we are becoming less willing to care for women and children. Everyone is out for themselves. What begins as an individual desire to enjoy some aspects of sex—pleasure and the expression of love—but not another—procreation—inevitably has social consequences. Rising numbers of broken families and children living in poverty are the social results of a decision to understand the nature of the body in a certain way.

Notes

1. Letter to Diognetus, in *The Didache, The epistle of Barnabas, The epistles and The martyrdom of St. Polycarp, The fragments of Papias, and The epistle to Diognetus* (Westminster, Md.: Newman Press, 1961).

2. Robert Jay Lifton, *The Nazi Doctors: Medical Killing and the Psychology of Genocide* (New York: Basic Books, 1986).

3. Karl Binding and Alfred Hoche, *Permission to Destroy Life Unworthy of Life: Its Extent and Form* (Leipzeig: Felix Meiner Verlag, 1920) as reprinted in *Issues in Law and Medicine* 8, no. 3 (1992): 231.

4. Rudolf Hess, as cited in Lifton, *Nazi Doctors*, 31.

5. Daniel V. Kelves, *In the Name of Eugenics: Genetics and the Uses of Human Heredity* (Cambridge, MA: Harvard University Press, 1985), 110.

6. *Buck v. Bell*, 274 U.S. 200 (1927): 207.

7. "A New Ethic for Medicine and Society," *California Medicine* 113, no. 3 (September 1970): 67. It should be noted that this editorial, while calling attention to the change, was not entirely against it. The editors urged readers to consider the role that physicians should play in this new environment.

8. "A New Ethic," 67.

9. Joseph Fletcher, *Situation Ethics: The New Morality* (Philadelphia: Westminster Press, 1966).

10. Fletcher, *Situation Ethics*, 33.

11. Fletcher, *Situation Ethics*, 31.

12. James Gustafson, "How Does Love Reign?" *The Christian Century* 83 (1966): 654-55.

13. Herbert McCabe, "The Validity of Absolutes," *Commonweal* 83 (1966): 439.

14. Paul Ramsey, preface to *The Patient as Person* (New Haven: Yale University Press, 1970), xii.

15. Ramsey, preface to *The Patient as Person*. Emphasis in original text.

16. Ramsey, preface to *The Patient as Person*.

17. Joseph Fletcher, *Humanhood: Essays in Biomedical Ethics* (Buffalo, NY: Prometheus Books, 1979).

18. This essay was earlier published as "Medicine and the Nature of Man," in *The Teaching of Medical Ethics*, ed. Robert M. Veatch, Willard Gaylin, and Councilman Morgan (Hastings on Hudson: Institute of Society, Ethics and the Life Sciences, 1973), 47–58.

19. "Medicine and the Nature of Man."

20. "Medicine and the Nature of Man," 12.

21. "Medicine and the Nature of Man," 16, 20.

22. "Medicine and the Nature of Man," 21–22. Here he uses the terms "idiot," "imbecile," and "moron" in a clinical way, referring to those with an IQ of

less than 25, between 26–50, and 51–75, respectively, as scored on a Stanford-Binet intelligence test.

23. Dianne Nutwell Irving, "Scientific and Philosophical Expertise: An Evaluation on the Arguments of 'Personhood,'" *Linacre Quarterly* 60 (February 1993): 18–46.

24. Peter Singer, *Animal Liberation: A New Ethics for Our Treatment of Animals* (New York: Avon, 1975), 20.

25.The three vows are *fides* (fidelity), *proles* (procreation), and *sacramentum* (permanency).

26. For now, we will only consider the "ideal" act of homologous in IVF that uses the gametes of the heterosexual married couple. We will consider other possibilities later.

27. Pius XII made this point in an address, "Fertility and Sterility," (May 19, 1956) in *The Human Body: Papal Teachings* (Boston: Daughters of St. Paul, 1960), 387–90: "The means by which one tends toward the production of a new life take on added significance inseparable from the desired end and susceptible of causing great harm to this very end if the means are not conformable to reality and to the laws inscribed in the nature of beings."

28. It is interesting to note that the courts have struggled mightily with this dilemma in surrogacy cases. The definition of motherhood was traditionally assumed to be that a mother is one who has given birth to a child. With donor gametes, this causality becomes confusing. Different courts have interpreted the meaning of motherhood to also include the donator of the ovum.

29. Paul Lauritzen, "What Price Parenthood?" *Hastings Center Report* Vol..20 (March-April 1990): 38-46.

30. *Gaudium et Spes* n. 4.

31. Congregation for the Doctrine of the Faith, *Donum vitae (Instruction on the Respect for Human Life in its Origin and on the Dignity of Procreation)* (Boston: Pauline Books & Media, 1987). An exceptionally articulate statement on the morality of in vitro fertilization may also be found in Bishop Sean O'Malley's (Fall River, MA) pastoral letter of November 9, 2001 (Boston: Massachusetts Catholic Conference, 2001).

32. Mark H. Beers and Robert Berkow, eds., *The Merck Manual of Diagnosis and Therapy*, 16th ed. (Rahway, NJ: Merck Research Laboratories, 1999).

33. According to the Centers for Disease Control, "Assisted Reproductive Technology Survelliance—2000," *Morbidity and Mortality Weekly Report (MMWR)* 52 (SS09- August 29, 2003): 1–16, the use of artificial reproductive technologies has an overall success rate of 31 percent for all procedures attempted in that calendar year. There were 99,629 procedures performed, with 25,228 live birth deliveries and 35,025 infants being born. Each attempted cycle of treatment costs between seven thousand and eleven thousand dollars.

34. Recently, Chinese scientists attempted to gestate five embryos that had the DNA of three different donors. They had replaced the nucleus of an oocyte with the nucleus from another oocyte and then fertilized it. The resulting em-

os thus had the DNA of three parents: two women and one man. In their procedure, they implanted five embryos and then aborted two. The resulting triplets eventually miscarried. Many nations have expressly prohibited such procedures.

35. *Donum vitae*, II, B, 5.

36.Obviously, a natural link between parent and child is to be preferred. This does not imply a criticism of adoption, which may be a wonderful experience for both the adoptive parents and for the child. It is simply to say that there is a preference for biological versus adoptive parenthood.

37. This procedure is sometimes also called ZIFT—Zygote Intrafallopian Tubal Transfer. If an embryo is transferred at the two-cell stage, it is referred to as TET—Tubal Embryo Transfer.

38. There are some variations of PROST where the physician accesses the fallopian tube through the use of ultrasound-guided catheters that are inserted vaginally.

39. IUI may also be performed by depositing the sperm intravaginally, intracervically, or pericervically.

40. See Peter J. Cataldo, "Gift as Assistance," *Ethics & Medics* 22, no. 12 (December 1997): 34, "Reproductive Technologies," *Ethics & Medics* 21, no. 1 (January 1996): 1–3, and "The Newest Reproductive Technologies: Applying Catholic Teaching," in *The Gospel of Life and the Vision of Health Care*, ed. Russell B. Smith (Braintree, MA: The Pope John Center, 1996), 61–94; Donald McCarthy, "Response to Catholic Moral Teaching and TOT/GIFT," in *Reproductive Technologies, Marriage and the Church*, ed. Donald McCarthy (Braintree, MA: The Pope John Center, 1988), 140–45.

41. *Donum vitae*, II B, 6.

42. Donald DeMarco, "GIFT as Replacement," *Ethics & Medics* 22, no. 11 (November 1997): 3–4, and *Biotechnology and the Assault on Parenthood* (San Francisco: Ignatius, 1991); John Haas, "Pastoral Concerns: Procreation and the Marital Act," in *Reproductive Technologies, Marriage and the Church*, ed. Donald McCarthy, (Braintree, MA: The Pope John Center, 1988), and "Gift? No!," *Ethics & Medics* 18, no. 9 (1993); William May, "Pastoral Concerns: Procreation and the Marital Act," in *Reproductive Technologies*; Nicholas Tonti-Filippini, "Donum vitae and Gamete Intrafallopian Tube Transfer," *Linacre Quarterly* 57, no. 2 (1990): 68-79.

43.Thomas W. Hilgers, "Answers for Infertility," *Celebrate Life* (May/June 1995):34.

44. See John T. Noonan, Jr., *Contraception: A History of its Treatment by the Catholic Theologians and Canonists* (Cambridge, MA: Belknap Press of Harvard University, 1965), 12–29. Noonan discusses at length the numerous laws and practices of contraception in the Roman Empire. He suggests that they "praised procreation as a civic duty" (22) and tried to encourage it through limiting inheritance rights for the childless. Contraceptives, however, were generally accepted except in cases where someone was harmed through their use. In Noonan's words, "The absence of reference to the subject in Roman classical

literature is perhaps best understood as due to a general calm acceptance of contraceptive practices" (28).

45. For an excellent overview of the development of Christian thought, see
Robert Wilken, *The Spirit of Early Christianity* (New Haven: Yale University
Press, 2003).

46. Genesis 1:28 (New American Translation).

47. Richard Batey, "The Mid Σαρξ Union of Christ and the Church," *New
Testament Studies* 13 (1966–67): 272.

48. Jeremiah 16:2.

49. Genesis 3:1–17; 2 Kings 11.

50. Noonan, *Contraception* 50.

51. Stanley Hauerwas, "The Family as a School for Character," *Religious
Education* 80 (Spring 1985): 272-85.

52. Ephesians 5:21.

53. Tertullian, "Apology," in *Tertullian: Apologetical Works and Minicius
Felix: Octavius*, ed Rudolph Arbesmann, trans. Rudolph Arbesmann, Sister
Emily Joseph Daly, and Edwin A. Quain. *Fathers of the Church Series*, Vol. 10
(New York: Fathers of the Church, Inc., 1950).

54. Hippolytus, "The Apostolic Tradition," in *The Apostolic Tradition of
Hippolytus*, ed. B.S. Easton (Cambridge: Cambridge University Press, 1934).

55. See, for example, Peter Gardella, *Innocent Ecstasy: How Christianity
Gave America an Ethic of Sexual Pleasure* (New York: Oxford University Press,
1985); John S. Grabowski, "Covenantal Sexuality," *Eglise et Theologie* 27
(1996): 229–252, and *Sex and Virtue: An Introduction to Sexual Ethics* (Washington, DC: Catholic University of America Press, 2003).

56. It is interesting to note that in recent polls of teenagers, the pro-life side
of the abortion debate is gaining ground. Clinical information about embryonic
and fetal development has trumped this language. A Gallup poll of August 2003
showed that 72 percent of teens surveyed believe that abortion is morally wrong.

57. An excellent analysis of this thinking may be found in Cormac Burke,
Covenanted Happiness: Love and Commitment in Marriage (San Francisco:
Ignatius, 1990), especially chapters two and three.

Chapter Four:
The Social Dimensions of Health Care

Choice is the modern American value. On television, in the newspapers, and on billboards, we are given a steady stream of messages that work to influence how we choose. Each advertising pitch plays on our desires for a future that we can shape and control. In the words of one of the early leaders of public relations, it involves the "engineering of consent."[1] Often, we are influenced to choose only for ourselves. The social effects of our choices are not always clear.

The twentieth century was the first time in human history where our ability to create our choices seemed to finally match our desires for them. We finally conquered many of the obstacles that lay in front of us. Science triumphed over sickness with penicillin and other antibiotics. Electricity became commonplace in our homes. Sophisticated communications and transportation inventions connected us to places that generations before us could only have imagined.

At the same time, our choices have also created an increasing gap between the rich and the poor. This is true not only internationally, between nations, but also within individual countries. Although the technology now exists to eradicate many of the diseases and chronic conditions that killed many previous generations, these advances are available only to those who have the money to pay for it. Many developing nations cannot afford vaccinations and other medical care. Even within the United States, there are millions of people who cannot afford medical care.

This chapter explores the rights and obligations that we have with regard to the distribution of health care. Is there a basic level of treatment that is required? What do we owe one another? Which economic systems are most likely to ensure that persons are able to receive the health care that they deserve? Catholic thought has consistently argued for both a natural right to have a basic level of health care and a corresponding obligation to care for our health. These two aspects of health care come together when we, as a society, have to decide what services we will support and those that we decide are the responsibility of the individual person. So, too, we must acknowledge the changing conditions of our world that make it difficult to create equitable systems for health care. In particular, the growing use of genetic information and changing demographics will have an increasingly important influence on the development of just health care systems.

Choice, or to put it more precisely, free will, is a power that God has given to human persons. Yet, the ability, as time has shown us, is not value neutral. In choosing, we desire something. Often, it seems as though the choice is only individual. What we choose for ourselves is the only aspect of free will that our society seems to focus upon. Yet, in order to fully understand choice, it must be placed within a broader structure.

Over time, there have been many competing concepts of social structure. Some have held that the needs of the society are more important than those of the individual. Others have argued that the individual person's needs take priority over those of the society. Catholic teaching argues for an integrated understanding of the person in the society. Neither the society nor the individual person may take precedence over the other. One concept that joins them together is the Common Good.

In his encyclicals *Mater et magistra* and *Pacem in terris*, John XXIII wrote that the common good was a set of conditions that enables each one of us to reach our perfection. It is the structure that allows each person to make the kind of choices that will allow us to be the person who God intended us to be. Individually, God calls us each to a vocation. We are given gifts that we are expected to use not only for ourselves, but also for others. We create the culture, the structure, which influences our understanding of the choices that we have. While children make their choices in a solipsistic way, in order to choose to know themselves, adults ought to choose for a broader social dimension. They create the culture that makes individual choices possible.

Defining Health

Few people would deny that there is a social dimension to health care. At some point, our individual freedom to be healthy is joined to the same obligation for others. The ethical difficulty is in finding the line that neatly separates one from the other. A further complication is in defining the mixture of individual, social, and governmental responsibilities and rights that will create the culture that is best for seeking health. Each part has a role to play in enabling the individual and the social goals of optimum health.

One place to start is in defining the meaning of the goal itself. What, exactly, do we mean when we say that there is a goal of health? Obviously, we cannot guarantee that every person will be completely healthy. Illness and disease do not neatly correspond with responsibility. Some persons are born with health problems that they themselves did not cause. Others live in poverty, where their available resources limit their choices. Even if we had an unlimited supply of resources, the reality is that we would be unable to cure everyone from every physical ailment. One's health is determined by a variety of factors that are out of individual, or even social, control. So, we can begin with a negative statement that it is impossible to achieve absolute health for everyone.

There have been many definitions of health. One popular definition comes from the World Health Organization. It states that health is "a state of complete physical, mental and social well-being and not merely the absence of disease or infirmity."[2] Positively, the definition emphasizes a holistic view of health. It does not limit itself to understanding health purely in terms of its physical nature. Instead, it also includes other human dimensions. Unfortunately, there are two flaws in it as well. First, it makes no mention of spirituality in health, and secondly, it assumes that a goal of "complete" health is even possible. The two criticisms are intertwined.

As was mentioned in earlier chapters, it is essential to link one's ethics to both an anthropology and to a system of absolute beliefs. The WHO definition does this, and in so doing, it invokes a view of the human person that is at odds with a Catholic understanding of health.

First, health clearly includes a spiritual dimension. Holistic care of the patient requires attention to this key human dimension. Lately, nursing has turned toward a more in-depth study of the relationship between spirituality and nursing care. Theorists have argued for the integration of spiritual assessment and treatment of patients by nurses.[3] In fact, as we highlighted in the earlier chapter on professionalism, health care has tried to care and cure physical illness with spiritual, as well as medicinal remedies. It has not been until the "scientific" revolution in medicine that the two aspects of health care, the spiritual and the physical, have become separable. The WHO definition reflects a more modernistic approach, which minimizes, and sometimes completely eliminates, a spiritual component to the human person.

Another element that is present in the definition is an implicit assumption that illness and disease are capable of being defeated. Although modern medicine has had some recent success in eradicating diseases (smallpox and poliomyelitis come to mind), the history of health care has been that this is an almost impossible task.

There are few, if any, "magic bullets" that will make a person completely physically healthy. As the history of antibiotics has shown, what we assume is an easy answer often becomes more complicated with time. The discovery of antibiotics has helped to extend the lifespan of many people. Yet, as we are finding, it has created a host of new problems. Bacteria have evolved into more virulent strains because over time they have developed defense mechanisms to antibiotics.[4] Repeated exposure to the antibiotics only succeeds in creating stronger microbes.

"Complete Health" is a chimera that fascinates us. Today, as a culture, we think that medicine is the panacea for illness. Whether it is antibiotics or elective cosmetic surgery, there is an assumption that medicine will find the cure and that we can defeat some illness or another. Time and money will supposedly solve the health problems that confront us. Perhaps the ultimate example of this is cryonics, or preserving one's body after death in liquid nitrogen or helium in the hope that a future generation will be able to reanimate the body.

Unfortunately, medicine cannot solve the greatest problem of all: our free will. Heredity, of course, plays a role in our health. Yet, oftentimes we create our own difficulties. Although we should not acquiesce in our search for scientific solutions, there is still a greater role that most of us could play in developing and maintaining our own health. We fill our bodies, and our minds and our souls, with choices that give us pleasure but not long-term health. Over time, these preferences also have an effect on our health.

One might argue that the greatest power for the preservation of health is actually free will. The health care professional may advise and offer scientific solutions, but these must be ultimately chosen and enacted by the individual person. The power to be healthy resides in the person and not in the professional.

If we examine the health of entire populations in more developed nations, it is clear that the cause of death for most people is related to their choices. In the United States, we tend not to die from lack of food, as in poorer nations, but from heart disease and cancer. Certainly, some of this disease might be explained by a genetic predisposition, but not all. Physically, we tend to be obese and not very fit. As a society, we encourage the consumption of inexpensive and nutritionally deficient food in greater and greater portions.[5]

So, the WHO definition errs on the side of excessive optimism. Health is the perfection of human functioning. Yet, as stated earlier, although free will is a power that we can use to gain or maintain health, it is a weak weapon that cannot solve all of our health problems. Even more, although we could theoretically make all of the right choices, by dieting and exercising, we still cannot stop the eventual deterioration of our bodies. Time wreaks its effect upon us, and although we struggle mightily, we can never escape our common end, death.

So if health is a goal, we must acknowledge that it is a temporary goal in the pursuit of some other good. We will all eventually die. At best, we can hope to preserve our health well enough to pursue the kinds of activities that will enable us to reach our own individual perfection. The end goal is not physical immortality, in the sense that this body is perfectible. Health serves the human person by enabling him or her to seek even greater goods. We do not live just so that our bodies become flawless. Rather, our physical health serves us by giving us the ability to seek what is ultimately good. The goal of health is at once, then, both a social and a personal goal. We desire some measure of the pursuit of life for ourselves, yet we must rely upon the community to enable us to seek it.

As adults, we have the most ability to maintain our health. We rely upon our families and the broader community to seek the goal for us in both our infancy and in our old age. At either end of life, we are in a dependent relationship with those who are healthier than we are. Obviously, this is a simplified explanation. There are, of course, some people who maintain their independence until their death and others who become dependent much earlier than at the end of their life. I doubt anyone would quibble with the dependency of an infant, so we can maintain that as a constant!

The broader point is that our health is never just an individual pursuit. To a greater or lesser degree, we need others to help us achieve and maintain health. Our individual ability to be healthy is limited first by our lifespan, which makes it likely that a significant part of our lives will be spent in some kind of dependency, and secondly by the fact that even when we do have the ability to choose, we often do not choose very wisely. Acting only upon our individual will, we have very limited abilities to be healthy.

Health and Social Responsibility

The broader community, then, must play a significant role in helping us to achieve health. The structuring of choices and the ability of everyone to join together in the pursuit of a common goal is significant. Our physical health is a gift, both from God and from other human persons who enable us to be born healthy, to develop our bodies in the way in which they are supposed to grow, and to maintain whatever abilities we can.

The community, then, has both rights and duties when it comes to health. We can assist the individual person in developing his or her physical, mental, and spiritual gifts. We cannot replace the individual free will, but we can mold it so that the correct choices are made, not in a deterministic way, but in a way that will allow each person to truly know what he or she does choose. For example, while individuals do have the free will to choose what they eat, food service businesses must also take the lead in offering an array of choices that support the ultimate goal of being healthy. While "supersizing" makes strong economic sense in the short term for an individual business, in terms of the broader social goods, we lose by the same measure. Obesity increases fuel consumption and health care spending and diminishes productivity. So while a business makes a quick profit, our society has long-term losses.[6]

The community has several obligations that it ought to fulfill. First, it has a duty to inform. Health education should focus upon empowering individuals to make the healthiest choices that they are able to. Second, where the evidence for certain kinds of healthy choices is clear, the community has the responsibility of enacting laws that will safeguard the community. Third, the community should devote its resources wisely in order to enable the greatest number of people to be able to be healthy. Decisions about the use of resources should emphasize low-cost, high-benefit needs. For example, immunizations should be preferred to cosmetic surgery. Finally, social responsibility demands that natural, human, and monetary resources should benefit the society as a whole and they should not only be used by the wealthy minority.

The first duty, then, of the community is to educate. By sharing objective knowledge about how different choices affect our health, the community empowers the individual person to make better decisions. The first teachers are, of course, the parents, who impart basic lessons. Obviously, they ought to also practice what they say! Family, schools, government, business, and other social groups will also teach lessons that are proper to their role.

When simply offering choices is not enough, there is also an obligation to then compel certain decisions. This should be done in a way that most indirectly compromises the decision-making of the individual person. The purpose is not to eliminate the person's free will, but to influence it. Most laws work not by direct intervention, but by influencing the culture in which decisions are made. By structuring choice, the society points the way toward self-sufficiency.

Recent social changes in American society point to these two approaches. Public service announcements, coupled with a change in public laws, have led to a shift in society about the health effects of cigarette smoking. Where forty or fifty years ago smoking was considered to have few health effects and was socially not only acceptable but encouraged (mostly by the advertising of the tobacco companies), it now is developing an increasing stigma. The educational approach was accomplished not only by formal education in schools but also by ad campaigns that contradicted the glamorous image of smoking. On the legal front, lawsuits were brought against the tobacco companies by the individual states. Laws were also changed to make public smoking less acceptable by, for example, limiting the areas in which smokers could light up. Both education and legal compulsion has begun to change the social acceptance of this addiction.

Laws can help to set the boundaries for good health, but they can never substitute for free will. As was noted in the earlier chapter on moral theory, people develop their sense of morality at different paces. However, relatively few people, even adults, move beyond a morality that is not heavily, or even totally, influenced by law. Used well, it can subtly and sometimes directly change behavior. Used indiscriminately, it will lose its power over time.

A third area in which the community exercises responsibility is in the use of resources. No society has an unlimited supply of resources on which to draw. Around the world, there are many people who have to live their daily lives in search of the basic necessities of life. So, there are two aspects of this use of resources that ought to be considered. First, every community has a responsibility to conserve what resources that it has and to use them only as needed. Second, there is another responsibility to share what one has with others. Resources are not evenly distributed around the world, and there is a need for resources in places where they do not naturally exist.

In terms of conserving resources, we should, when possible, minimize our use of available resources, and try to develop new methods of using resources that conserve. Although minimizing resources will often be cost-effective, at other times, it may not be. At that point, both governments and businesses need to carefully consider the long- and the short-term benefits that could be achieved through minimizing resources.

As to sharing resources with those less fortunate, an excellent example of this is the distribution of vaccines by the pharmaceutical company, Merck. In the 1980s, Merck was attempting to develop a new treatment for cancer. Although researchers did not find what they were looking for, they did discover a drug that was highly effective for treating onchocerciasis, or Nile River Blindness. For about fifty dollars per dose of Mectizan, patients could be cured of the disease.

The Merck research scientists felt obligated to help the African and Latin American people suffering from river blindness because they knew they had found a cure. Merck executives explored third-party payment options for Mectizan with the World Health Organization, the U.S. Agency for International Development, the U.S. Department of State, and the U.S. Congress that would finance a low-cost delivery system of this needed medication. Every attempt failed. Knowing that the drug was effective and that it was needed, Merck decided to underwrite the financial costs of the program itself. Today, over thirty million people in thirty-two countries have been treated with the drug, and the World Health Organization has announced that it may be possible to completely eradicate the disease.[7]

This is an excellent example of meeting the needs of the poor, even though there is no profit for the corporation. Obviously, governments, nonprofits, and for-profit businesses do have to operate efficiently. All have to show some gain in investment or they will cease operations. Yet, the goal of any economic system is to meet other needs of the community. Profit is not a goal in and of itself. This is why Catholic social teaching does not explicitly favor one economic system over another. Rather, it focuses upon the end point and rightfully acknowledges that there may be several ways of reaching the same goals.[8]

Although it may be argued that capitalism does an excellent job of maintaining efficiency, the overall good of meeting basic human needs must also be kept in mind. In this case, Merck saw this and responded, although there was no profit to be made through selling the drug. Merck's corporate mission statement explicitly highlights this approach: "Our business is preserving and improving human life," and "We expect profits, but only from work that satisfies customer needs and benefits humanity."[9]

Health Care Systems

The United States has one of, if not the, most developed health care systems in the world. The federal government has spent huge amounts of money on research and development of medicine. Private businesses, like pharmaceutical companies, have been able to use this social resource and to also then invest their own money in the development of new technologies and pharmaceutical solutions to various health problems.

American health care is modeled on a mixed economic system of capitalism for those with financial resources and socialism for the poor and elderly. Although we give capitalism much latitude to make the exchange of goods and services cost-effective, there are times at which the government also steps in and requires that certain social goods be obtained. For example, although most individuals pay for their health care through third-party medical insurance that is offered as a product by for-profit corporations, there is another program that is financed through the federal government to give minimal coverage to individuals who cannot either afford or who fail to qualify for this coverage.

Catholic health care also fulfills this niche. Approximately 13 percent of community hospitals in the United States are Catholic. Yet, they often provide a greater percentage of public health and specialty services than for-profit, government-sponsored, and other non-profit health care facilities. For example, in areas like social work services, hospice, palliative care, and HIV/AIDS treatment, Catholic health care facilities nationally offer more services.[10]

In the past twenty years, Catholic health care, like its for-profit competitors, has moved from stand-alone facilities into the development of large health care systems. Today, there are sixty systems, which reach every state.[11] Geographically, individual systems sweep up the east and west coasts of the United States and over large areas of the Midwest. Economically, there are great benefits that can be made through a consolidation of services. Most individual Catholic health facilities throughout the United States now belong to one of these systems. There are various models for how the systems work, but the essential characteristic that we will focus on is that the systems allow a shifting of resources from the wealthy to the poor.

Many Catholic health care facilities are in the poorest parts of the inner city. At the same time, there are other hospitals, nursing homes, and clinics in more affluent neighborhoods. Originally, Catholic health care owes its founding to the dedicated orders of sisters who were missionaries in America. They were, and are, the thread that binds these different kinds of care together. They, personally, provided a link between these two diverse communities. Although sometimes there was a transfer of financial help, more often it was the moral connection that made possible the continued services in the poorer neighborhoods. Community leaders who came to know the sisters served alongside them in fundraising. Today, that same link continues to provide health care to the poorest people in the United States.

Clearly, some of these economically depressed areas, whether they are rural or inner city, simply cannot jumpstart themselves easily. They do not possess either the human or the natural resources with which to improve their conditions. So, these need to be given and nurtured so that they someday can do so. Education and the shifting of resources are necessary for their development and their survival.

By favoring the gift of resources to poorer communities, we are making a decision that the strict structures of capitalism should not be followed. Although aspects of a free market system work to the benefit of the society, if we follow classical capitalism to its logical extreme, we establish a society in which the least fortunate are left to their own abilities to survive. It reinforces a broad kind of Social Darwinism that is opposed to Christian values.

In Catholic teaching, the principle is called the Preferential Option for the Poor. That is, whenever decisions are made for the society, we ought to choose in favor of what provides advantages for the poorest members of society. We need to make explicit decisions that will help them to be self-sufficient, productive members of the community. In other words, we should prefer the choice that benefits those who do not have the power to choose for themselves.

This points us toward another issue: how our limited resources ought to be spent. If we favor the poor, then we ought to fund those kinds of health care that will serve them. Low-cost, effective, preventive health care should therefore be at the top of whatever list of spending priorities we have.

In the American health care system, our resources are oriented toward highly technical, acute care. Although we do fund programs in public health, most of our resources are spent on providing technological solutions to health problems. Organ transplants, ICU care, and cosmetic surgery are all expensive technologies. Although they are very effective at what they attempt, there is an inherent conflict. As a society, we must make choices about how the limited resources that we have will be spent.

Over the twentieth century, as medicine was able to develop new drugs and treatments, more and more was spent on research and care. In the first half of the twentieth century, American medicine was transformed. There were very few limitations on spending. The benefit was that new breakthroughs were made on a consistent basis and that many hospitals were established or expanded. The liability was that the spending was financed through a favorable World War II economy, whose effect lasted for about twenty-five years after the war.

In the past forty years, an emphasis upon maximizing the benefit to be derived from these resources has transformed American medicine. Since 1983, when the federal government, who pays for most of the medical spending in the United States, instituted a cost control system, called the Medicare Prospective Payment System, there has been a movement toward standardizing care. Prior to the institution of the Medicare Prospective Payment System, health care facilities were reimbursed for the costs of their services. The then-Department of Health and Human Services established a medical coding system that would reimburse health care practitioners at standard rates for the same procedure. One author has noted the "reimbursement environment from the late 1960s until the early 1980s made it difficult not to make money operating hospitals, so long as they were located away from concentrations of low-income populations and in states that did not regulate hospital income."[12] Not coincidentally, as the medical infrastructure grew, so did for-profit hospital companies. By the early 1980s, there were six large for-profit hospital chains operating in the United States.[13]

Since that time, medical coding has defined medical practice. Insurance companies use modified forms of the original program, and physicians must bill using those codes. The effect has been that there has been a standardization of care and a limitation on physicians in how they practice medicine. Although there are some benefits to this approach, including establishing a more efficient use of resources for health care, it has also placed a financial burden on the health care providers, who must spend more time documenting care and seeking reimbursement.

Our health care system is now geared mostly for acute care. We have sophisticated ICUs and many wonderful pharmaceuticals that have radically transformed our life span. The difficulty is that other types of medical care have been de-emphasized. Since we have devoted our resources toward acute care, the funding mechanisms are oriented toward it. Most people, for example, have limited insurance coverage for hospice treatment, although it is likely that a majority of the present population will have need of this service in the future. As previously mentioned, Catholic health care facilities provide a disproportionate amount of health care services that are not very profitable.

Another difficulty is that we have invested in an economic system that favors those who are employees of large businesses. As unions gained power after World War II, they included health care as a bargaining point. Businesses began to add health care insurance as a benefit to their employees, and eventually the health insurance company became the means by which medical bills were paid. Today, the majority of persons in the United States who are covered by health insurance do so through employer-sponsored plans. Self-employed persons and those who work for small businesses, who make up the backbone of the American economy, are hard-pressed to get coverage.

Health care is thus paid for by third parties, either the federal government or private insurers. For those who do not qualify for entry into those systems, it becomes more and more difficult to afford not only disease and trauma treatment, but also preventative care. We are in a difficult position because many people both want the best care, and they would like to have little cost to their coverage. Since the insurance companies did most of the medical spending, until recently people did not see the rising costs. Premiums remained steady and coverage continued as it had before.

Now, the costs are being shifted back toward the consumer. Insurance carriers are limiting the total lifetime amount of coverage, increasing deductibles, and limiting the kinds of drugs that will be covered. Year after year, the price tag for medical insurance is going up, and it is a constant task for human resource managers to negotiate new policies.

The situation is even more difficult for those who are self-employed or who have some kind of underlying health condition. Those whose insurance coverage is not offered through a group plan pay much higher rates. If the person who seeks the insurance has a documented health condition, his or her coverage will be very high, if he or she can get coverage at all. In one recent article, a woman described how the delivery of her child under a self-insured plan was billed to her at $22,000, even though she thought that she was covered under her policy![14]

As resources become more and more strained, there has been increased public pressure to change our present health care funding system away from a strict capitalist model to one that is controlled by the federal government. Although there are some national health care models that emphasize a strong national control of health care through the government bureaucracy, like that of the United Kingdom, this is not the only model.

The first such national health care system was implemented in Germany in the late nineteenth century. Named for the German chancellor who proposed it as a political move to disempower the growing Socialist party, the Bismarck model attempted to strengthen the German monarchical political system by admitting the criticisms of the Socialists but solving them under the prevailing political system.[15] In the opinion of one author, Germany's social insurance system was perhaps Bismark's greatest triumph, having had its effects permeate successive generations.[16] The Bismarck health care model is a mixture of private insurance and national control. Private insurers, called "sickness funds," are paid jointly by workers and their employers. Unlike the U.S. system, insurers are required to cover everyone, and they do not make a profit. Medical care is provided by independent physicians and hospitals. The government regulates costs and reimbursement rates. France, Belgium, the Netherlands, and Switzerland also follow this model.

The United Kingdom's National Health System uses what is called the Beveridge model, after Sir William Beveridge, the economist and social reformer. Shortly after the beginning of the Second World War, Beveridge was charged with chairing the Interdepartmental Committee on Social Insurance and Allied Services in order to assess how the nascent welfare programs that were administered by the British government could be more efficiently run. Having advocated a greater governmental role in addressing what he called the five "giants"— want, idleness, sickness, squalor, and ignorance—Beveridge used the committee to argue for a national system of social security, health care, full employment, and educational benefits. Working from a Keyensian economic model, he argued that in times of economic hardship, the government should increase rather than reduce social spending in order to stimulate the economy. Although all of the pieces that he envisioned were not eventually adopted, the establishment of national health care was one of the lasting effects of his report. In fact, there are multiple examples of how a national health care system can strike a balance between private businesses and national control. The Beveridge model has been influential in many other nations besides the United Kingdom. Spain, most of Scandinavia, New Zealand, Hong Kong, and Cuba use this model.

Canada, Taiwan, and South Korea offer yet another model that takes parts of both the Beveridge and Bismarck models. Instead of having the government offer all of the services, as in the Beveridge model, or leaving the funding to controlled private insurers, as in the Bismarck model, the National Health Insurance model uses private-sector providers, and the government provides payment through a national insurance program into which every citizen pays. As the sole payor, the government negotiates rates with the private health care companies and the practitioners. So, fees for services and costs for pharmaceuticals tend to be lower than in a system like that of the U.S. Companies in Canada, for example, have made tidy profits by undercutting the costs of identical drugs offered in the United States.

When the subject of national health care is debated in the United States, the tendency is to demonize any proposed system as an overreaching exercise of federal power. To be fair, it also seems as though many such proposals lean heavily toward the Beveridge model, and thus the criticism rings at least partially true. However, as we have just seen, there are several different ways of approaching a government-private sector jointly run health care system.

Catholic thought has been very supportive of moving American health care toward a national model. In 1993, the U.S. Catholic bishops approved the publication of *A Framework for Comprehensive Health Care Reform: Protecting*

Human Life, Promoting Human Dignity, Pursuing the Common Good. In that document, they wrote that

> Our approach to health care is shaped by a simple but fundamental principle: "Every person has a right to adequate health care. This right flows from the sanctity of human life and the dignity that belongs to all human persons, who are made in the image of God. Health care is more than a commodity; it is a basic *human right*, an essential safeguard of human life and dignity.[17]

They called for the reform of what they judged to be an unjust system because resources were unfairly distributed, access to care was either outright denied to the poor or severely limited, and the rising costs of the present system would continue to diminish the ability of the present system to care for the majority of Americans.

The bishops urged that any health care reform should conform to eight principles:

1. *Respect for Life*—whether it preserves and enhances the sanctity and dignity of human life from conception to natural death.
2. *Priority Concern for the Poor*—whether it gives special priority to meeting the most pressing health care needs of the poor and underserved, ensuring that they receive quality health services.
3. *Universal Access*—whether it provides ready universal access to comprehensive health care for every person living in the United States.
4. *Comprehensive Benefits*—whether it provides comprehensive benefits sufficient to maintain and promote good health; to provide preventive care; to treat disease, injury, and disability appropriately; and to care for persons who are chronically ill or dying.
5. *Pluralism*—whether it allows and encourages the involvement of the public and private sectors, including the voluntary, religious, and non-profit sectors, in the delivery of care and services; and whether it ensures respect for religious and ethical values in the delivery of health care for consumers and for individual and institutional providers.
6. *Quality*—whether it promotes the development of processes and standards that will help to achieve quality and equity in health services, in the training of providers, and in the informed participation of consumers in decision-making on health care.
7. *Cost Containment and Controls*—whether it creates effective cost-containment measures that reduce waste, inefficiency, and unnecessary care; measures that control rising costs of competition, commercialism, and administration; and measures that provide incentives to individuals and providers for effective and economical use of limited resources.
8. *Equitable Financing*—whether it assures society's obligation to finance universal access to comprehensive health care in an equitable fashion, based on ability to pay; and whether proposed cost-sharing arrangements are designed to avoid creating barriers to effective care for the poor and vulnerable.[18]

The Catholic Health Association has also been a strong proponent for a transformation of our present system. In its statement of principles, called *Continuing the Commitment: A Pathway to Health Care Reform*, members stated that:

> Distinct Catholic values, including protection of human life from conception to natural death, a preferential option for the poor, and a sense of responsible stewardship, have always provided a solid foundation and starting point for all of CHA's advocacy efforts. Combined with an intentional focus on responding to the health care needs of individuals, families, and communities, these values have been and will continue to be the driving impetus for CHA's reform initiatives.[19]

Contemporary Challenges to Health Care

The delicate balance of our present funding system is also being threatened by other developments. Two of the most significant are the use of genetic information and also demographic population trends. In the 1997 film *Gattaca*, the fortunes of the citizens of a futuristic society are dictated by the vicissitudes of their genetic code. The genetically superior are guaranteed a comfortable life, while the rest are allowed a minimal existence. While we are not today at such a level of diagnostic sophistication, nor are we living in a society that proposes such a blatant sorting of the population, the specter of the misuse of genetic information is rapidly emerging.

The Human Genome Project, a scientific research study that is funded by the National Institutes of Health in order to "create an encyclopedia of the human genome—a complete map and sequence," has already begun to affect our lives.[20] Recent discoveries have shown a relation of genetic abnormalities to cystic fibrosis and other diseases.

With the ability to have such information also comes the potential for misuse. Particularly within American society, insurance is one area where genetic information can have serious repercussions, both for the private citizen as well as the private corporation. Genetic information is, after all, information, and that is the basis on which funding decisions for health care must be made. Individuals desire insurance coverage in order to adequately prepare for unforeseen events. At the same time, insurance is also a business. Private corporations provide coverage only when it is to their economic advantage. If companies are not permitted to make rational decisions regarding a level of appropriate risk, insurance cannot be offered. There is, therefore, an ethical conflict between the insurance companies and the consumer about this medical information and how it is to be used.

There is a conflict between the right to privacy for the patient, a duty of confidentiality for the health care professional, and the justice of access to genetic information for insurance companies. The use of the term "privacy" may be misleading. In the United States, the term connotes not only a right to non-interference in personal liberty but also a limitation on the use of information. In Europe, the preferred legislative term for privacy rights in relation to information has been "data protection."[21]

Within Catholic ethics, there is no absolute right to privacy (except in Confession) with regard to medical information, but justice and prudence demand appropriate safeguards of the person's best interests. Although many persons would like an absolute right to privacy, it does not exist. Due to our nature as social and individual beings, a conflict will always exist between personal desires and social needs. While most of us would wish for some degree of control over our own lives, we recognize compelling social needs that override our individual right to self-determination, free speech, and many other basic human rights. The same applies to the issue of access to medical information.

To interpret the present situation in light of Catholic social teaching, it will be necessary to understand how "privacy" as a concept both converges and diverges from its common use. The Second Vatican Council, for example, addresses the right to privacy in *Gaudium et Spes*. In the context of defining the nature of the common good, the Council Fathers wrote of the right of the human person "to his good name, to respect, to proper knowledge, the right to act according to the dictates of conscience and to safeguard his privacy."[22] In the postconciliar instruction, *Communio et Progressio*, The Pontifical Commission for the Means of Mass Communication also makes reference to this right when it speaks of the responsibilities of news organizations: "But the right to information is not limitless. It has to be reconciled with other existing rights. There is the right of truth which guards the good name both of men and of societies. There is the right of privacy which protects the private life of families and of individuals. . . . This right to information is inseparable from freedom of communication."

A Catholic understanding of a right to privacy must be understood within the broader categories of the nature of the human person and his or her relation to the common good. In this context, the meaning of freedom is also a critical focal point. Implicit in American concepts of the term is the belief in the almost absolute autonomy of individual liberty and self-determination.[23] The philosophical basis of American claims about rights differs greatly from the Catholic use of the same terms. As David Hollenbach, S.J., has noted:

> Catholic rights theory is far removed from individualistic or libertarian rights theory. The theory presented in the encyclicals is personalist, and not individualist, and it recognizes that persons are essentially social and institution building beings. Because of this fact, the personal rights which belong to every human being in an unmediated way create duties which bind other persons, society and the state."[24]

The Catholic understanding of the right to privacy, then, is founded upon a theological understanding of personhood that differs from that of American society. One of the hallmarks of the present pope, John Paul II, has been to consistently address this understanding of the human person and to apply this concept to compelling issues.[25] In his first encyclical, *Redemptor Hominis*, he began his pontificate with a clear statement of the nature of the person:

> The man who wishes to understand himself thoroughly-and not just in accordance with immediate, partial and often superficial and even illusory standards and measures of his being-he must with his unrest, uncertainty, and even his weakness and sinfulness, with his life and death, draw near to Christ. He must, so to speak, enter into Him with all his own self, he must "appropriate" and assimilate the whole of the reality of the Incarnation and Redemption in order to find himself. If this profound process takes place within him, he then bears fruit not only of adoration of God, but also at deep wonder of himself.[26]

It is only through Christ, through a reflection on the Incarnation and the Redemption that the profound meaning of the person may be understood, he argues. The Incarnation and the Redemption point both to our creation by God in his image and the unconditional love that he has for us, which saves us from our own sinfulness.[27] "The person in the community . . . as a fundamental factor in the common good, constitute(s) the essential criterion for all programs, systems and regimes," John Paul II said elsewhere.[28]

Our inability, or unwillingness, to recognize that the person is one, if not *the*, weakness of our contemporary society. Speaking to bishops in Puebla, Mexico, in 1979, John Paul II said:

> Perhaps one of the most obvious weaknesses of our present day civilization lies in an inadequate view of man. Without doubt, our age is the one in which man has been most written and spoken of, the age of the forms of humanism and anthropocentrism. Nevertheless, it is paradoxically also the age of man's abasement to previously unsuspected levels, the age of human values trampled on as never before.[29]

A proper anthropology, then, sees the human person as both individual and social by nature. Created in the image and likeness of God, we find our purpose in community. Any right to privacy supposes that the right must be interpreted in light of the common good. The freedom to act one way or another, then, is conditioned by the natural goals that have already been given to us by God. We may not act in a way that violates our individual or our social nature.

The growing development of computer technology in medicine has forced us to more carefully delineate the origins and applications of limitations to privacy and confidentiality and their influence on the justice of providing adequate access to health care. Computers enable us to collect and to manage information more productively, which also allows persons to make decisions that were impossible in past years.

In the case of insurance, this means that the process of underwriting some types of policies, which involves assessing the potential risk of loss with the prospective profit, can be profoundly influenced by additional information. Individually underwritten polices, in which a person must be "qualified" in order to complete the contract, as opposed to simplified issue policies, where a class of persons are given a group policy, will be most affected.[30] In the former, specific personalized information is used to more assess the potential risk to the insurance company. In simplified policies, this information is not required. With the increased risk for the insurance company comes an increased cost for the prospective insured person. Yet, even this simple distinction between individual and simplified policies understates the varieties of ethical conflict that are inherent in insurance coverage. As one source figures it, when we consider that there are three basic forms of insurance (health, life, and disability), and three categories for each (private, group, and social), with four additional criteria on one's genetic risk, there are possibly "fifty-four different situations where there are (potentially) different ethical, social and legal problems" in insurance coverage.[31]

Underwriting such risks involves assessing four criteria: a sufficient number of homogenous risks, a definite and measurable loss, a fortuitous loss, and a non-catastrophic loss.[32] When these criteria are thrown into imbalance, insurance no longer presents a profitable business. The first means that a pool of similar people must share the risk. If, for example, a group of persons are tested and are shown to be genetically positive for a particular form of cancer, it would not be in the insurance company's best interest to insure them since the risk is not shared equally by all. Actuaries provide a statistical basis for the second criterion. The third means that the loss and subsequent payment of benefits should be random. Finally, the nature of the loss should be such that it will not bankrupt the company.

At the heart of the issue from the insurance company's point of view is what is known as "adverse selection."[33] This is when a person is aware of information that would indicate that he or she is more likely to make an early claim on his or her policy but withholds such information from the insurance company. Obviously, widely available genetic testing would also make it possible for a person who receives a positive report on his or her susceptibility for a particular disease or condition to make such an "adverse selection" much more accurately. In essence, in order for insurance to be both profitable and obtainable, both parties must be aware of the risks and the prospective benefits of the insurance policy.

The relationship between an individual policyholder and the insurance company will be significantly affected by the availability of genetic information. In many ways, it resembles the relationship between a card dealer and a player at a blackjack table. The house and the dealer know that the odds are in their favor. The player, however, is willing to take a small risk in order to achieve certain possible benefits. If either the player or the dealer has additional information, it is impossible to play the game in the same way. Genetic information creates an imbalance of power between the insurance company and the person.

Whoever has access to the information would have an advantage over the other party.

Changing the nature of the relationship between the person and the insurer would have significant social implications in the United States, which relies upon a free market mechanism to insure some degree of adequate health care. The conditions for access to medical information is thus at the heart of the issue. As medical databases become more common, it will be technologically possible (and probable) to link many different kinds of information very accurately. Individuals, as well as companies and possibly even the government, will want access to the information. Already today there are ethical conflicts concerning the use of medical information, which will be exacerbated by genetics.

Laws that protect patient health confidentiality on the state level tend to be applications of broader principles that recognize a professional privilege. The record itself is not protected, only the information that is gained in a privileged relationship. When the information is placed in the record, it is "privileged" because of the way in which the information was obtained. In and of itself, the record is not considered to be confidential, but the means of obtaining it is, and thus the record becomes protected vicariously.[34]

The difficulty with this method of assuring confidentiality is that there is no broad principle of the confidentiality of a record. As a society, we have not yet tackled the issue of who should have access to health information and how it should be used. The implications become most apparent when one considers the blanket consent form that most insurance companies require of their prospective policyholders. The Medical Information Bureau (MIB), a private association that is sponsored by approximately five hundred insurance companies, contains vast amounts of medical information that is obtained by the use of blanket consent forms. In order to apply for insurance, an applicant must agree to the release of information to the MIB. Information obtained by the insurance company by applicants is not routinely given to the individual unless a specific request for it is made in writing. According to Turkington, the MIB maintains records on approximately fifteen million Americans.[35] For the most part, the exchange of information by the MIB is unregulated on either the federal or the state level. Although the individual gives "consent," it is so broad that its only purpose is to legally protect the insurance company. The discretion of who has access to the information is left to the insurance company. In no sense is the information subject to the control of the person.

Individuals are very concerned about the growing ability to access all kinds of personal information. While one can clearly see that some of this fear may be due to ignorance about the technology, there is a legitimate issue that underlies this problem. Americans are very wary of intrusions into their private lives. As the film *Gattaca* dramatically illustrates, we can envision a world where information can become prejudicial to the individual. Any resolution to the question of who may access health care information will ultimately need to balance the need for privacy with legitimate social concerns. To move too much in one direction or another without a radical overhaul of the American health system to a national model will result in an imbalance of power. Persons have a right to ordinary health care, and insurance companies need to make just economic decisions on how they can provide social benefits while maintaining profitability.

The U.S. Congress has taken steps to regulate the use of genetic information. In 2008, President Bush signed into law the Genetic Information Nondiscrimination Act (GINA). This legislation prohibited the use of genetic information for insurance underwriting, among other provisions. It also prohibited insurance companies from using genetic information to establish pre-existing health conditions in order to exclude persons from coverage.[36]

Another looming issue is the demographic shift in the average age of the American population. Due to the success of medicine in the twentieth century, individuals are much healthier than in previous generations. Two trends have emerged as a result. First, we are living longer. The life expectancy of a child born in the United States in 1900 was 47.3 years. By 2006, one could expect to live to be 77.7 years old.[37] Second, fertility rates have slowly declined. American women who are between the ages of forty and forty-four years presently have an average of 1.9 children each, which is below replacement-level fertility rates. That is, we are not having enough children to replace our present population.[38] In order to do so, there needs to be slightly more than two births per woman during her lifetime. In the United States, the declining fertility rate has been mitigated by the increasing number of immigrants, as well as the fact that the Hispanic population has a higher-than-average fertility rate. However, in Europe, and other developed nations like Australia, the declining fertility rates are an even greater cause for concern.[39]

According to Kohler et al., European nations over the past fifteen years have seen "the emergence of unprecedented low fertility levels with a total fertility rate (*TFR*) at or below 1.3 children per woman."[40] He calls these patterns "*lowest-low fertility* to emphasize the dramatic implications of these unprecedentedly low levels of fertility: for instance, if they persist over a long time in a contemporary low-mortality context, *TFR* levels at or below 1.3 imply a reduction of the annual number of births by 50% and a halving of the population size in less than 45 years."[41] In 1961, Australia's TFR was 3.55 babies per woman. In 2001, that percentage had dropped to its lowest rate of 1.71 babies.[42]

So, the United States, as well as other Western industrial nations, is facing a population that is becoming more elderly, along with a decline in the number of persons who will replace them. Financially, this will have a significant effect. Presently, our funding mechanism for health care, especially for social welfare programs like Social Security, Medicaid, and Medicare, rely upon a stable, if not slightly increasing, number of full-time workers who provide the resources that allow these programs to fund care of the elderly. As the population ages, there will be an increased demand for services that are funded by a shrinking pool of workers. In the words of the Congressional Budget Office, "The retirement of the baby-boom generation portends a significant, long-lasting shift in the age profile of the U.S. population, which will dramatically alter the balance between the working-age and retirement-age components of that population."[43]

In January of 2008, the first person in the baby boomer generation, Kathleen Casey-Kirschling, became eligible to collect social security benefits. In the twenty years following, approximately eighty million persons, or about ten thousand a day, will become eligible for social security.[44] The Congressional Budget Office has forecast an unprecedented growth in federal spending for the three entitlement programs of Social Security, Medicare, and Medicaid. In 2005, together they accounted for approximately 8.6 percent of the gross domestic product (GDP). By 2050, spending is anticipated to rise to 19.9 percent of the GDP.[45] In short, it will be all but impossible to continue to fund these three programs under the present system. With a shrinking workforce and an aging population, there simply will not be enough money to sustain these programs.

If there is a right, as the Catholic Church believes, to ordinary health care, we should also look carefully at the means by which we accomplish it. Our present health care system cannot continue to sustain the needs of our society. While it does some things well, like provide an infrastructure for research and innovation, it also fails to provide care for all members of the society. Also, the system is in danger of collapsing financially, as genetics and demographics take their toll. There is an immense challenge to reconstruct our health care system in a way that is both just and financially sustainable. Anyone who has studied the issue will attest that something *must* be done.

Our social responsibility is to help each person become the best person that he or she can be. There are many economic models that will enable us to meet some of our present needs. Unfortunately, it would be impossible to meet every need. So, we must try to be as equitable to each person as we can. The eight principles offered by the U.S. Catholic bishops provide a structure for assessing some of those models. By seeking a health care system that ensures universal coverage; is oriented toward the poor; utilizes public/private partnerships; emphasizes preventative, chronic, and critical care; provides quality; seeks cost containment; and has equitable payment mechanisms, we will at least include in the discussion the key goods that must be met. While we are obligated as individuals to be as healthy as we can, this is not just a solitary task. There is a social responsibility for health care that we also all share.

Notes

1. Edward L. Bernays, "The Engineering of Consent," *The Annals of the American Academy of Political and Social Science* 250, no. 1(1947): 113–120. Bernays, the nephew of Sigmund Freud, was the first person to apply Freud's psychological theories to business. He is generally considered to be the originator of modern public relations.

2. Preamble to the Constitution of the World Health Organization as adopted by the International Health Conference, New York, 19–22 June, 1946; signed on 22 July 1946 by the representatives of sixty-one states (Official Records of the World Health Organization, no. 2, p. 100) and entered into force on 7 April 1948.

3. Mary Elizabeth O'Brien, *Spirituality in Nursing: Standing on Holy Ground* (Sudbury, MA: Jones and Bartlett, 1999). O'Brien develops a theology of nursing care and describes various models and applications of spiritual care for nursing.

4. See Michael Shnayerson and Mark Plotkin, *The Killers Within: The Deadly Rise of Drug-Resistant Bacteria* (Boston: Little, Brown, 2002).

5. Robert J. Kuczmarski and Katherine M. Flegal, "Increasing Prevalence of Overweight among US Adults," *JAMA: Journal of the American Medical Association* 272, no. 3 (1994): 205.

6. Andrew L. Dannenberg, Deron C. Burton, and Richard J. Jackson, "Economic and Environmental Costs of Obesity: The Impact on Airlines," *American Journal of Preventive Medicine* 27, no. 3 (2004): 264.

7. See http://www.who.int/mediacentre/news/releases/2009/river_blindness _200907 21/en/index.html

8. See John Paul II, *Centessimus Annus*, Encyclical, (1 May 1991), especially § 12–13 and 33–34.

9. See http://www.merck.com/about/mission.html

10. The Catholic Health Association of the United States, *Catholic Healthcare in the United States* (St. Louis, MO: Catholic Health Association, 2009).

11. Catholic Health Association, *Catholic Healthcare.*

12. Bradford H. Gray, *The Profit Motive and Patient Care: A Twentieth Century Fund Report* (Cambridge, MA: Harvard University Press, 1991).

13. Gray, *The Profit Motive.* Gray lists these as the Hospital Corporation of America (200 hospitals), American Medical International (115 hospitals), Humana (87 hospitals), National Medical Enterprises (47 hospitals), Charter Medical Corporation (41 hospitals), and Republic Health Corporation (24 hospitals).

14. See http://www.doublex.com/section/news-politics/health-insurance-woes-my-22000-bill-having-baby (August 5, 2009)

15. See Melchior Palyi, *Compulsory Medical Care and the Welfare State* (Chicago: National Institute of Professional Services, 1949), 21–23.

16. Walter Sulzbach, *German Experience with Social Insurance* (New York: National Industrial Conference Board, 1947) 5-6.

17. National Conference of Catholic Bishops, *A Framework for Comprehensive Health Care Reform: Protecting Human Life, Promoting Human Dignity, Pursuing the Common Good* (Washington, DC: U.S. Conference of Catholic Bishops, 1993), n.p.

18. Conference of Catholic Bishops, *Framework for Comprehensive Health Care Reform*.

19. The Catholic Health Association of America, *Continuing the Commitment: A Pathway to Health Care Reform* (St. Louis: The Catholic Health Association, 2000). Other significant statements of policies and strategies for health care reform may be found in the 1984 report of the CHA Stewardship Task Force, *No Room in the Marketplace* (1986), and *Setting Relationships Right: A Proposal for Systemic Health Care Reform* (1993).

20. V. McKusick, "Mapping and Sequencing the Human Gene," *New England Journal of Medicine* 320 (1989): 910.

21. An excellent survey of the American notion of privacy may be found in Philip A. Smith, O.P., "The Right to Privacy: *Roe v. Wade* Revisited," *The Jurist* 43 (1983): 289–317. Smith outlines the diverse meanings of the term and how it has been judicially adjucated from the time of Louis Brandeis and Samuel Warren's foundational article— "The Right to Privacy," *Harvard Law Review* 4 (1890): 190–96—until the time of the article.

22. Vatican II, "*Gaudium et Spes*, Pastoral Constitution," in *Vatican II: The Conciliar and Post-Conciliar Documents*, 1988 Revised Edition, ed. Austin Flannery (Grand Rapids, MI: Eerdmans, 1988), 26, p. 927.

23. How these rights are understood is, of course, a matter of great controversy. See, for example, Ralph F. Gaebler, "Is There a Natural Law Right to Privacy?" *American Journal of Jurisprudence* 37 (1992): 319–336, and Walter Murphy, "The Right to Privacy and Legitimate Constitutional Change," in *The Constitutional Bases of Political and Social Change in the United States* (New York: Praeger, 1990): 213–14.

24. David Hollenbach, *Claims in Conflict: Retrieving and Renewing the Catholic Human Rights Tradition* (New York: Paulist Press, 1979), 97.

25. Much has been written on John Paul II's understanding of the person. His writings, both before and after his election to the papacy, are voluminous, numbering over one hundred articles and seven books. According to George H. Williams, *The Mind of John Paul II: Origins of His Thought and Action* (New York: Seabury, 1981), 354, the definitive pre-papal bibliography on Karol Wojtyla was edited in Polish by Barbara Eychler in *Chrzescianin Swiecie* 74 (February 1979): 67–91. Another bibliography was edited in 1980 under the title *Karol Wojtylaw swietle publikacji: Karol Wojtyla negli scritti*, ed. Wiktor Gramatowski, S.J. and Zofia Wilinska (Vatican City: Liberia Editrice, 1980). Representative articles and books that deal with John Paul II's understanding of the person are J. Brian Benestad, "The Political Vision of Pope John Paul II: Justice through Faith and Culture," *Communio* 8 (1981): 3–19; Ronald Lawler,

John Paul II (Chicago: Franciscan Herald Press, 1982); George Hunston Williams, "John Paul II's Concepts of Church, State and Society," *Journal of Church and State* 24 (Autumn 1982): 463–96; and *The Mind of John Paul II*; Elzbieta Wolicka, "Participation in Community: Wojtyla's Social Anthropology," trans.Alice Manterys, *Communio* 8 (1981): 108–118; and Andrew Woznicki, *A Christian Humanism: Karol Wojtyla's Existential Personalism* (New Britain, CT: Mariel, 1980). Obviously, however, Karol Wotjyla's works before he became pope would afford a much more nuanced appreciation for his ideas. Yet, given the immense discussion of his pre-papal conception of the person, particularly with regard to his book, *The Acting Person* (see George H. Williams, "John Paul II's Concepts of Church, State and Society," 468, fn. 17, for a sense of the debate about three competing English translations of the meaning of chapter 7 in that book), it will be necessary to limit this analysis.

26. John Paul II, Encyclical, *Redemptor Hominis*, 4 March 1979, English translation, (Boston, MA: Daughters of St. Paul, 1979), 18–19, §10; original Latin text published in AAS 71 (1979): 257–324.

27. John Paul II, *Redemptor Hominis*, 17, § 9.

28. John Paul II, *Redemptor Hominis*, 36, § 17.

29. John Paul II, Address, *Amados Hermanos*, 28 January 1979, English translation in *Origins* 8 (8 February 1979): 534; original Spanish text in AAS 71 (1979): 195.

30. Robert J. Pokorski, "A Test for the Insurance Industry," *Nature* 391 (26 February 1998): 835-8

31. Ray Mosely, Lee Crandall, Marvin Dewar, David Nye, and Harry Oster, "Ethical Implications of a Complete Human Gene Map for Insurance," *Business and Professional Ethics Journal* 10 (Winter 1991): 73.

32. Mosley et al., "Ethical Implications," 75.

33. Pokorski, 835.

34. Pokorski, 117.

35. Pokorski, 115.

36. The full text of the bill, HR 493: Genetic Information Nondiscrimination Act of 2008, may be found at the Library of Congress website at this address: http://thomas.loc.gov/cgi-bin/query/D?c110:6:./temp/~c110n04ox8::

37. Centers for Disease Control/National Center for Health Statistics, *Life Expectancy at Birth, 65 and 85 Years of Age, US, Selected Years 1900-2006*, http://205.207.175.93/HDI/ReportFolders/reportFolders.aspx. (Accessed 1 October 2009).

38. Jane Lawler Dye, *Fertility of American Women: 2006* (Washington, DC: U.S. Census Bureau, 2008), 1.

39. See Hans-Peter Kohler, Francesco C. Billari, and José A. Ortega, "Low Fertility in Europe: Causes, Implications and Policy Options." in *The Baby Bust: Who Will Do the Work? Who Will Pay the Taxes?* ed. F. R. Harris (Lanham, MD: Rowman & Littlefield Publishers, 2006): 48–109.

40. Kohler et al., "Low Fertility in Europe," 48.

41. Kohler et al., "Low Fertility in Europe."

40. Kohler et al., "Low Fertility in Europe," 48.

41. Kohler et al., "Low Fertility in Europe."

42. Susan Linacre, "Australian Social Trends: 2007," Catalogue 4102.0. (Canberra, Australia: Australian Bureau of Statistics, 2007), 9.

43. Congressional Budget Office, *A CBO Study: The Long Term Budget Outlook: 2005* (Washington, DC: The Congress of the United States, 2005), 4.

44. Mark Lassiter, *Nation's First Baby Boomer Files for Social Security Benefits—Online!* (Baltimore: Social Security Administration Press Office, 2007).

45. Congressional Budget Office, "Long Term Budget: 2005," 4, 19, 27–28.

Chapter Five:
Invasive Medical Procedures

The human body is a gift from God. It is not simply a thing, an object. Instead, we are embodied persons, and our identity is bound to our body. Its shape, health, color, gender, and abilities are significant aspects not just of the physicality of the body, but also its identity. We live not just as spiritual but also as physical beings.

In considering the morality of medical procedures that will involve a significant entry into the body, some degree of caution is appropriate. The initial stance of a Christian is that since the body is holy and is intimately attached to who we are, we should not perform acts that would diminish that sacredness. Any alteration of the body is serious, potentially harmful, and should be considered only after a careful deliberation of what it is that is to be done and how it will relate to the overall purpose of our body.

The human body is not a machine. We, as humans, have the tendency to minimize parts of the body and only consider them instead of the whole being. The principle that reflects this belief and that guides ethical actions in invasive procedures is the principle of totality. It states that any procedure that invades the bodily integrity of a person must be considered in light of the complete nature of that person. So, even if a procedure might be efficacious, it must still be justified by the overall effect that it will have on the person. While human life is sacred, there is no absolute obligation to always keep someone alive, nor to always correct what are natural occurrences in the body.

In this chapter, we will examine the development of Christian thought on the morality of invasive medical procedures. We will first discuss the development of practices and beliefs about dissection and vivisection from the Ancient Greeks to the development of modern science. This will then allow us to examine more carefully how the principles for assessing the morality of different kinds of interventions have been understood. Then, we will examine some contemporary surgical practices in the light of these principles.

The History of Dissection

It has not been until relatively recently that most invasive medical procedures were even possibly considered moral. The Greek view (and one could say ancient cultural view in general) of the encounter with the internal human body was one of unease. While it would be reading too much into the medical traditions to say that the dissection of the human cadaver was absolutely prohibited, we can at least note that there was at a minimum a discomfort about working with a dead body. The opening of a dead body was dissuaded by cultural prac-

97

tices that were reinforced by religious beliefs. It was a desecration.[1] According to Von Staden:

> In many ancient Greek sacred laws, every human corpse is considered a significant source of pollution for all who, in any fashion whatsoever, come into contact with it or stand in a relation of kinship to it. An especially common expression of the belief that corpses entail religious and civic pollution is the prohibition against the following activities on the terrain of a sanctuary or in a temple: dying, abandoning or burying a corpse, giving birth, having sexual intercourse, urinating, defecating, and, in the Hellenistic period, menstruating."[2]

One interesting aspect of this idea about the ability of a corpse to pollute was that pagan priests were prohibited to attend to, or even to be near, a corpse. The dead body would profane them. One can see that this attitude is, in fact, quite opposite from later Christian practices of having the priest be present at the moment of death and to be involved in the burial of the dead.

Therefore, very few invasive procedures were performed, and those that were, were done with some reluctance. Aristotle, for example, in justifying the use of animals for dissection and study wrote, "If someone should consider unworthy the observation of other animals, similarly, he should regard that of his own species; it is not in fact without great disgust that we see what comprises the human being: blood, flesh, bones, veins and similar parts."[3] While pointing toward animal models as being worthy of study, and expressing a certain revulsion, Aristotle at least tacitly accepts viewing the interior of the human body. This cannot be used to justify an interpretation of ease with regard to dissection but merely an acknowledgement of its limited usefulness.[4]

This reluctance to open the body had both a philosophical and a practical foundation. Pragmatically, as we now know from science, infections will quickly take hold when there is a disturbance of bodily integrity, unless adequate safeguards are taken. It is likely that many early surgical patients died as much from the infections as from the procedure itself. Over the centuries, some practices became accepted, like bloodletting and craniotomies, but these were not indicative of a general rule of practice. Most often, they were instances of having to deal with accidental events.

In one instance, for example, Galen mentions his success at treating a slave who had been injured while wrestling. After repeated, non-invasive treatments, the wound always became re-infected. Galen reported how his understanding of anatomy permitted him to diagnose the possibility of a bone that protruded into the chest cavity. After intervening and removing the bone, the slave returned to health. In this instance, the surgery was required by the circumstances.[5] Even with these situations, physicians were likely to hand them off to specific practitioners rather than to do them personally. Philosophically, attitudes about dissection were rooted in different perceptions of how medicine should be practiced.

Let us examine the development of different approaches to medicine, beginning with Hippocrates, who is often thought of as the "Father of Medicine."

He practiced on the island of Cos in the Aegean, around the fifth century B.C. Much of the Hippocratic Corpus, or the body of writing attributed to him, has been shown to have been written by others. This was not an unusual situation, as many documents in the ancient world are identified with the founder, rather than the disciples, of a school of thought. For simplicity's sake, however, we will refer to Hippocratic medicine to include all of the works that are part of our collection.

In the works that are thought to be genuine, Hippocrates is more often wrong than right on anatomical details. The structures that he correctly identifies are largely the skeletal system. However, he identifies the brain as a large gland that secretes mucus, the heart as a muscular organ of pyramidal shape, and the circulatory system as being composed of only four pairs of vessels in the body.[6] One author noted that "his descriptions were probably made from the inspection of the surface of the human body and chance observations of human wounds."[7]

Hippocrates did not dissect corpses. Instead, he argued that physicians should diagnose through observation: "If the nature of a disease cannot be perceived by the eye, its diagnosis will involve more trouble and certainly more time than if it can. What escapes our vision we must grasp by mental sight."[8] Hippocrates aimed to make medical practice consistent and reliable. According to the Hippocratic works, physicians should treat patients in a consistent way, based upon experience, and through an analysis of symptoms.

Ultimately, Hippocratic medicine believed in the existence of four foundational elements: earth, air, fire, and water. These corresponded to four humours, or substances, within the human body: black bile, yellow bile, blood, and phlegm. Medical treatment aimed to maintain a balance of these humours in the body. To be in "good humour" was to have an equilibrium of these forces. The influence of this theory is still felt today on our own vocabulary. To be "melancholy" is to have too much black (*melas*) bile (*cholera*), and to be sanguine is to have an abundance of blood, which would make one cheerful, and reddish in the face. The theory of the humours dominated all medical knowledge at the time. In fact, this approach continued to influence medicine until the seventeenth century.

Celsus was a Roman author who is notable for his compilation of the ancient Greek medical information. The scholarly consensus is that he was probably not a physician. However, his descriptions of medicine are generally regarded to be accurate and representative of the state of medicine in the first century A.D. According to him, the first physicians after Hippocrates treated patients in three ways: by diet, by medications, and by hand. Of these three methods, the first, diet, was given the greatest respect. Eventually, a dispute arose among Hippocratic practitioners that led to the development of four different "schools" of thought: Dogmatism, Empiricism, Pneumatism, and Methodism.

While both Dogmatism and Empiricism tended to agree on many treatments, they did not agree on how one could know what health was. The trajectory of Hippocratic medicine was toward uncovering the hidden origins of sickness. This eventually led some of his followers to accept the morality of dissection and even vivisection. The Dogmatists believed that in order to know how to treat disease, one must know have a philosophical knowledge of nature itself in order to then apply the knowledge to treatment. The Empiricists declared that only practice and experience could lead to the most beneficial treatments. In Celsus' words, "there is a primary difference of opinion, some holding that the sole knowledge necessary is derived from experience, others propounding that practice is not sufficient enough, except after acquiring a reasoned knowledge of human bodies and of nature."[9] The Dogmatists thought that dissection would allow the physician to discover the true nature of the body, while the Empiricists believed that one should learn by testing treatments.

Pneumatism and Methodism were later theories of medicine. The first believed that all existence was connected to a universal pneuma, which translates as both "breath" and also as "spirit." Developed from the work of Erisistratus, the Pneumatists treated disease by trying to establish good breathing and balance. A later practitioner was Galen. The second, Methodism, arose in the first century B.C. Identified mostly with the Roman physician Soranus, it argued that the Dogmatists and the Empiricists had made medical practice too complicated. Illness, they thought, was related to the tenseness or the relaxation of the body. Once that could be determined, then the "method" of treatment would be clear. Unfortunately, most of what we know about Methodism comes through the pen of Galen, who was not a fan.

Each of these approaches to medicine had slightly nuanced judgments on the morality of surgery, the dissection of animals and humans, and vivisection. By tracing the different medical authors, we can see the outlines of how they assessed these acts.

For a brief period in ancient history, anatomical studies of both corpses and live persons were carried out by the Dogmatists.[10] The enormity of this small historical lacuna of anatomical dissection cannot be underestimated. Ancient taboos against not only handling corpses but also cutting into them were well established throughout the ancient world.[11] Under the patronage of the Ptolemaic Egyptian kings in Alexandria, two physicians, Herophilus and Erasistratus, are said to have carried out as many as six hundred dissections of corpses, in both public and private settings in the fourth century B.C. Herophilus was also thought to have performed vivisections and dissections of live human beings. Herophilus' articulation of two human skeletons attracted students from afar, possibly including women.[12]

The discoveries of Herophilus and Erasistratus are mentioned in texts that are both supportive and dismissive of their practices. Tertullian, a second century Christian author, Celsus, Augustine, and Galen all mention their practices. These authors tended to uniformly condemn the practice of the vivisection of condemned criminals that was attributed to Herophilus.

The brief acceptance of dissection and vivisection was the result of a shift from an analogical, or symbolic, to a "hands on" method of understanding the human body. As we have already discussed, Hippocratic medicine originally emphasized the study of the human body through a comparison with the animal world, or through philosophical analysis. To know about the human body, one would make comparisons with what one could observe about the world. The acceptance of dissection was a turn toward validating what one knew through observation of the body itself. It was only when the Dogmatists turned their attention to the particulars of human anatomy that dissection became theoretically possible. According to Ludwig Edelstein, the difference between the two approaches is that those who favored dissection focused upon the body itself, without any link to extraneous information.[13]

These two schools of thought are reflected in the work of the Roman writer Celsus, who was an Empiricist. In his work *De Medicina*, we find carefully described distinctions between Dogmatism and Empiricism. The former "propound as requisites, first a knowledge of hidden causes, after these of natural actions also, and lastly of the internal parts."[14] The Empiricists "do indeed accept evident causes as necessary; but they contend that inquiry about obscure causes and natural actions is superfluous because nature is not be comprehended."[15] In advancing this Empiricist position, Celsus condemns dissection and vivisection. Cutting into a live person is not only cruel and violent, but the very act itself changes what will be seen. Similarly, a dead body is not the same as a living one, so what one sees is not what exists in the living. He does believe that one should take advantage of chance opportunities through injury to see how the body works.

The early Christian authors uniformly condemned dissection and vivisection. Tertullian echoes Celsus' view that such acts are pointless. He describes Herophilus as "the well known surgeon, or (as I may almost call him), butcher, who cut up no end of persons in order to investigate the secrets of nature, who ruthlessly handled human creatures to discover their form and make."[16]

Augustine, too, condemned the practices. In *The City of God*, he discusses the contrast between the utility and the beauty of the human body. He concludes, "Assuredly, no part of the human body has been created for the sake of utility which does not also contribute to its beauty."[17] It is precisely this appreciation for beauty that he then invokes against the Alexandrian physicians:

> For although, with a cruel zeal for science, some medical men, who are called anatomists, have dissected the bodies of the dead, and sometimes even of sick persons who died under their knives, and have inhumanly pried into the secrets of the human body to learn the nature of the disease and its exact seat, and how it might be cured, yet those relations of which I speak and which form the concord (*coaptatio*), or as the Greeks call it, harmony, of the whole body outside and in, as of some instrument, no one has been able to discover, because no one has been audacious enough to seek them.[18]

Without a proper sense of the inner structure and beauty of the body, then, anatomy is bound to fail because it assumes that discovering the physical structures will lead them to where they need to begin. In his work *De Anima*, or *On the Soul*, Augustine repeated this criticism, writing that it was useless to try to unveil what is meant to be concealed from view.[19]

Other early Christian writers like Prudentius and Fulgentius also made passing references to the immorality of surgery and dissection. In a poem concerning a martyred deacon, Romanus of Ceasearea, Prudentius describes surgery as "Hippocratic butchery."[20] Fulgentius uses the same description of butchery in his *Mitologicorum Libri Tres*, calling the Court of Galen in "the narrow streets of Alexandria . . . many butcher shops of surgeon-executioners."[21]

This prohibition did not extend, however, to discarding the information gained by Herophilus and Erisistratus. Their discoveries, both accurate and erroneous, served as the main source of anatomical information until the Renaissance, in the sixteenth century. Other writers on medicine made comparisons with this material with information gleaned from animal dissection and observation.

Galen, a second-century Roman physician, was notable for his extensive writings on anatomy, as well as on other subjects. He synthesized his knowledge of anatomy from the works of the Alexandrians, his dissection of animals, and his own observations. He was a surgeon as well as a physician. He gained information from his studies of an intact human skeleton in Alexandria, as well as his examination of bodies in his professional practice and others that he happened upon. He reported various encounters with dead bodies, at different stages of decomposition. These included bodies from destroyed tombs and the decaying body of a robber whose flesh was eaten away by birds.

Galen represents a synthesis of the earlier analogical tradition with that of the Alexandrians. Following the Roman prohibition against dissection, he did none himself, although in his role as surgeon, he obtained specific information about human anatomy. He was talented enough at surgical techniques to be named as the physician to the gladiators at Pergamon in 158 A.D. for a period of thirty-five months, during which he was reappointed a total of five times.[22] Galen, using the work of his predecessors, organized and then expanded upon the information from his own experience. He firmly believed that good medical practice required a thorough knowledge of human anatomy. Even in his comparison with animal models, he adopts the position that any parts that are used must be made with those animals that are most like humans. His influence was so great that his writings were required of medical students from his lifetime until they were superseded in the sixteenth century.[23]

One should note, however, that even though there was a general agreement that the body was not to be dissected, popular practices worked against this ideal. In the early Church, and later in the Middle Ages, the bodies of dead saints were often partitioned. Individual relics were distributed among several churches. Body parts were often stored in specially made vessels, called reliquaries, that were shaped like the piece that was inside. body must always remain intact. For example, from the early into the late Middle Ages, as the cult of the saints grew, relics became sought-after items. The completeness of the saint's body, in

the sense that his holiness was retained within the relic itself, points to an acceptance for parturition of the body.[24]

Second, medieval burial practices tended to reinforce the belief that what
counted in terms of the grave was that it be located near a holy place, like the
tomb of a saint. Our modern concept of a permanent place of rest in an individual grave was not a common expectation, unless you were of royal blood or you
were a particularly venerated and holy person. The majority of the dead, who
were mostly poor, were eventually stored in spaces that were within the pre-
cincts of the consecrated ground. But, they were sometimes simply stacked with
parts that were alike.[25] Graves were often exhumed when they became too full,
or bodies were put into one place until they had sufficiently decomposed. Then
they were moved. Their final resting place was in ossuaries, where skeletal parts
were stacked in piles. For the more adventurous, it is possible to gain access to
these crypts even today. In many of the major cities of Europe, like Paris, the
ossuaries remain.

Still, there was hesitancy among theologians to condone the practice of par-
titioning the body. They struggled with how to apply the doctrine of the resurrection of the body. They debated how our mortal bodies were related to our
resurrected bodies, whether all parts of the person will be resurrected (since
some thought that the resurrected body would not have either internal or sexual
organs), and how the divided bodies of the saints would be resurrected.
Throughout all of the writings, however, it would be fair to say that they maintained a respect for the intrinsic totality of the body, even as they struggled with
the practicalities of popular practices.[26] Christian insistence that cremation was
not acceptable and that the body be kept reasonably intact were reflections of a
respect for the sanctity of the body.

It was not until the thirteenth century, with the rise of the medieval university, that anatomy once again became a sustained topic of study and dissection
returned, with, as we shall see, the approval of the Church. It was accompanied
by a cultural reticence to wholly approve of the practice. The first evidence for
renewed dissections was autopsies carried out at the Italian universities, in particular the University of Bologna and the University of Salerno in the thirteenth
century. Frederick II, the Holy Roman Emperor, granted permission to carry out
dissections for medical study. Additionally, he mandated that all surgeons study
anatomy for a year and that they demonstrate their competence to a member of
the medical faculty.[27]

The historical record does not give clear evidence for how the transition occurred so that dissections became acceptable. Looking back to the early Church
sources, the condemnation of dissection is rooted in a belief that such an act
usurped divine knowledge. What was hidden by God's providence should be
respected. In effect, dissection was prideful. With the emergence of modern science, there is a cultural shift toward an exploration of the complexity of the natural world. The early scientists saw in the world a validation of Christian belief.
So, perhaps the shift has more to do with a changed attitude about the human

ability to know the world than a change in basic beliefs. Throughout the tradition, it was a constant belief that the human body was something good. In fact,
the prohibition against dissection reflected this belief. The same conviction then
became the justification for exploring anatomy.

One particular text that both reflects this Christian attitude toward the body
and that has paradoxically given rise to some erroneous perceptions that all anatomical studies were condemned because of it is the papal bull, *De Sepulturis*,
by Pope Boniface VIII in 1300 A.D. The purpose of the bull was to condemn the
practice of boiling the bodies of those who had died in a place that was far from
their home.[28] For members of the nobility who were engaged in the Crusades or
in other travel that would make it impossible to return their bodies home quickly, it was starting to become the practice that the dead body was disemboweled
and then dismembered. The resulting parts were then boiled until no flesh remained on the bones. These, in turn, would then be carried home. The body of
Louis IX of France and his relatives, who died on a journey to Egypt in 1270
A.D., and the German emperor Frederick Barbarossa were treated in this way.

Pope Boniface condemned the practice, writing, "Now, this is not only
abominable in the sight of God, but extremely revolting under every human
practice."[29] Those who engaged in such a practice would be excommunicated,
with forgiveness given only by the Pope, unless they were imminently dying.
Needless to say, this effectively thwarted the act.

It is fair to say that there was a nuanced approach to the treatment of the
dead human body, from the available thirteenth century and later sources. Dissection was practiced with the approval of both the secular and the religious
authorities. Yet, there still remained a respect for the dead, as shown both by
Pope Boniface's condemnation of that particular treatment of the body and other
texts. The bodies of those who were to be dissected were usually condemned
criminals, yet they were still to be given respect, even if they were to be used for
medical study.

In Rome, for example, in the fourteenth and fifteenth centuries, a private association, the *Arciconfraternita di San Giovanni Decollato*, engaged in "charitable work toward providing comfort and moral and material assistance to persons
condemned to death."[30] The members counseled the prisoners, attempted to have
them repent, and would provide a companion for their journey toward death.
They helped them to write their last wishes and delivered any final messages to
their families. For our particular interests, they also disposed of the bodies once
the sentence was carried out. Ordinarily, the dead body was left exposed on the
scaffold after the execution until the evening. The brothers then took the bodies
down and brought them to their church, where burial was to take place. Under
an order signed by a senator or the governor, some of those bodies would be
given over to the physicians for dissection. At the end of the process, which was
normally five to seven days, all of the parts of the body were placed in a chest
and brought back to the confraternity for burial and funeral rites.

In that the dissection was an act that in some manner was an intrusion into
the sacredness of the body (and in some instances could even be considered sac-

rilegious), it is significant to note that special efforts were prescribed to ensure the salvation of those who were dissected. Although the confraternity promised at least one memorial Mass for the repose of the soul of the condemned, the guidelines for the dissected dictated that twenty Masses should be said for them. Likewise, the physicians and the medical students also performed penitential acts, like giving alms to the poor from the fees paid by persons who attended a public dissection, making donations to the confraternity for candles, and celebrating additional Masses for the repose of the souls of those who dissected.[31]

In 1315, Mondino de Luzzi carried out a human dissection that has been accorded great importance because some suppose that it represents a change in practice toward acceptance of dissections. Yet, as we have indicated above, dissections that predate this by a century were already documented. At this time, dissections for medical knowledge were actually moving toward becoming commonplace parts of medical education.[32] One public human dissection every five years satisfied the requirement for many medical students.[33] Gradually, the Italian models of medicine spread to the other great universities of Europe.

Mondino's contribution to medicine was found more in his notoriety with regard to dissection than in adding to the known anatomical literature. He authored a book, the *Anathomia*, which gave instructions for the proper method of dissection. Mondino and other anatomists continued to rely upon Galen's anatomical models, which were supplemented by Arabic medical texts, like those written by Avicenna and Averroes. They also continued the imprecise comparison between animals and humans. Few physicians still had accurate anatomical information. Partly, this had to do with the purpose of the dissection. Essentially, it was a demonstration of Galenic principles, rather than an investigation into the body itself.

With the dawn of the Renaissance and the increasing practice of human dissection, physicians and artists began to study the form of the human body more deeply. Emphasis was placed not only on an accurate anatomy but also on the mathematical and geometric proportions of the body.[34] Artists such as Albrecht Dürer, Michelangelo, and Leonardo DaVinci approached their depictions of the human body from a mathematical perspective, attempting to perfect the dimensions of perfect beauty.

DaVinci (1452–1519), in particular, intensely studied anatomy. Familiar with the work of Galen and Mondino, he embarked upon his own study of the human body and produced countless precise drawings and commentaries of human anatomy. DaVinci carried out many dissections, probably about thirty, which he recorded in his notebooks. Although it was never completed, it seemed clear that he planned to eventually publish his own anatomical text. Although his texts did contain some factual errors, they were far superior to the other works that were known at the time. The truly sad postscript to his life is that his work remained unknown for over three hundred years, since he was never able to publish it, and his private papers were passed on from heir to heir with little recognition of their importance.

Apart from DaVinci's unknown manuscripts, it was not until the sixteenth century that there began to be a concerted effort to accurately represent human anatomy. In the two hundred years after DaVinci, miscellaneous texts by numerous authors incrementally moved the study of anatomy forward, but none were vastly different from the glosses that preceded them, except for Andreas Vesalius.

In the sixteenth century, Andreas Vesalius began his own dissections and publications on human anatomy. Educated at the University of Paris, the University of Louvain, and the University of Padua, Vesalius was appointed as professor of surgery at the University of Padua in 1537. In a series of public autopsies, Vesalius quickly gained a reputation for painstakingly tracing every sinew, bone, and artery in the human body and then reproducing them in a series of drawings that became the standard anatomical textbook for centuries. What set Vesalius apart from his predecessors was his approach to the subject of anatomy. Rather than seeing anatomy as a justification for treatment, Vesalius used anatomical studies to reassess the medical knowledge that had preceded him. He was not content to simply prove Galenic medicine. Instead, he relied upon his own experience of the human body to suggest a new approach to medicine. Instead of simply verifying previous sources, anatomy was oriented toward the discovery of the structures of the body.

Vesalius' *De Humani Corporis Fabrica* was published in 1542. It was immediately recognized as a monumental work that differed greatly from the previous works that were based upon the works of Galen. In particular, Vesalius' rejection of some of Galen's medical opinions set him against other physicians who continued to support the prevailing medical attitudes. Only a few months after the publication of his *Fabrica,* Vesalius relinquished his academic appointment. Considering that he was only thirty years of age at the time, and that his work refuted the prevailing obedience to Galen, it is not surprising that Vesalius did not immediately gain favor with his superiors.

In spite of his contemporary critics, Vesalius' approach to medicine, and the *Fabrica*, exerted a profound influence on the later development of anatomy. With the rise of modern science, the approach that Vesalius pioneered became the standard for medicine. Physicians followed him into the body, dissecting it as a way of understanding how it worked.

This new study of the human body had the continued support of the Church. One of Vesalius' first public dissections took place in 1540 at the Church of San Francisco in Bologna. So long as those involved retained a respect for the body, then it would likely be acceptable to the Church. It is clear that the advances in medicine (and science in general) had the support of the Church.[35]

For example, Vesalius pointedly remarks in introducing the human skeleton in the *Fabrica* that "God, the supreme maker of things, rightly made its substance of this temperament so as to supply the entire body with a kind of foundation." In the preface, he writes:

So as it is inescapable that you are uniquely interested in the science of the universe, so you would sometimes be delighted to ponder the construction of the most perfect of all creatures, and take pleasure in considering the lodging place and instrument of the immortal soul—a domicile which, because it admirably resembles the universe in many of its names, was fitly called a microcosm by the ancients.[36]

The human body, he argues, reflects the perfection of the universe. Although some of his contemporaries disagreed, Vesalius places his work within the accepted theology of the time.

The seventeenth century brought with it more focused examinations of different parts of the body, as in William Harvey's description of the circulatory system.[37] The public, for the most part, continued to regard dissection as abhorrent. Secrecy with regard to selection of the bodies and when they were obtained was essential.[38] It is interesting to note that because of the general disapproval of dissecting bodies, medical schools, especially those in the Renaissance in Italy, often were not under the direct control of municipal authorities. Instead, they were under the authority of either the Church or, in rare cases, the king. In this way, they avoided the necessity of requesting permission to examine dead bodies.

For the most part, then, research and teaching of anatomy were done quietly but with official approbation. The public authorities intervened only when a public scandal emerged, as in the infamous nineteenth-century Scottish case of Burke and Hare, who murdered in order to get the bodies to sell.[39] As medical schools proliferated, they increasingly turned toward anatomical study as a principal part of their curriculum. Eventually, in some schools, it was required that aspiring physicians acquire a corpse in order to complete their course of studies.[40] Professional body snatchers, or resurrectionists, would steal the recently deceased for a small payment. This provided a fairly regular supply of bodies.[41] It is fair to say that by the eighteenth century, anatomical studies were commonplace and that modern science had found it essential to understand the intricate workings of the human body.

Mutilation and Totality

Another issue in medical practice dealt with what was called mutilation, which can be defined as the destruction of some part or the suppression of some function of the body. Assuming that our bodies are ultimately under the authority of God and that we have a responsibility to care for this gift, are there situations in which it would be moral to destroy a part or to suppress a function of one's body?

Theologians have answered that it was moral to perform a mutilation if it was necessary to preserve the body. This was expressed in what has become known as the "principle of totality." Thomas Aquinas stated this principle this way:

> A limb is part of the whole body and therefore it exists for the sake of the whole, as the imperfect for the sake of the perfect. The individual limb must therefore be dealt with in the way the benefit of the whole demands. Now the limbs of the <u>human</u> body, are as such conducive to the proper functioning of the whole body, even though they become detrimental thereto, as where a gangrenous limb poisons the whole body. A limb that is healthy and functioning well cannot, therefore, in principle be removed without the whole suffering.[42]

So, physicians could destroy aspects of the body in order to alleviate some medical condition because it is useful to existence of the body as a whole. For example, in cases of a gangrenous limb, it would be standard medical practice to cut off the diseased part so that the entire body was not infected.

In the case of disease, then, the principle of totality is rather straightforward. Applied in other instances, however, it becomes more complex. One topic with which some have struggled is castration and sterilization. According to Eusebius, in the second century A.D., Origen interpreted Matt. 19:12 literally and castrated himself to make himself more holy.[43] He also wished to teach women, and this would make him above suspicion. Also, beginning in the sixteenth century, young boys were castrated in order to preserve their unique singing voices. Obviously, both of these instances involved the destruction of healthy organs. Interestingly, the Church condemned the first but tolerated the second. Men who voluntarily castrated themselves, according to the canons of the Council of Nicea, were not permitted to be ordained or, if they were already ordained, to function as priests. The rule did not hold for those who had involuntarily been castrated.

As for the castrati singers, although there were various attempts to stop it, it was clear that broader cultural demands made that difficult. Many families paid to have their sons castrated, in the hope that they would become rich through patrons of the arts. In 1589, Pope Sixtus V reorganized the Sistine Chapel Choir to include castrati. They remained until 1913, when the last castrati, Alessandro Moreschi, retired.[44]

Theologians distinguished between varying levels of mutilatory actions, based upon how they related to the total functioning of the body. They saw a difference between an action that destroyed a diseased part, an action that destroyed a healthy part, and actions that were directed at parts of the body that were not considered to be principal "members" of the body.

In the first instance, as we have stated, the severing of a diseased or dysfunctional organ or a body part is permissible since allowing it to remain could adversely affect the healthy working of the body as a whole. One may think here of surgery to remove a burst appendix, or even one that is not yet completely compromised but is likely to fail. Obviously, if there are other treatments that would be less radical interventions, they would take precedence.

The destruction of a part that is still able to function is not morally acceptable, unless it is probable that it will fail imminently. Into this category we can
place medical procedures like ligation of the vas deferens, also known as a vas-
ectomy, in men, or a salpingectomy, or removal of the fallopian tube, in women,
in order to prevent unwanted conception. Any destruction of otherwise healthy
organs is thought to be an intervention that subverts the healthy functioning of
the body. In other words, if it works as it should, then we may not simply destroy it for what is arguably a good purpose. The same purpose would be served
in another, less destructive way by controlling one's actions rather than by destroying a healthy body part. There are other instances that could be included
like plastic surgery for breast enlargement, penile implants, and gastric bypass
operations to control one's weight.

One would contrast these interventions with those that are more superficial.
Cutting fingernails or hair would differ in the degree of manipulation that is
done. By "manipulation," what is literally meant is "changing by hand." In other
words, manipulation is the extent to which one actively attempts to cause an end
or goal that is not natural. Since our bodies naturally grow hair and nails, cutting
them would not be considered wrong. In fact, to not do so might be considered
unhealthy.

Decorative alterations of the body like tattooing and piercing would tend to
fall between the range of techniques that we have just outlined. In some instances, these might be considered to be innocuous. Given proper technique, with ear
piercing or a small tattoo, there is a minimal expectation of infection or interfer-
ence with the healthy functioning of the body. Piercing of the genitals or the
tongue, however, would seem to involve a much greater degree of risk.

Similarly, one should consider the motivations for wanting to use one's
body as a "canvas" for expressing thoughts and desires. Too often, what one
thinks is a perfect form of self-expression in our youth becomes an embarrassing
and permanent remembrance later on. Ultimately, Christians believe that the
body is already beautiful. One should think carefully before choosing to make
permanent changes to it.

Organ Donations

Here we will consider the morality of the surgical aspects of organ donation. In
the previous chapter, we discussed the social costs of donating organs. Here we
will focus in on whether it is morally permissible to give away a part of your
body, either while you are still alive, or after death.

Until relatively recently, organ donation was not a practical solution to organ failure. It was not until December 23, 1954, that the first successful kidney
transplant took place in Boston. Very rapidly after that, drugs were developed
that assisted patients in combating the rejection of organs by their immune sys-

tems. Within a decade, Dr. Christian Barnard of South Africa successfully transplanted the first human heart.

While medically these operations were successful, they did present challenges for the Catholic principles that guided choices about the morality of surgery. If the reader will recall, the operative guideline had been the principle of totality, which permitted diseased organs, but not healthy ones, to be removed from the body. In the instance of a kidney transplant, a live donor had to give one of his or her organs to the other person. In fact, in the very first transplant, the donor was a brother of the patient who received the transplant.

According to the received application of the principle, it seemed that the charitable act of giving one of one's organs to another person would be prohibited because it involves the removal of what would be a healthy organ. In the two decades that preceded the first successful organ transplant, the Catholic condemnation of the mutilation of a healthy organ was vigorously applied to the prevailing cultural ascendancy of eugenic sterilization.

In the United States, laws were enacted that legalized the forced sterilization of mental institution patients. Led by Indiana in 1907, the practice eventually spread to thirty states. Although today we tend to identify such laws with Germany's racial purity laws of 1933, a recent study suggests that the American laws were as far-reaching. In fact, American sterilizations continued until 1964.[45]

In the midst of these eugenic developments, Pius XI issued his encyclical *Casti Connubii* in 1930. Within the context of marriage, he stated that "private individuals have no other power over the members of their own bodies than that which pertains to their natural ends; and they are not free to destroy or mutilate their members, or in any way render themselves unfit for their natural functions, except when no other provision can be made for the good of the whole body."[46] He explicitly condemned governments who do this, stating that "where no crime has taken place and there is no cause present for grave punishment, they [public magistrates] can never directly harm, or tamper with the integrity of the body, either for reasons of eugenics or for any other reason."[47] This encyclical was followed by a condemnation of sterilization for either eugenics or for birth control by the Holy Office in 1936.[48]

Given the clear statement of the principle of totality, it is unsurprising that many theologians condemned organ transplants when they were first performed.[49] At first glance, this act would seem to fall under the prohibition of excising a healthy organ. Two statements, first in 1952 and then again in 1954, by Pius XII also seemed to lead to this conclusion. The first, to the First International Congress of Histopathology, rejected the application of the principle of totality to the community at large: "The [political] community, considered as a whole, is not a physical unity which subsists in itself. Its individual members are not integrating parts of it."[50] He repeated this interpretation of the principle in an address two years later to a group of ophthalmologists, saying that "individuals insofar as they are members of this organism [of humanity] are only functional parts . . . the total organism which is humanity has no right to impose on individuals demands in the domain of physical being on the grounds of any natural right of the 'whole' to dispose of the parts."[51]

However, not all moral theologians were so quick to dismiss the possibility that organ transplants could be moral under some conditions. Fr. John Connery, SJ, noted in *Theological Studies* that the issue was not easily resolved simply by the application of texts against sterilization.[52] In particular, Fr. Bert Cunningham, CM, and Fr. Gerald Kelly, SJ, made the case for the morality of transplants.[53]

Writing in 1944, before transplants were even a possibility, Fr. Cunningham argued that the principle of totality could be extended to permit transplants by reframing the principle in reference to the Mystical Body of Christ. Using St. Paul's analogy that we are all members of the Body of Christ, he wrote that this relationship could be understood to mean that individuals are able to act charitably by donating their organs to those who are in need. This interpretation received Connery's approval when he wrote, "Personally, I am in favor of Fr. Cunningham's position."[54]

Justification for organ transplants by using the principle of totality reached its full development in two articles by Fr. Gerald Kelly.[55] In the first article, he reviewed the texts that we have discussed earlier. His conclusion was that they must be understood in light of world events at the time of their promulgation. In essence, the texts reflect a "papal attack on the totalitarian concept of society."[56] No individual is to be subordinated to the greater good of society. Therefore, he concluded, Pius XII did not condemn all organ transplants. Instead, he rejected the idea that a person's body is subject to the absolute will of the state.

The second article considered at length the history of the morality of mutilation, a statement of the present theological opinions, and an analysis of specific problems. Using Cunningham, Kelly argued that organ *donation* is a laudable act because it is a charitable gift of self. Rather than being self-destructive, as some theologians believed, Kelly wrote that it expresses the desire of the donor to a good of a higher order, the virtue of charity. The organ is not taken, or forced from the person. Rather, it is *given* by one person to another in need.

Understanding transplantation as a charitable gift reoriented the act from something done by society to an individual person to something done by one person to another in need. Recent papal teaching reflects this. John Paul II wrote that "transplantation presupposes a prior, explicit, free and conscious decision on the part of the donor, or someone who legitimately represents the donor. . . . In this sense, the medical act of transplantation make's possible the donor's act of self-giving, that sincere gift of self which expresses our constitutive calling to love and communion."[57]

The present Catholic teaching, then, emphasizes that transplants are gifts. Neither human tissues nor organs should be bought or sold because this "lead[s] to a merely instrumental use of the body, and therefore of the person."[58] Ordinarily, organs should be donated after death, although the donation of paired organs, like kidneys, can be moral.

Surgery on Conjoined Twins

The last topic that we will consider in this chapter on invasive medical procedures is that of the separation of conjoined twins. Conjoined twinning is a rare congenital malformation that occurs with a frequency of between one and two per million live births.[59] Cases have been reported from ancient times. The earliest reference seems to be found in the works of Pliny, and particular cases throughout history have achieved some notoriety.[60] These cases are often popularly referred to as "Siamese twins," after the Bunker twins, Eng and Chang, who were born in Thailand, formerly Siam, in 1811 and who toured with the P.T. Barnum circus for many years. They eventually retired as farmers on a Pennsylvania farm, married two women, and between them sired twenty-two children, dying at the age of sixty-three. Other famous instances of conjoined twins include the Blazek twins, the Binnenden Maids, and the Lakeburg twins.[61]

Depending upon where they are predominantly joined, these sets of twins are identified by different clinical descriptions, all of which use the Greek word "pagus," which translates as "that which is fixed." The most common form is thoracopagus twins, who share a thorax, with a 74 percent incidence. The potential shared organs include the heart, liver, and intestine. Pygopagus twins, with a 17 percent incidence, are the next most common form. They may share the spine, rectum, and genitourinary tract. Other conjoined twins are ischiopagus, craniopagus, and omphalopagus, who are joined at the pelvis, brain, and liver, respectively. They are relatively rare, at 6 percent, 2 percent, and 1 percent incidence rates.[62]

Not surprisingly, given the dearth of cases for the surgical separation of conjoined twins, there has been little analysis in Catholic moral theology on how one should proceed. Several cases, however, have received some consideration. The first is the separation of an unnamed pair of conjoined twins at Children's Hospital in Philadelphia by Dr. C. Everett Koop in 1977. The second is the separation of Amy and Angela Lakeburg at that same hospital in 1993, by a different team of physicians.[63]A more recent example was a pair of twin sisters in the United Kingdom. Their case, which we will look at in more depth, is notable for the published comments of the Archbishop of Westminster at the time, Cormac Murphy-O'Connor.

Mary and Jodie were born in Manchester, England, on August 8, 2000, to Catholic parents from Malta who traveled to the United Kingdom for medical care after an ultrasound indicated the probable condition. Local resources would not be sufficient for care, so their government arranged for the mother to be cared for in Manchester. The father was approximately forty-four years old and the mother thirty-four. They had no other children. According to court records, the father had been unwillingly unemployed for over eight years and the mother's job ended during her pregnancy.

The combined birth weight of the twins was 6 kg. At delivery, they were immediately taken to a resuscitation unit, and medical notes indicated that the health status of each twin was quite different. Jodie was "crying and active . . . making respiratory effort. Easily intubated. . . . Baby making spontaneous breathing effort." Mary, on the other hand, was not as well. Although she too was making a spontaneous respiratory effort, the team noted that she was "stiff to ventilate," and that they had difficulty in placing an airway. The consulting neonatologist indicated that because of fetal scans that were performed before delivery, these were expected results. In those tests, Mary's chest had a large quantity of fluid where the lungs should be and her heart was quite large. The consulting anesthetist indicated that at delivery, he could not detect any gasway at all and that because there was no evidence of carbon dioxide, he doubted that Mary had ever breathed for herself. Each twin had her own brain, heart, lungs, and other vital organs, with the exception of a shared bladder and an interconnected circulatory system.[64]

Jodie and Mary were classified as ischiopagus tetrapus (i.e., having four feet) conjoined twins. The judges who were later involved in this case described them as follows from a photograph and consultants' reports:

The lower ends of their spines were fused and the spinal cords were joined. There is a continuation of the coverings of the spinal cord between one twin and another. The bodies are fused from the umbilicus to the sacrum. Each perineum is rotated through ninety degrees and points laterally. . . . Jodie's head seems normal but Mary's is obviously enlarged, for she has a swelling at the back of the head and neck, she is facially dysmorphic and blue because she is centrally cyanosed. Between these two heads is a single torso about forty centimeters long with a shared umbilicus in the middle. Two legs, Mary's right and Jodie's left, protrude at an acute angle to the spine at the centre of the torso, lying flat on the cot but bending to form a diamond shape. The external genitalia appear on the side of the body. The consultant's report reads: "The nature of the conjoin produces a grossly abnormal laterally placed vulval configuration on each side and a markedly splayed perineum. The vulva for each twin is composed of two halves, each coming from the other twin. There is a single orifice in each vulva, which drains urine and meconium, and each twin has an imperforate anus. Each twin has two hemi-vaginae and two hemi-uteri. Such ano-urogenital disposition is consistent with a cloacal abnormality. . . . Internally, each twin has her own brain, heart, lungs, liver and kidneys, and the only shared organ is a large bladder which lies predominantly in Jodie's abdomen but which empties spontaneously and freely through two separate urethras. . . . Jodie's aorta feeds into Mary's aorta and the arterial circulation runs from Jodie to Mary. The venous return passes from Mary to Jodie through an inferior vena cava and other venous channels in the united soft tissues."

Based upon this anatomy, both twins' physical development continued on predicted paths. Jodie continued normally, reaching expected milestones. Mary did not continue to develop, but her condition did stabilize because she received artificial nutrition and her sister continued to provide oxygenation through the combined circulatory system. Consulting physicians, however, warned that the situation would not remain stable for an extended period of time because Jodie's heart could not continue to provide such an output without severely depleting her strength. At three months, for example, Jodie appeared markedly thinner than Mary because her body was doing the work of sustaining both lives, a condition that is often present in conjoined twins. Specialists were not in agreement, however, on the timeframe when heart failure might occur. Some said that it would occur in three to six months, and others believed that it could be years away.

All of the physicians did agree that given Mary's physiology, she would not have survived birth. The undeveloped state of her organs would have meant that if she were not born as a conjoined twin, she would not have had the means to sustain herself. In the judges' words, "She would not have lived but for her connection to Jodie. She lives on borrowed time, all of which is borrowed from Jodie. It is a debt she can never repay."[65] Since she did not have the ability to survive on her own, and Jodie did, the ethical issue that arose was whether it was permissible to separate these two girls when one of the inevitable results would certainly be the death of Mary.

The parents objected to the separation, believing that it would be equivalent to killing one of their daughters. The issue became a cause of legal review when the hospital decided to seek an opinion from the court as to the legal course of action. In the initial decision by Justice J. Johnson, the hospital's view that the operation ought to proceed prevailed, and the subsequent review by the court of appeals affirmed the ruling. Johnson's conclusion was that he understood the nature of the operation to be analogous to withdrawing (artificial) food and hydration: "It is of course plain that the consequence for Mary is one that most certainly does not represent the primary objective of the operation."[66] In the latter review, the court sought out many different authorities, including Cormac Murphy-O'Connor, Archbishop of Westminster, who submitted an *amicus curiae* brief that concluded that the surgery was impermissible under Catholic teaching.[67]

To begin our analysis, let us quickly acknowledge that the press coverage of this unfortunate situation in the United Kingdom was facile and even, perhaps, deeply prejudicial to Catholic beliefs. The reporters quickly surmised that the best story was one of "science v. a backward religion" and contrasted the heroic physicians against the ignorant parents.[68] We shall also reject the position of Justice Johnson and some of the physicians in this case who believed that the separation of the twins was a deliberate act to terminate Mary's life and it was justified because of her underlying condition.[69]

The court of appeals' decision, in short, was that although the parents would have been justified in their decision to not treat the condition with surgery and to allow the twins to eventually die, because the case was now before the court, it had the jurisdiction to decide what should be done. The resulting decision was nuanced and comprehensive. Ultimately, the decision of Justice Ward was decided on the basis that those who have to decide "simply have to choose the lesser of their inevitable loss."[70] Moreover, although he rejected the language of repelling an unjust aggressor, he justified the action of killing Mary by characterizing her as sucking the blood from her sister. She was, in effect, a parasitic murderer from whom the physicians were legitimately able to protect Jodie.[71]

It will remain for others to analyze the legal basis for the ruling.[72] Suffice it to say that Catholic moral theology would reject this blatant utilitarian calculation that was then forced upon the parents. Here, we will concentrate upon Archbishop Murphy-O'Connor's statement that the separation is morally wrong from a Catholic perspective.

In this instance, it is possible to reach an opposite position, though not on the grounds that the justices used. However, since the physiology of conjoined twins varies widely, and this anatomical detail directly affects the morality of what one does in the surgery, one may not say that acceptance in this situation applies to every instance of conjoined twin separation.

An additional factor to consider in this discussion is that although the separation of conjoined twins is exceedingly rare and therefore might seem to be but a footnote to other more prevalent bioethical dilemmas, properly understanding the values associated with determining a moral course of action here will help us to more carefully argue other kinds of cases where a similar relation is present. The conflict that lies at the center of this discussion is the limit of care for a person who is dependent on another for his or her continued existence. The most obvious situation that parallels this is the relation between the mother and the fetus, especially in cases where the continuation of the pregnancy causes a threat to the life of the mother. By carefully analyzing the morality of separating conjoined twins, we will be better able to be aware of the consistencies in our ethical thought in what is admittedly a very complex area.

In his brief to the Court, Archbishop Cormac Murphy-O'Connor highlighted five essential points that led him to counsel against the separation:

1. Human life is sacred and one may never aim to kill to cause an innocent person's death by act or omission.
2. A person's bodily integrity should not be invaded when the consequences are of no benefit to that person.
3. Though there is a duty to preserve life, no such duty exists when the only available means is a grave injustice. (The good end will not justify the means.)
4. There is no duty to act when it imposes an excessive burden.
5. Respect for the natural rights of parents requires that the courts override these rights only when there is clear evidence that they are acting contrary to what is owed their children.

Clearly, one can easily agree with Archbishop Murphy-O'Connor that these five principles are expressions of Catholic teaching and that we should consider them in reaching a decision. It is also clear that should the parents have followed through on their decision that nothing should be done in this instance, it would have been a moral decision in the light of the desire to avoid extraordinary treatment for their children. In fact, if we follow that final guideline, the courts would not have been involved, as the appeals court rightly noted.

In much of his statement, the Archbishop is precisely correct. We should reject language that indicates that a direct killing is morally acceptable. Yet, his analysis of what is being done in the surgery is also not an accurate description of the act. He writes that some might argue that "one might embark on such an operation without having Mary's death as part of one's aim, and that her death would then be a foreseen, but unintended consequence of a morally justifiable operation aimed at saving Jodie." Yet, he goes too far when he argues that "what is not possible is that one could embark on such an operation without foreseeing that it would do Mary no good, but only lethal harm." The surgery, he argues, is inevitably a "violation of Mary's bodily integrity" and is therefore wrong. While it is admittedly difficult to establish where the physical dividing line lies that would distinguish Jodie's body from Mary's, one may not say that Mary's body is synonymous with Jodie's.

I would suggest that an analogous situation is that of an ectopic pregnancy, where the mother has a growing embryo within her fallopian tube that will inevitably rupture and kill her. Moral theologians have agreed that the surgical solution to this dilemma, excising the fallopian tube and removing that section with the growing embryo, meets the criteria for the principle of double effect and is a moral choice.

In this instance, the action that one undertakes is to perform surgery in order to restore the bodily integrity of each twin. The good effect here, preserving Jodie's life, cannot be accomplished without the evil effect of Mary's death. Yet, Mary is not deliberately killed in order to bring about the good effect of preserving Jodie's life. True, it is foreseen that she will probably die as a result of the operation, but that is not what is intended. Her death is the result of her physical defects. It might be heroic of Jodie, were she able to consent to have her twin remain fused to her own body, to continue to provide that life support to her sister, yet one would be hard-pressed to claim that she has an obligation to do so.[73]

The principle of totality is significant here as well. Surgery that aims at restoring the functioning of the body is good. While separating the twins did mean that Mary would not be able to sustain her own life, that did not mean that permitting Jodie to do so was therefore immoral.

Certainly, this analysis would not hold for all cases of conjoined twinning because the degree to which twins are fused together and the presence of shared organs could have a significant effect. In this instance, both girls had all of their own organs. In other cases, like the Lakeburg twins, they share an organ, like a heart. If one is forced to choose to take an organ away from one or another twin, that would significantly change the conclusion. I would argue that such a circumstance would then fall under Archbishop Murphy-O'Connor's description of this operation, that one directly intends to kill one of the children in order for the other one to survive, and thus it would be morally wrong.

Conclusion

The Catholic tradition on invasive medical procedures has been consistent with regard to its belief that the human body is to be treated with reverence and with care, whether it is dead or alive. The body is never to be considered just a thing or an object to do with as we please.

The condemnation of dissection and vivisection by the early Church fathers was accompanied by this attitude. They responded to what they perceived to be a desecration of the body by the early anatomists, like Herophilus. The intricacy of the body was a sign of God's omniscience, and to attempt to understand it was prideful because the very act of opening the body made what one saw not what it was that would normally occur there. In pragmatic terms, it was impossible to understand what happened under the skin because opening up the body changed what was there.

It was not until the thirteenth century that we have strong evidence of a change in this view. First bodies were used as teaching aids for the known medical knowledge that was handed down since Galen. Then, in the sixteenth century, modern medicine in the person of Andreas Vesalius succeeded in mapping the anatomy of the human body. With the support of the Church, scientific medicine emerged.

The transition from condemnation to acceptance of dissection was a shift not only for the Church but also for the broader Western culture. It would be fair to say that although most contemporary persons would acknowledge that dissection of cadavers or even surgery of living persons is a necessary task, there remains in us a visceral remnant of repulsion that pervades our confrontation with what lies beneath our skin.

Theological discussions of invasive practices have centered upon maintaining a reverence for the body. Mutilation of the body, organ transplantation, and the separation of conjoined twins, the three topics that we examined at the end of this chapter, are similar in that they all consider the effect that a particular medical act has in objectifying the body. All interventions should have as their standard that they maintain or enhance the dignity of the person. Acts that destroy a healthy body or that treat a body as a thing to be used either by individuals or governments are objectively immoral. In our technological age, it is essential that we remain focused upon the ultimate goals of any therapeutic techniques; otherwise, we risk destroying the very goods that we seek through our efforts.

Notes

1. See Ludwig Edelstein, "Der Geschicte der Sektion in der Antike," in *Ancient Medicine: Selected Papers of Ludwig Edelstein*, trans. O. and C.L. Tempkin (Baltimore: Johns Hopkins University Press, 1967), 247–301,

2. Henrich von Staden, "The Discovery of the Body: Human Dissection and Its Cultural Contexts in Ancient Greece," *The Yale Journal of Biology and Medicine* 65 (1992): 225. See also n. 15, p. 238, where he cites the Greek inscriptions as evidence.

3. Aristotle, "De Partibus Animalium," 645a 24–25.

4. For a fuller discussion of the possible interpretations of this Aristotelian text, please see Andrea Carlino, *Books of the Body: Anatomical Ritual and Renaissance Learning* (Chicago: University of Chicago Press, 1999), 156–57.

5. Galen, *De facultabibus naturalibus* 3.4 and *De anatomicis administrationibus* K2 632–34. Cf., Von Staden, Herophilus 147, n. 20.

6. J. Chadwick and W.N. Mann, *The Medical Works of Hippocrates* (Oxford: Blackwell, 1950): 183–84, 192, 209–210. See also G.E.R. Lloyd, ed., *Hippocratic Writings*, "On the Heart," trans. I.M. Lonie (London: Penguin, 1978), 347–53.

7. T.V.N. Persaud, *Early History of Human Anatomy: From Antiquity to the Beginning of the Modern Era* (Springfield, IL: Charles C. Thomas, 1984): 34–35.

8. Chadwick, *Medical Works of Hippocrates*, "The Science of Medicine," 87.

9. Celsus, *De Medicina, Prooemium* 12–15 in *De Medicina With an English Translation in Three Volumes*, Vol. I, trans. W.G. Spencer (Cambridge, MA: Harvard University Press, 1960), 9. See also Heinrich von Staden, "Celsus as Historian?" in *Ancient Histories of Medicine: Essays in Medical Doxography and Historiography in Classical Antiquity*, ed. John Scarborough (Leiden: Brill, 1999), 251–94.

10. Ludwig Edelstein argues that the time period was not more than five hundred years. It began in the third century B.C. and extended, at the latest, until the second century A.D. See Owsei and C. Lilian Tempkin, eds., *Ancient Medicine: Selected Papers of Ludwig Edelstein* (Baltimore: Johns Hopkins University Press, 1967), 251.

11. Von Staden, "The Discovery of the Body," 225–231.

12. The evidence for this is not clear. One second century B.C. author, Hygnius, notes in his work, *Fabula*, the story of a woman, Hagnodice, who disguises herself as a man in order to study with Herophilus. When she is later accused of improper conduct with her female patients, she disrobes in court, revealing that she is female. This kind of story, where a woman disguises herself only to reveal her true nature by exposing her breasts or genitalia is also found elsewhere in ancient literature. Its formulaic structure diminishes its probable accuracy. See Heinrich von Staden, *Herophilus: The Art of Medicine in Early*

Alexandria (Cambridge: Cambridge University Press, 1989), 36–9, for a discussion of the text.

13. Edelstein, *Ancient Medicine*, 293.

14. Celsus, *De Medicina*, 9.

15. Celsus, *De Medicina*, 15–17.

16. Tertullian, "*De Anima* (On the Soul)," 10:4 in Alexander Roberts and James Donaldson, eds., *The Ante-Nicene Fathers, Vol. III: Latin Christianity: Its Founder, Tertullian* (Grand Rapids, MI: Eerdmans, 1951), 189. Tertullian again briefly mentions Herophilius in conjunction with his condemnation of a medical device to kill a live infant in the womb by cutting it into pieces. See De Anima 25:5 in Roberts 206.

17. Augustine, *The City of God* (22:24) in *A Select Library of the Nicene and Post-Nicene Fathers of the Christian Church*, Vol. II, St. Augustine's City of God and Christian Doctrine, ed. Philip Schaff, trans. Marcus Dods (Grand Rapids, MI: Eerdmans, 1988), 503.

18. *The City of God*, 503–04.

19. See Augustine, "The Immortality of the Soul," in *Writings of St. Augustine*, Vol. 2, trans. Ludwig Schopp (New York: Cima Publishing, 1947), 22–31.

20. Prudentius, *The Book of the Martyr's Crowns (Liber Peristephanon)* "Discourse of the Martyr St. Romanus against the Pagans" 10: 498 in Roy Deferrari, ed. *The Fathers of the Church: A New Translation*, Vol. 43, *Poems of Prudentius*, Sr. M. Clement Eagan, trans. (Washington, DC: Catholic University of America Press, 1962), 212.

21. Fulgentius, *Mitologicorum libri tres* 1:16–17 in Fabii Planciadis Fulgenti, *Opera*, ed. R. Helm (Leipzig: Teubner, 1898), 9, as translated and cited by Andrea Carlino, *Books of the Body: Anatomical Ritual and Renaissance Learning* (Chicago: University of Chicago Press, 1999), 165.

22. Luis H. Toledo-Pereya, "Galen's Contribution to Surgery," *Journal of the History of Medicine and Allied Sciences* 28, no. 4 (1973): 357–375.

23. W.L.H. Duckworth, trans., *Galen: On Anatomical Procedures. The Later Books*, M.C. Lyons and B. Towers, eds. (Cambridge: Cambridge University Press, 1962).

24. For an infinitely more detailed examination of this topic, see Caroline Walker Bynum, *The Resurrection of the Body in Western Christianity, 200–1336* (New York: Columbia University Press, 1995), especially chapters 2 and 5. The division of the body was sometimes accepted, and other times not. Some sources tell of saints' bodies that miraculously reunited body parts that had been taken as relics.

25. Philippe Ariès, *Western Attitudes Toward Death from the Middle Ages to the Present* (Baltimore: The John Hopkins University Press, 1974), 18–22.

26. For a detailed and masterful analysis of these questions, see Caroline Walker Bynum, *The Resurrection of the Body in Western Christianity, 200–1336* (New York: Columbia University Press, 1995).

27. For the text of the law, see J. Walsh, *The Popes and Science*, 419–423. It is also important to acknowledge that at this time, surgeons were generally not physicians. Surgeons were more technicians who amputated, or bled. Still, they were required to attend dissections so that they could learn not to do harm.

28. In fact, this new method was preferable to the old one that involved removing various parts of the body to be deposited at shrines on the way home. The body of Henry I of England was carried from Rouen, France, home to Reading, England. Beforehand, the body was "cut into pieces, heavily salted and packed in oxhides against the smell, which according to the chronicler [Henry of Huntington], had already killed the man responsible for extracting the brain. By the time the funeral procession had reached Caen, the corpse was exuding a liquid so foul that its attendants could not drain it without what Henry of Huntington called 'horrors and fainting'" (Katharine Park, "The Life of the Corpse: Division and Dissection in Late Medieval Europe," *The Journal of the History of Medicine and Allied Sciences* 50 [1995]: 112). Park quotes Henry of Huntington, *The Chronicle of Henry of Huntington*, trans. Thomas Forester (London: Henry G. Bohn, 1853), 262–263.

29. James J. Walsh, *The Popes and Science: The History of the Papal Relations to Science during the Middle Ages and Down to Our Own Time* (New York: Fordham University Press, 1913) 32–33. Walsh also provides the complete Latin text of the bull on pp. 413–418. Walsh's book is essentially a refutation of Andrew D. White, *On the History of the Warfare of Science with Theology in Christendom* (New York: Appleton, 1898). White, the first president of Cornell University, argued that the bull impeded scientific investigation of the human body through dissection. It is fair to say that Walsh annihilates White's argument, both by providing the actual text of the papal bull and by demonstrating how the work of the Italian universities that carried on anatomical studies in the fifteenth and sixteenth centuries were supported by the Church. Walsh was clearly supported, and thus White was also refuted, by Mary Niven Alston's article, "The Attitude of the Church Towards Dissection before 1500," *Bulletin of the History of Medicine* XVI (1944): 221–238. Alston wrote that "in Italy dissection began earlier than 1240, at Montpelier by 1340 at the latest, and in France proper probably prior to 1400, certainly by 1407. We have no testimony that anatomy was hindered in Italy at any time, unless the prohibition against boiling be taken as a hindrance. But Guy de Chauliac, a papal chaplain, did not interpret it that way" (232).

30. Andrea Carlino, *Books of the Body: Anatomical Ritual and Renaissance Learning*, trans. John Tedeschi and Anne C. Tedeschi (Chicago: University of Chicago Press, 1999), 99.

31. Carlino, *Books of the Body*, 100–119.

32. Walsh, *The Popes and Science*, 61–119.

33. Persuad, *Early History of Anatomy*, 80–83, 89–100.

34. Artists like DaVinci used scientific principles to show how aesthetic beauty is reflective of the ordered nature of existence. DaVinci's art, for example, reflects the use of the "Golden ratio," or phi, where perfection is expressed

as the relation of the numbers 1:1.618. The Acropolis, as well as the measurement of a beautiful body (as in, for example, the distance between the three segments of the human finger), reflect this proportion.

35. See Walsh, *The Popes and Science,* generally. A more recent work, by David Bentley Hart, *Atheist Delusions: The Christian Revolution and its Fashionable Enemies* (New Haven: Yale University Press, 2009), does an admirable job of exposing the many falsehoods connected with a Christian denial of scientific progress. Both Walsh and Hart argue convincingly that modern science is indebted to the Church for its development.

36. Andreas Vesalius, *De Humani Corporis Fabrica,* trans. Daniel Garrison, and Malcolm Hast, *Vesalius Translation Project at Northwestern University,* http://vesalius.northwestern.edu/flash.html (accessed October 29, 2004).

37. It is worth noting that Harvey refrained from publishing his work on the circulatory system for twenty-five years, since he believed (correctly) that his views, being contrary to accepted knowledge, would be hard for many to accept.

38. Carlino, *Books of the Body,* 104.

39. Burke and Hare were infamous for sixteen murders beginning in 1827, in Edinburgh Scotland. The pair sold their victims to the local medical school to use as anatomy cadavers. Bodies were in short supply since the only legal corpses that could be used were those of criminals convicted of a capital crime.

40. According to one author, Ruth Richardson, *Death, Dissection and the Destitute* (London: Routledge and Kagan Paul, 1987), some Scottish schools in the 1700s accepted corpses for tuition payments.

41. For the most part, the governmental authorities tacitly condoned the practice, except when the body snatchers murdered in order to get the bodies.

42. Thomas Aquinas, *Summa Theologiae* (II,IIae, Q. 65, art. 1) in *Summa Theologiae,* Vol. 38, [Blackfriars] trans. Marcus Lefébure (New York: McGraw Hill, 1975), 48–51.

43. Eusebius, *The Ecclesiastical History II,* trans. JEL Oulton (Cambridge: Harvard University Press, 1957) (Bk. VI, VIII), 28–33.

44. See Sixtus V, *Cum Pro Nostri Temporali Munere* (1589) and Pius X, *Tra le Sollecitudini* (1903).

45. See André N. Sofair and Lauris C. Kaljian, "Eugenic Sterilization and a Qualified Nazi Analogy: The United States and Germany, 1930–1945," *Annals of Internal Medicine* 132, no. 4 (2000): 312–319, and also Robert J. Lifton, *The Nazi Doctors: Medical Killing and the Psychology of Genocide* (New York: Basic Books, 1986), 21–44.

46. Pius XI, *Casti Connubii,* Encyclical, 31 Dec. 1930, in *Seven Great Encyclicals* (Glen Rock, NJ: Paulist, 1963), 97.

47. *Casti Connubii* § 70, 96–97.

48. Heinrich Denzinger and Adolf Schönmetzer, *Enchiridion symbolorum* (Barcinone: Herder, 1973), 3760–3765.

49. See, for example, L. Bender, OP, "Organorum humanorum trensplantatio," *Angelicum* 31 (1954): 139–60.

50. Pius XII, "Allocution to the First International Congress of Histopathology," (Sept. 13, 1952), in *The Human Body, The Monks of Solesmes,* (Boston: Daughters of St. Paul, 1960), 204.

51. Pius XII, "Allocution to a Group of Eye Specialists," (May 14, 1956) in *The Human Body*, 375–76.

51. John Connery, SJ, "Notes on Moral Theology," *Theological Studies* 15 (1954): 602–06.

53. See Fr. Bert Cunningham, CM, *Morality of Organic Transplantation* (Washington, DC: Catholic University of America, 1944), and Fr. Gerald Kelly, SJ, *Medico-Moral Problems* (St. Louis, MO: Catholic Hospital Association, 1958), 246–47.

54. Connery, "Notes on Moral Theology," 603.

55. Fr. Gerald Kelly, SJ, "Pope Pius XII and the Principle of Totality," *Theological Studies* 16 (1955), 373–96, and "The Morality of Mutilation: Towards a Revision of the Treatise," *Theological Studies* 17 (1956): 322–344.

56. Kelly, "Pius XII and the Principle of Totality," 395.

57. John Paul II, "Many Ethical, Legal and Social Questions Must Be Examined in Greater Depth" (June 20, 1991) *Dolentium Hominum* (Vatican City: Vatican Press, 1992) § 3, p. 12. See also "Blood and Organ Donors," (2 Aug. 1984) *The Pope Speaks* 30 (1985): 1–2.

58. Ibid.

59. The incidence of conjoined twins in pregnancy is approximately one per fifty thousand to one hundred thousand pregnancies. Of those who survive long enough to become separated, there is a 3:1 ratio of females to males.

60. James J. O'Neill Jr., "Conjoined Twins," in *Pediatric Surgery 1925–1938,* and A.F. Guttmacher, "Biographical Notes on Some Famous Conjoined Twins," *National Foundation* 3 :10

61. The Blazeks were pygopagus twin females born in Bohemia in 1878, the Binnendens were born in Kent, England, in 1100, and the Lakebergs were thoracopagus twins born in Chicago, Illinois, USA, in 1993. An extended discussion of the Lakebergs is included later in this essay.

62. O'Neill, "Conjoined Twins," 1926–27.

63. Children's Hospital of Philadelphia has performed the majority of conjoined separations in the United States.

64. These, and the ensuing clinical assessments, were compiled by the Justices of the Law Lords of the House of Lords Court of Appeal in their decision concerning the separation of the twins. Lord Justice Ward et al., "A (children), Re [2000] EWCA Civ 254 (22 September 2000) Case B1/2000/2969, Sec. II, 11. Retrieved from www.bailii.org 2 November 2009. Sec. II, 6–8

65. Ward, Sec. II.7

66. Ward, Sec. II 16.

67. Cormac Murphy-O'Connor, "A Submission by Archbishop Cormac Murphy-O'Connor, Archbishop of Westminster to the Court of Appeal in the Case of Central Manchester Healthcare Trust V. Mr. And Mrs. A and RE a Child (By her Guardian ad litem, the Official Solicitor)" 14 September 2000,

http://www.rcdow .org.uk/cardinal/default.asp?content_ref=45 (accessed November 1, 2009).

68. See, for example, the summary of the news stories by Libby Purves, "A Question to Break the Heart," *Human Life Review* 27 (Winter 2001): 45–47.

69. See, for example, the testimony of a neonatologist on the case, who said that "I think I come back to the fact that the quality of any life that she will have will be so poor that, yes, I feel that it is appropriate to terminate her life." Lord Justice Ward et al., "A (children), Sec. II, 11.

70. Ward, III, 9.3.

71. Ward, II, 10.4.

72. One such analysis that finds the legal ruling wanting is that of George Annas, *American Bioethics: Crossing Human Rights and Health Law Boundaries* (Oxford: Oxford University Press, 2004), 81–94.

73. The analogy of the double effect and ectopic pregnancy and the separation of conjoined twins has been discussed briefly in M. Therese Lysaught, "Is it Killing?" *Human Life Review* 27 (Winter 2001), 48–52, and JJ Paris and AC Elias-Jones, "Do We Murder Mary to Save Jodie? An Ethical Analysis of the Separation of the Manchester Conjoined Twins," *Postgraduate Medical Journal* 77 (2001): 593–598.

Chapter Six:
Ethics at the End of Life

The nature of the relationship between medicine and death has changed remarkably in the nineteenth and the twentieth centuries. Decisions at the end of life have assumed greater and greater importance, not only because of our growing technological abilities, but also because of greater social changes in our culture. As we have developed the ability to extend life, we are also confronted with the very real loss of a language and a framework in which we can understand how it is that we confront death. Our approach to death, as has been said many times, by many people, is really a reflection of how we view life, and more to the point, how we view ourselves.

Where previously medicine fought valiantly against death, and was sometimes successful, today medicine has the capacity to prolong life almost indefinitely. Perhaps the greatest changes have overtaken us in the past sixty years. Where once physicians were only able to alleviate pain and stop some disease processes, they now have the ability to transplant and to actually cure a great number of diseases. Medical historians tend to link this technology of medicine to the advent of antibiotics. From the 1930s, when antibiotics first began to achieve success, the modern medical establishment has seen a great increase in drugs, facilities, and theory.

While the ability to truly heal is a relatively recent phenomenon, the capacity to kill is not. By virtue of their knowledge of the human body and the treatments to alleviate distressing symptoms, physicians have always had the ability to kill. That they have not is due to a number of factors, some of which can be traced back to the Hippocratic Oath itself. In light of Greek ethical considerations that saw human life as being less important than the aims of the state, the Hippocratic Oath was a reform movement that stressed the intrinsic sanctity of life. The Judeo-Christian view of the person complemented this view and embedded it in Western culture.

Direct killing, whether through medical technology or other means, has always been proscribed as murder, unless the person who is killed has clearly violated the order of society. In the ancient world, murder was considered wrong not because of the intrinsic sanctity of life but rather because it denied the king the use of one of his subjects. Judaism and Christianity also prohibited murder, but on different grounds. For them, it was an offense against God, who is the good Creator. Individual persons are valuable because of their relation to God and not for their social contribution.

Indirect killing, however, may sometimes be justified. Ethicists and physicians have long recognized the principle of double effect, which we discussed earlier in chapter two. It allows a physician to aid a dying patient through the use of palliative care that might have as an effect the death of the patient. So long as the death is indirect, that is, not intentionally caused, the use of pain medication has been seen to be acceptable. Of course, there are several elements to the principle of double effect, but I would like to focus here upon the claim that one can intend an act that has negative consequences without intending those particular consequences. In fact, as we know, the principle of double effect is really an examination of the object, the intention, and the circumstances to determine if they are properly considered.

This acceptance of assistance in pain control was seen as morally licit because of presuppositions that included faith in God and a recognition of a moral framework in which it is possible to differentiate between object, intention, and circumstances. Based upon the natural law, ethicists claimed that certain kinds of actions were intrinsically immoral. One such clear prohibition was murder. The intentional killing of a person who had done nothing to deserve it as a punishment was clearly proscribed.

Suicide was thus seen to be a clearly immoral act by virtue of its object. Euthanasia, physician-assisted death, and autonomous suicide were considered by most to be actions that were intrinsically immoral. The suicide victim in medieval times, for example, was refused burial in consecrated ground, and his or her body was instead placed beside a crossroads in the hope that the shape of the roads would dissuade the Devil from interfering with that person who had acted in a mortally sinful way. No justification for suicide was thought possible.

Today, the world is different both technologically and morally. Our scientific abilities have created a host of new ethical dilemmas. With the power to prolong life also comes the ability to end it. Recent legislative and judicial decisions have slightly opened the door to suicide, albeit suicide with a "professional," technological bent. The justification for such a cultural acceptance of physician-assisted suicide has deep theological roots. Epistemologically, our world has also changed. Cultural conflicts today are not simply about conclusions. More fundamentally, they are about presuppositions. Within the larger debate about physician-assisted suicide is a disagreement about how we know what we know, and how that knowledge is itself to be applied in making difficult decisions in trying circumstances. We have a plethora of ethical theories that will result in different conclusions that are dependent upon their presuppositions.

An acceptance of physician-assisted suicide is itself founded upon an Enlightenment conception of natural law and optimism about the ability of modern medicine to cure. Essentially, physician-assisted suicide and euthanasia are technological cures for the human condition, and they point to a basic cultural conflict about the meaning of medicine as a profession. Both seek to eradicate suffering through the death of the person, which is acceptable only in light of an epistemology in which the ability of human persons to choose what they will is also the freedom to do so. Scientific death is the inevitable conclusion of a medical ethic that focuses primarily upon technology and its application to disease.

The alternative to an ethics of cure is an ethics of care. Here, the emphasis is focused upon not simply the cure of disease and clinical symptoms but rather on how medicine can treat the entire person. Sometimes, the ethics of care means that one must accept when it is impossible to cure. Our power to treat the physical body is limited and inadequate to deal with the human suffering that sometimes accompanies death.

This chapter examines moral questions at the end of life. We will accomplish this through an examination of the Christian theology of death and care for the dying, and its application to several issues: determination of death, withdrawal of nutrition and hydration, and physician-assisted suicide. By examining a theology of death, we can then see how it will apply to the hard decisions that we have to make at the end of our own life, or the life of those we love.

The Christian Understanding of Death and Care for the Dying

The first book of the Bible, Genesis, tells us that the world as we know it is not the world that was intended for us. God made a creation that is good, and in which there is an order and a purpose. Yet, Adam and Eve, images of us, turned their back on this gift by choosing their own reality instead of the one offered to them by God. The result of their choice is a fractured world of alienation, suffering, and death.

This fallen world is not a punishment in the sense that God is out for vengeance, torturing us until we give in. A more apt way of understanding this is that our relationship with him is now damaged in such a way that we are unable to return to the innocence of love that characterized humanity before this bad choice.

Think for a moment of a married couple. On their wedding day, they are filled with joy at the thought of living a life together. They offer themselves to one another and pronounce their vows. Shortly after their marriage, one of the spouses commits adultery. Even if the innocent spouse forgives, the adulterous act forever changes the relationship of the couple. They are no longer in that state of innocent love that they were before the adultery.

In the same way, Adam and Eve's fall from grace has irrevocably changed the innocence of our relationship with God. Yet, even in the midst of our violation, God still calls us back to him. In Deuteronomy, God makes the choice clear: "See, today I set before you life and prosperity, death and disaster. If you obey the commandments of Yahweh your God, that I enjoin on you today, if you love Yahweh your God and follow his ways, if you keep his commandments, his laws, his customs, you will live and increase, and Yahweh your God will bless you in the land which you are entering to make your own."[1] As children of Adam and Eve, we are wounded by their choice. Just as the effects of adultery extend beyond the spousal relationship to the entire family, so too does that original turning away from God leave its inheritance in our own lives. Yet, even though we have acted unfaithfully, we are offered that relationship with God over and over again.

St. Paul echoes the Genesis stories in his description of sin in Romans 5:1–21. Our lives are under the control of sin and death. Adam's choice (and Eve's, I would add) brought sin and death into the world, and we are unable to escape from it. Death is the consequence for all of our sins. However, just as one man brought death, so another, Christ, brings the gift of freedom from sin.

The choice to prefer evil to good brings with it a radical loneliness and disconnection. Death is finally, in its true form, an alienation from what is real. In this context, then, hell is our actualized choice to choose our own constructed world, rather than the real life of being in relationship with God. In C.S. Lewis' fictional work on heaven and hell, *The Great Divorce*, he illustrates this truth by depicting hell as an ever-expanding town, where persons move further and further from one another.

So, the scriptural teaching on death is about our existence as beings who were created to be in relationship with God but who have failed to do so. While it is probably true that the early Church would link biological death to this theological belief, we need to be careful about confusing one with the other. Too often, we lose our way toward God because we misinterpret this teaching as sickness and death are punishments from God for our own personal sins. I was bad, some people think, so God gave me cancer.

The Christian belief in the resurrection of the body is a claim that there is a transformation of our frailties into perfection. Dying is thus an act of opening ourselves to that interconnection with God. Only by risking love does death have any significance. As the contemporary poet and undertaker Thomas Lynch has written, "Grief is the tax we pay on our attachments, not on our interests or diversions or our entertainments. We grieve according to the emotional capital we invest in the lives and times of others, that portion of ourselves we ante up before the cards are dealt. We only grieve our losses when we play for keeps -- real love, real hate, real attachments broken."[2] At the same time that we mourn the dead, we, as Christians, also focus on our hope of the resurrection. We celebrate the promise made to us by God that we will be able to overcome death and not have to grieve anymore.

So, as a community, we care for the dying and the dead as an act of solidarity with them. Where they go, we follow. We travel the journey with them, out of love. For those who have been chronically ill, disabled, or incapacitated in their life, such generosity and love is a precious gift that they receive. The nurses in my family (especially my beautiful wife!), and the nurses who I have had the privilege of teaching, have also shared with me that at such moments, to be the one who is able to give such comfort and care can be an awesome gift. Health care professionals know suffering and death firsthand and are our hands and our hearts for the sick and the dying. They witness for us by what they do.

So, as we consider specific issues related to ethics at the end of life, we can summarize several points that define Christian teaching on death and dying. Death is not ultimately meant to be. It is a condition of our present existence, but it was not part of God's creation. Instead, it was introduced by our misuse of freedom. Our present experience of death also points us toward what we have corrupted. Ultimately, we are meant to live in loving relationship with God, and with one another. So, our actions toward the dead and the dying should work toward assisting them to live well as they die. We should neither push them toward death prematurely nor prolong their dying indefinitely.

What then, do we owe the dying? In short, we are obligated to walk with them as they move toward death. We should provide appropriate treatment that allows them to manage their symptoms, especially pain, and to alleviate disease whenever we can. There is an old saying from the Middle Ages that should epitomize our priorities: physicians should cure sometimes, relieve often, and comfort always. Unfortunately, we often become so focused today on curing often or always, that relieving and comforting fall by the wayside. Beyond the observation that we are not able to offer every resource that is desired to prolong life, it is also prideful to assume that we can completely control our physical existence. This is not to say that we should adopt a kind of "Luddite" ignorance to scientific progress. It is just a cautionary comment that our faith does not ultimately reside in science, but in God, and that our central concern ought to be to manifest the love of our neighbor in our care for the dying.

There is clearly a disconnect between contemporary medicine and the care for dying patients. Many persons fear that the end of their life will be filled with pain and suffering and that they will have little control over their own death.[3] Unfortunately, those concerns are not unfounded.

In 1995, the results of the SUPPORT study were published.[4] The investigators followed 9,015 terminal patients for a period of four years. The first phase of the study began in 1989. Through patient and physician interviews and a study of medical records, researchers documented the conditions under which the patients were treated during their terminal illnesses. What they found was that there were significant differences of opinion between patients and their physicians.[5] Approximately one-third of the patients wanted to forgo resuscitation. Physicians disagreed with patient preference at about the same rate. In instances where the physician did not know the choice of the patient, CPR was more likely to be done, at a higher cost.

In the second phase of the study, nurses intervened by providing information to the primary care physicians on the patients' desires and their prognosis. They also arranged meetings with the patients and their caregivers in order to assist them in making treatment decisions in a collaborative way with their physicians. They measured progress through five indicators: the time between the writing of a DNR (Do Not Resuscitate) order and the patient's death, the percentage of physicians who agreed with a patient's choice with regard to having a DNR, days spent in an ICU prior to death, percentages of patients who died in pain, and relative costs of end-of-life treatment. In spite of an active intervention with patients and physicians, the investigators reported, "The intervention had no impact on any of these designated targets. . . . The study certainly casts a pall over any claim that if the health care system is given additional resources for collaborative decision-making in the form of skilled professional time, improvements will occur."[6] They concluded that trying to change treatment decisions would require an approach that is different from intervening with individual patients and physicians who have volunteered. Instead, they pointed to the need to change the culture of dying, and perhaps to have more "proactive and forceful interventions."[7]

From a Christian point of view, there is a definite conflict between technology that is thought of as a tool by which we are able to escape from the human conditions of death and suffering and one that sees this same technology as a tool that can assist us as we compassionately accompany the dying. Any interventions are wrong that seek to control death and fashion it into a "right" to be exercised by an autonomous human person who alone determines the meaning of death. The aim of the SUPPORT study was to enable patients to be active participants in treatment decisions at the end of their lives, and this is to be commended. We should be wary, however, of overemphasizing either patient or physician "control" of dying. Ideally, both should be exercised within a culture that understands the parameters of both. As we move to a consideration of specific treatment decisions at the end of life, this will be an underlying theme. In order to make good moral choices, it is essential that these decisions be understood in the light of more fundamental ideas about the nature of the person and the meaning of death.

The Determination of Death

Until recently, knowing that someone was dead was fairly uncomplicated. Checking to see if someone was breathing and if his or her heart was still pumping was simple. Certainly, there was always some fear that a particularly tragic condition might make it appear that these cardio-pulmonary signs might be masked. But, in general, these were fairly reliable indicators of the biological cessation of life. After a while, rigor mortis and the process of decomposition itself would be even more definitive signs that death had occurred.

Modern technology has changed this traditional assessment. Now, with respirators that will breathe for us and defibrillators that will shock our hearts back into a normal rhythm, we can extend life in ways that were unimaginable even fifty years ago. As we neared this threshold of being able to sustain life for longer and longer periods of time, a discussion began among physicians about whether other criteria beyond cardio-pulmonary functions might also be accurate measurements for when death occurs.

In 1968, the Ad Hoc Committee of the Harvard Medical School to Examine the Definition of Brain Death published its conclusions in *JAMA* (the *Journal of the American Medical Association*).[8] For patients in an irreversible coma, they believed that specific criteria associated with the brain could be used to determine whether death had occurred for those patients who were being artificially sustained. Although the report did not use these terms, the physicians had to choose between two competing definitions: whole brain death and higher brain death.

The former defines death as the cessation of all functioning of the brain, while the latter only focuses upon the ability of the person to have the actual or potential capacity to be self-conscious. These definitions are rooted in competing concepts of personhood that we discussed earlier in relation to the emergence of personhood in neo-natal development. The Harvard Committee recommended that the whole brain definition be adopted.

Proof that the whole brain was not functioning could be established, the committee thought. Unresponsivity to pain, no spontaneous movements or breathing, lack of reflexes, and a flat electroencephalogram (EEG), would all be confirmatory tests, provided that the physician could rule out the presence of barbiturates and hypothermia. When these tests were carried out twice, with at least a twenty-four-hour period between, they could be considered conclusive that the condition of brain death was irreversible.

Shortly after the Harvard committee's recommendations, the American legal definition of death changed to include brain death. Kansas was the first state, in 1970, to legally permit the inclusion of brain death criteria for the determination of death. Its statute, however, was criticized because it seemed to establish two definitions for death: one definition was cardio-pulmonary, and the second was brain death. Leon Kass and Alexander Capron proposed a model statute that clarified the definition of death and suggested instead that there were two sets of criteria to establish death.[9]

For approximately a ten-year period, individual legal cases attempted to clarify the definition of brain death, with some states passing legislation. On the federal level, Congress established the President's Commission for the Study of Ethical Problems in Medicine and Biomedical and Behavioral Research in 1978. They took as their first task to define death, submitting their report to Congress on July 9, 1981.[10]

In that report, the President's Commission recommended the adoption of a common statute by every state that would reflect the Capron/Kass provisions. This model law was known as the Uniform Determination of Death Act (UDDA). In the years following this proposal, about half of the states adopted the precise wording of the statute, while the rest passed some variation of it. Around the world, a majority of nations have also adopted these criteria. A recent study of eighty nations reported that 88 percent of those surveyed had brain death criteria in addition to cardio-pulmonary criteria as a way of determining death.[11]

Catholic teaching supports the use of whole brain criteria for the determination of death, and it is fair to say that the general theological consensus is in favor of the definition. Both Pius XII and John Paul II have stated that the Church takes no position on the technical aspects of the tests to determine brain death. Pius XII wrote that "it is for the doctor to give a clear and precise definition of

'death' and of the 'moment of death' of a patient who lapses into a state of un-
consciousness. That is the province of medicine."[12] John Paul II wrote, "Here it
can be said that the criterion adopted in more recent times for ascertaining the
fact of death, namely the *complete* and *irreversible* cessation of all brain activity, if rigorously applied, does not seem to conflict with the essential elements of
a sound anthropology."[13]

Although the higher brain proponents argued stringently for their definition,
no state or medical society has ever sided with them.[14] This is not to say, however, that the definition of brain death is not without problems. The optimism with
which the criteria for assessing the "cessation of the vital functions of the entire
brain" were proposed by the President's Commission has not been completely
realized.

With either the cardio-pulmonary or the neurological criteria, one of the
practical difficulties is that although we tend to understand death as a particular
point in time at which the soul is separated from the body and transformed into a
new embodiment of the person, in practice it is impossible to definitively fix that
point only on the basis of biological criteria. Biologically, it might be more apt
to say that death is the disintegration of the unified integrity of the body. What
this means is that we can surmise that the fixed point has occurred because the
internal processes of the human body irreversibly disintegrate after that fixed
point. We can delay the effects of this disintegration with technology, but it is
impossible to reverse the process.

In clinical practice, then, it is possible to delay the disintegration that inevitably follows death. Patients who are declared dead by neurological criteria can
still demonstrate biological signs of "life" like a beating heart, hair growth, the
healing of wounds, or the sustenance of a growing embryo or fetus. If the respi-
rator were to be removed, these bodies would advance more rapidly toward disintegration. What is occurring here is a delay, rather than a reversal, of that de-
cay.

Opponents of brain death criteria counter with several arguments. Some authors, like Robert Truog, use the evidence of ongoing physiological functions to
argue that we should therefore embrace the "higher brain" definition since it is
clear that the person is not truly dead, since the body exhibits these functions.
He argues, for example, that since blood pressure rises when a body thus maintained responds to the surgical incision for organ harvesting, it is clear that the
person is not truly dead under the current criteria.[15] While pragmatically he is
correct in observing that there is not a complete synthesis between our definitions and the clinical signs, we must take a step back and remind ourselves that
the criteria are guidelines in determining whether the disintegration of the body
has begun. Death, as a process that proceeds from an initial point, may manifest
residual signs of life that with time will eventually cease.

Other opponents, like Martyn Evans and Michael Potts, argue that a "narrative" case can be made against the definition. They contend that there is a kind
of human disgust that we have when we are told that a patient whose heart is

still beating but who is not breathing is dead: "The only way . . . [this] initial reaction could be changed is if the 'higher brain death' advocates 'educated' it out of . . . [us]."[16] They contend that the emphasis that is placed on the inability of the patient to breathe on his or her own is an arbitrary sign that does not reflect a human emotional response to the encounter with a body that still retains its ability to maintain a heartbeat. Evan and Potts write that "for the vast majority within at least Western culture (if not elsewhere) the heartbeat within a warm human body *counts for life,* whether or not its rate is controlled by the brain."[17]

In response, other authors believe that this same narrative approach works for the whole brain criteria. Kenneth Iserson notes that in the case of decapitation, the heart continues to beat, but "there is no question that person is irreversibly dead. Even in ancient times the Talmud said 'the death throes of a decapitated man are not signs of life anymore than is the twitching of a lizard's amputated tail.'"[18] There is, of course, a counter response to this. David Jones, O.P., has documented a case presented by D.A. Shewmon at Cambridge University in 1997 of a child who suffered brain damage due to meningitis. Tests showed a flat EEG, no spontaneous respiration, no intracranial blood flow, and an MRI scan that showed "ghost-like tissues and proteinaceous fluids in the cranium." Yet, the child's body continued to be maintained for fourteen years, as of the writing of the article.[19]

Essentially, instances like this point toward some suspicion that the conditions for whole brain criteria are sufficient for a declaration of death. The significance that is attached to the disparate signs of life that are stated here is the core of the issue. Is it sufficient to say that the irreversible cessation of the brain means death? If so, is it possible to be completely sure that this has occurred? Again, the consensus of physicians and theologians alike is that the cessation of the brain is sufficient and that it can be proven with a degree of certainty that would permit physicians to then remove organs from a dead body. Yet, it must be conceded that there still is some doubt.

The Persistent Vegetative State and Artificial Nutrition and Hydration

Patients who are diagnosed as being in a persistent vegetative state (PVS) have suffered severe damage to those structures of the human brain that enable them to be conscious. They do not meet the criteria of being dead because they do not have a total cessation of all functioning of the brain. In fact, the brainstem, the structure at the base of the skull that controls autonomic nervous system responses, is still operative and may be for years after the destruction of the higher brain structures. The Multi-Society Task Force on PVS defined the condition in this way:

The vegetative state is a clinical condition of complete unawareness of the self and the environment, accompanied by sleep-wake cycles, with either complete or partial preservation of hypothalamic and brain-stem autonomic functions. In addition, patients in a vegetative state show no evidence of sustained, reproducible, purposeful, or voluntary behavioral responses to visual, auditory, tactile, or noxious stimuli; show no evidence of language comprehension or expression; have bowel and bladder incontinence; and have variably preserved cranial-nerve and spinal reflexes. We define persistent vegetative state as a vegetative state present one month after acute traumatic or nontraumatic brain injury or lasting for at least one month in patients with degenerative or metabolic disorders or developmental malformations.[20]

A sustained study of this condition by the Multi-Society Task Force resulted in the several conclusions regarding the ability of these patients to recover from their injuries and their life expectancy. Patients who don't emerge from the state after three months are very unlikely to regain function, or consciousness. If the condition remains after twelve months, the study concluded, the condition should be considered permanent. The benchmarks at one year after the onset of PVS were as follows: "thirty-three percent had died, fifteen percent were in a persistent vegetative state, twenty-eight percent had severe disability, seventeen percent had moderate disability, and seven percent had a good recovery. Of the seven percent of patients who had a good recovery, over half showed signs of improvement within three months after injury, and almost all within six months after injury."[21] The mortality rate for an adult patient in PVS was eighty-two percent at three years and ninety-five percent at five years. In terms of recovery from PVS, children had more promising recovery and mortality rates, although generally, the longer the condition remained, the more unfavorable the outcome.

PVS is a frustrating condition for family and practitioners alike. Patients in a PVS are unlikely to recover and thus everyone—patient, family, and health care providers—are in a kind of suspended animation, where true progress toward recovery becomes less and less likely as time passes. The inevitable result will be the death of the patient, but the moment when that will occur is very unclear. The family members mourn the loss of the relationship that they had with this person and are left with the care of this living, uncommunicative individual.

What are our obligations? Catholic teaching will quickly dismiss the idea that this person is no longer someone who is worthy of our care. The PVS patient is not just a body. He or she remains a person with dignity and rights. Otherwise, we fall into the dualist trap of separating out the person from his or her body.

Our first duty is to provide ordinary care to this person. The clearest statement of what ordinary care means was given by Pius XII in 1957, in his allocution, "The Prolongation of Life." He explained it in this way:

Normally, one is held to use only ordinary means—according to circumstances, of persons, places, times and culture—that is to say, means that do not involve any grave burden for oneself or another. A more strict obligation would be too burdensome for most men and would render the attainment of the higher, more important good too difficult. Life, health, all temporal activities are in fact, subordinated to spiritual ends. On the other hand, one is not forbidden to take more than the strictly necessary steps to preserve life and health, as long as he does not fail in some more serious duty.[22]

To place his remarks in context, it will be helpful to remember that at the time, the world was witnessing the explosive success of medicine. There were emerging solutions to many of the problems of disease and death. Transplants were also just on the horizon.

In his address, Pius XII is recalling the tradition. As far back as the sixteenth century, theologians like De Vitoria had defined the difference between ordinary and extraordinary obligations to sustain one's life. The question for their age was whether a person who had a condition, like asthma, that could improve if he or she were moved from his or her birthplace to another climate that was healthier should give up friends and family just to add time to his or her life. De Vitoria did not think that one had to do that.

Pius XII recalls this and applies it to the questions of his day. Are we obligated to pursue all means of continuing our life? Pius responds that we are not obligated to pursue those means that are excessively burdensome. Even though some of the new medical advances could prolong life, it did not mean that one had to do everything possible to sustain one's life.

So, we come to the contemporary question of how we are to treat those persons in a PVS. More pointedly, the question about treatment has been focused on a particular issue: Are we obligated to provide nutrition and hydration to these persons? Can nutrition and hydration be considered extraordinary treatment for PVS patients?

When the question first arose, there were some Catholic bishops and theologians who argued that nutrition and hydration was a form of medical treatment, and therefore it could sometimes be considered extraordinary. Others took an opposing position, stating that so long as the person was able to metabolize the nutrition and hydration, we were always obligated to provide it. The latter group argued that even though nutrition and hydration was delivered to the patient by means of some technology, the means of delivery was often used because of its ease in care. If the feeding tube was not present, for example, we would still be obligated to feed a patient who could eat.

One of the main proponents of the arguments in favor of understanding artificial nutrition and hydration as sometimes falling within the category of extraordinary treatment is the Dominican bioethicist, Fr. Kevin O'Rourke, O.P. He does not deny the personhood of PVS patients. Rather, he has contended that the preservation of their biological existence may not be of benefit to them. He wrote, "If it is morally certain that persons cannot or will not perform acts of this nature [human acts of cognitive-affective function] now or in the future, then the moral imperative to prolong their lives no longer is present."[23] Fr. O'Rourke believes that in some cases of PVS patients, it is better to allow patients and their proxies to weigh the "hope of benefit" and the "degree of burden" that artificial nutrition and hydration has and decide whether to continue the treatment.

The article quoted above was an attempt to Fr. O'Rourke to further clarify his position in relation to a papal allocution by John Paul II on artificial nutrition and hydration. In March of 2004, the Pope spoke specifically on the topic. He took the position that artificial nutrition and hydration should be considered, in principle, ordinary comfort care and ought to be provided to all patients. He wrote that:

> the administration of water and food, even when provided by artificial means, always represents a *natural means* of preserving life, not a *medical act*. Its use, furthermore, should be considered, in principle, *ordinary* and *proportionate*, and as such morally obligatory, insofar as and until it is seen to have attained its proper finality, which in the present case consists in providing nourishment to the patient and alleviation of his suffering.[24]

Physician-Assisted Suicide and Euthanasia

John Paul II has written that we are now confronting a "culture of death." The clearest indications of such an identity are found in the growing acceptance of physician-assisted suicide. We will begin by assessing the impact that Dr. Jack Kevorkian has had on the discussion. Kevorkian, a former pathologist, has raised the issue to new heights, or depths, depending upon one's point of view. To date he has admitted to involvement in the deaths of approximately forty-five people in Michigan.[25] He does not shy away from the term "killing." In fact, he created a term for his work—"Medicide: the termination of life performed by professional medical personnel."[26] The number might be much higher than this because at one point when he was being prosecuted, he "appeared" to not be assisting in any more deaths, but several bodies were discovered that had "kevorkianesque" characteristics. More recently, one newspaper source put the number at approximately sixty-two deaths, while Kevorkian's lawyer, Geoffrey Fieger, has indicated that the number is probably closer to one hundred.[27] Clearly, however, Kevorkian was assisting people to die, and the number was sufficient for the Detroit Area Owners of Motels to ask him to stop leaving bodies in their rooms.

Kevorkian was prosecuted four times in Michigan. The first two trials charged him with assisting in a suicide, a violation of a temporary, four-year Michigan statute. The third time, he was prosecuted with assisting in a suicide under Common Law. In all three trials, he was acquitted. The prosecutor, the district attorney of Oakland County, Michigan, was defeated in his bid for reelection by David Gorcya, a candidate whose main campaign issue was a promise not to attempt prosecution for a fourth time. However, Gorcya was forced to press the issue after Kevorkian appeared on the CBS television show

60 Minutes. Kevorkian videotaped the death of Thomas Youk, a fifty-two-year-old man who suffered from ALS, or Lou Gehrig's disease. In the video, he is clearly seen to be performing an act that resulted in the death of Youk. Kevorkian was convicted of second-degree murder and delivery of a controlled substance. He was sentenced to ten to twenty-five years, of which he served eight years. He was released on parole in 2007.

Kevorkian brought the issue of physician-assisted suicide to the forefront of public discussion. However, he has been able to do so only because of a cultural schizophrenia that permits killing because of a fear of not having control at the end of one's life. With the media spin that his lawyer, Fieger, so ably performed, Kevorkian was seen as a benevolent friend of the terminally ill, as well as a proponent of a "right to die." Kevorkian has written about his own vision of end-of-life care that places much more emphasis on the role of the physician to kill. He proposes an entire industry of death that is founded upon the joining together of an absolute autonomy of the patient to decide the length of his or her life with the absolute power of the physician to enact that desire by killing the patient.

Internationally, the Dutch experience has also played an influential role. In the Netherlands, physicians have practiced euthanasia for about twenty-five years. Although technically illegal, euthanasia is tacitly accepted so long as the physician observes guidelines that were jointly developed by the Dutch legal and medical communities and approved by the Dutch Supreme Court, or Hoge Raad. These guidelines have influenced similar proposed sets of criteria elsewhere.

A sustained study of the nature and extent of euthanasia and physician-assisted suicide was conducted in 1991 by the Dutch government. The resulting report, by the Remmelink Commission, documents 2,300 actual cases of euthanasia and 400 cases of physician-assisted suicide. In about one thousand cases, the patient made no request to die. In approximately 50 percent of these cases, the patient raised the subject of euthanasia. In 87 percent of the cases, the patient's value system was discussed with the family. One must be wary, however, of making too much of this report, since it is extremely likely that some of the cases of involuntary euthanasia that are reported might likely meet the conditions for a just use of the principle of double effect. Furthermore, in 2005, two physicians at University Medical Center, Groningen, the Netherlands, Eduard Verhagen and Pieter J.J. Sauer, published an article in the *New England Journal of Medicine* in which they outlined what has become known as the Groningen Protocol. These guidelines permit the euthanasia of newborn infants with birth defects.[28]

The authors write that there are circumstances "in which, despite all measures taken, suffering cannot be relieved and no improvement can be expected. When both the parents and the physicians are convinced that there is an extremely poor prognosis, they may concur that death would be more humane than continued life."[29] The authors estimate that fifteen to twenty newborns are reported as killed each year in this way, and they suspect that others go unreported.

The chilling aspect about the contemporary Dutch development of advocating euthanasia is that historically, they were significantly opposed to the same justifications when they were tied to Nazism. While it is true that one should be wary of throwing that label around indiscriminately since it tends to lose its force when suggested too facilely, the current Dutch protocol is eerily reminiscent of the T-4 program of the Nazis that legally permitted them to euthanize infants with congenital deformities.[30] Public support for the program was gained through the infamous case of an infant, Baby Knauer, who was born blind and with a missing leg and forearm in 1938. Upon receiving a personal letter from the father of the baby, Adolf Hitler sent his personal physician, Karl Brandt, to examine the baby to verify its condition. In finding it to be as described, Brandt promised the child's physicians that there would be no legal penalty if the child were to be killed, which happened shortly afterward.[31]

German physicians were intimately connected with the genocide of Nazism. In the words of Dr. Viktor Brack, head of the Chancellery's "Euthanasia" Department II, "The syringe belongs in the hand of a physician."[32] After 1938, Nazi physicians experimented with various methods of killing infants and psychiatric patients. At first, they injected each patient, but eventually they moved toward more efficient ways of murdering many people at once. Gas chambers were first attempted at mental asylums in Germany. Dr. Irmfried Eberl was trained by the SS to kill mental patients in his position as head of the psychiatric hospital at Brandenburg-Gürden, one of the six main killing centers in Germany itself. He was later appointed as the Commandant of Treblinka, in July of 1942. Dr. Eberl did not do well there, however, and his command was short-lived.[33]

There is clearly a comparison to be drawn between the Dutch advocacy of euthanasia and the historical record. The Germans invaded the Netherlands in May of 1940. In 1941, after attempting to control the Dutch medical society, the Netherlands Society for the Advancement of Medicine (Nederlandsche Maatschappij tot Bevordering der Geneeskunst, NMBG), by barring Jews from its membership, the appointed Reich Commisar, Dr. Arthur Seyss-Inquart, demanded that Dutch physicians join a newly formed organization, the Chamber of Physicians (*Artsenkamer*) under Nazi patronage. Implicit in this order was the expectation that Dutch physicians would participate in euthanasia. Of the 6,500 physicians in the Netherlands at the time, only 500 participated with the Nazis. The others acceded to the demand that they not be identified as physicians and treated their patients privately throughout the occupation. The majority of the physicians evolved into a well-organized resistance movement in which virtually every doctor in the Netherlands would take part. To this day, the in-house journal of the Royal Netherlands Society for the Advancement of Medicine is called *Medisch Contact*. Among other things, the movement was able to influence the results of medical examinations on workers conscripted to forced labor, to resist and sabotage German measures against Dutch Jews (such as sterilization), to withhold information from the German authorities (e.g., about wounded resistance fighters), and to help improve the food situation for the civilian population. One of its most important actions was the doctors' strike of March 24, 1943. Its immediate cause were the fines imposed on eighty doctors who had failed to register with the Chamber of Physicians. As well as being fined, they were ordered to register within two weeks. Under the terms of the decree establishing the Chamber, however, doctors were free to renounce the practice of their profession at any time. So, more than 6,000 of the country's 6,500 doctors submitted a "statement of renunciation." They also demonstrated this publicly by removing any reference to the word *doctor* from their nameplates, prescriptions, and labels. Under Dutch law, however, they remained qualified and so did not abandon their patients. This action was not a strike in the true sense of the term but a demonstration—a public stand to make clear whose side the medical profession was on.[34]

It is disturbing that in a fifty-year span, the Dutch have moved from bravely risking their lives to prohibit euthanasia to endorsing it, in the name of compassion.

Although one can rightfully condemn the Dutch emphasis on euthanasia, one must also observe that the Dutch have an integrated approach to end-of-life issues. Patients with terminal illness are offered hospice care, and there is a real concern about how to provide meaningful palliative care. All this is good, of course. Yet, allowing the killing of patients, especially those who have not even requested death, is an incongruity with a broader ethic of care for the dying.

In the past fifteen years, Dr. Timothy Quill, M.D., an associate professor at the University of Rochester Medical School, has become a leading proponent of physician-assisted suicide. Quill achieved notoriety after an article of his appeared in the *New England Journal of Medicine*. In the article, he documented how he had helped a patient of his, Diane, who was diagnosed with acute leukemia. With a 25 percent chance of surviving, she elected not to initiate chemotherapy and asked Quill to assist her in dying when she was closer to death. After much discussion and hesitation, Quill helped Diane in her desire to commit suicide by prescribing enough barbiturates by which she could end her own life. After the article was published, Quill was under consideration for a variety of criminal charges, including tampering with a death certificate and manslaughter, but a grand jury in New York refused to indict him. Subsequently, the New York State Health Department reviewed the case and found no cause for professional misconduct. Largely because Diane performed her act alone, Quill was not charged with any wrongdoing, by his own admission.

Since those events, Quill has written and spoken widely on the issue of physician-assisted suicide. Unlike Kevorkian, who appears reckless, Quill enjoys great respect from his supporters and critics alike for his persuasive arguments to legalize physician-assisted suicide.

Partly his success may be attributed to his background. He is a psychiatrist who was for eight years the director of a hospice program. Quill's concerns are with the hard cases that medicine cannot help. He argues for the handful of cases in which pain relief is not possible. He believes that for the most part, the American medical system is unable to deal with death because it is a failure. He has argued passionately for better methods of palliative care and a concerted effort to enable people to use hospice services. On these issues, it is clear that he is right.

Federal oversight on the abuse of narcotic drugs has sometimes scared physicians away from prescribing proper amounts to control suffering. If a physician gives a large quantity of morphine, for example, he or she is likely to be reviewed. Fear of losing a medical license is an effective cause of insufficient palliative care at the end of life. Couple this with the fact that most people who die in the United States do not avail themselves of hospice services, which have as their mission comfort care, and we have a difficult system that tends to treat the dying without a view to controlling suffering. We will come back to Quill in a little bit and look a little more carefully at his arguments.

Another factor in this debate is the legislative decisions about physician-assisted suicide. In the United States, Oregon was the first state to approve a law legalizing physician-assisted suicide. Shortly after its passage in 1996, a judge issued an injunction to prohibit its enactment. In early November 1997, Oregon voters again approved the legalization of physician-assisted suicide by defeating a measure that would have invalidated the first vote. The injunction has now been lifted, and Oregon is the first, and only, state to have a law that allows physician-assisted suicide. In the first year that the law was enacted, 23 patients received lethal drug prescriptions. It is not coincidental that Oregon is also one of the least religious states in America.

Before Oregon approved its measure, other states had defeated similar measures in favor of physician-assisted suicide. In California and Washington State, narrow majorities defeated the referendums. Other states, including New York, have passed clear statutes prohibiting physician-assisted suicide. In the time since Oregon's approval, ballot measures to provide similar measures in other states have been defeated every time that they have been proposed.

Finally, before we move into the specific arguments of Kevorkian and Quill, I would like to mention some of the judicial challenges with regard to physician-assisted suicide, in particular the decisions in *Quill v. Vacco* and *Compassion in Dying v. State of Washington*. While of course such cases as Cruzan have a relationship to this issue, the two cases just mentioned are more directly related. Both were challenges to approved statutes prohibiting physician-assisted suicide, the first in New York and the second in Washington. The U.S. Supreme Court decided the final outcome of these two cases in the summer of 1997. The Supreme Court ruled that states have a compelling interest in this issue and that they may enact legislation to prohibit it.

What was particularly interesting about these cases was not their eventual disposition by the Supreme Court but rather the language of the decision at the appeals court level. *Quill* was decided in the U.S. Court of Appeals, Second Circuit, while *Compassion in Dying* was decided in the Ninth Circuit.

In *Quill*, the majority opinion of the appeals court argued that restrictions on physician-assisted suicide were unconstitutional under the equal protection clause of the Constitution. New York State, the court ruled, does not treat similarly situated persons—those in the final stages of terminal illness—alike. Those who are on respirators or other types of technological care can choose to "hasten their deaths" through the removal of life-sustaining equipment while those who are not dependent on such machines may not hasten their deaths.

The removal of life-sustaining equipment has traditionally been allowed under the principle of double effect. The court argued that since both acts result in death, then the intention is the same. One is not certain in this decision whether the justices rejected the principle or were simply ignorant of it.

The *Compassion* decision had another interesting argument. The judges argued that because of *Roe v. Wade*, all persons have a right to privacy, which extends to the right to determine what will be done with one's body. It is logical, they argued, that if a woman has a right to do with her body as she wishes in the case of abortion, then so too does an individual have a right to die if he or she wishes.

While both of these decisions were overturned, they give insight into the epistemological issue that was raised earlier. Both, implicitly at least, deny a moral methodology that would see a clear differentiation between object, intention, and circumstances. They tend to see the moral decision as more of an experiential decision, in which the agent cannot know with certainty the objective content of the act, and thus whatever is chosen becomes much more subjective, with the will of the agent determining his or her own ends. The judicial arguments for physician-assisted suicide rest upon the same foundations as Kevorkian and Quill.

Let us move to a more precise analysis of Kevorkian and Quill. Although both Kevorkian and Quill appear to be dissimilar, they are, in fact, arguing from similar premises concerning autonomy and personhood.

Kevorkian is controversial for a number of reasons in this debate. His reasons for assisting people to die are extreme, and yet unknown to most. There are several reasons for this. First, Kevorkian's aim of physician-assisted death is part of a larger fascination with death that appeared early in his career. His residency as a physician was terminated because of his attempt to research death in different ways. He reportedly photographed the eyes of dead and dying patients in order to ascertain the moment of death. In his first post-residency job, he transfused blood from corpses to live volunteers. He has publicly suggested that condemned prisoners be made to donate organs so that some good can come from their deaths. Alternatively, he thinks that they could be used for scientific study. In speaking about the Nazi medical experiments, he noted that they were wrong not in their aims but in the way that they did things. Lately, he was trying to arrange the suicide of an emphysema victim so that the man could donate his liver to a teenage girl who needed a liver to survive.

A second difficulty with Kevorkian is that he will assist just about anyone to die, for whatever reason he sees fit. Several of his cases have been of people who were not suffering from terminal disease. Sherri Miller, who died in 1991, had severe multiple sclerosis. Marjorie Wantz, who died the same night, had chronic pelvic pain, was probably addicted to Halcyon, and had severe depression. Another case, that of Judith Curren, was particularly troubling. Curren, the wife of a psychiatrist, suffered from severe depression but no other condition.

The Curren case also points to his inability or unwillingness to carefully assess the conditions of the people whom he helps to die. Curren, who had a number of underlying problems, had been beaten by her husband only two weeks before this meeting with Kevorkian. Several commentators have suggested that her conditions were the result of severe psychological problems that might have been solved.

Third, Kevorkian states that his aim is to alleviate suffering. Therefore, all means that help him to obtain this end are justifiable. In Sherri Miller's case, because he could not find a proper site to put an IV in, he used carbon monoxide gas instead. Clearly, carbon monoxide is not a medical treatment for any known disease.

Kevorkian's justification for physician-assisted suicide is centered upon his contention that autonomy is the highest good. Although he claims that he aims for the relief of suffering, what is significant about Kevorkian is the centrality of the physician in all of this. The physician ultimately holds the key to life or death in Kevorkian's world. She or he decides the fate of one who requests assistance in dying. Kevorkian's world is one in which the physician determines who gets what and why and how. Ultimately, he claims that he wants "a rational policy for planned death for civilized society." The physician, of course, does the planning.

Kevorkian stands as the logical end point of a medical establishment that sees itself mainly in terms of cure. If the purpose of medicine is to cure, then physician-assisted suicide seems to be the way that the discussion ought to go. To focus so centrally on cure has the possibility of allowing science to determine the values and to make them up as we go along. If society needs to be cured, who better than the physician?

In a sense, Kevorkian has turned the Nazi model of medicine into a thoroughly American version. As Robert Jay Lifton has noted, the Nazi doctors were focused upon the calling to be the physicians for the state. They had to ensure the health of the nation. Therefore, life that was not worthy of living, *lebenuswert leben*, could be terminated. The handicapped and mental ill were all not worthy of life because they infected the whole. In Kevorkian's world, the absolute is not the state, but the autonomous physician.

Next to Kevorkian, Quill seems quite promising. He rejects the Kevorkian aims in favor of a dignified death. He focuses upon the idea of comfort care and the need for patients to be able to choose how they wish to die. In that, Quill is the complete opposite of Kevorkian. He advances the autonomy of the patient in the decision-making process. Where Kevorkian idealizes the physician, Quill idealizes the patient.

In his article in *The New England Journal of Medicine*, he expresses his reservation about assisting a patient in taking her own life:

> I have long been an advocate of active, informed patient choice in treatment or nontreatment, and of a patient's right to die with as much dignity and control as possible. Yet there was something about her giving up a 25% chance of long-term survival in favor of almost certain death that disturbed me. I had seen Diane fight and use her considerable inner resources to overcome alcoholism and depression, and I half expected her to change her mind over the next week. Since the window of time in which effective treatment can be initiated is rather narrow, we met several times that week. We obtained a second hematology consultation and talked at length about the meaning and implications of treatment or nontreatment. She talked to a psychologist she had seen in the past. I gradually understood the decision from her perspective and became convinced that it was the right decision for her. [35]

The essential characteristic for Quill is ultimately that the patient be allowed to choose the manner of his or her death. He does not think that there are many instances where one would have to help a person to commit suicide if appropriate options were given. Yet, he believes that patient autonomy is essential. This leads him to state that one of the true obligations of the physician is nonabandonment of the terminally ill patient.

Quill is well intentioned and for much of what he says, I believe that he enjoys the support of many ethicists. Yet, although one can agree with many of his conclusions, the basic difficulty is his premise of patient autonomy. For Quill, the patients' decision is the final word. So long as they determine their eventual outcome, the act should be respected, if not supported, by the physician.

There are several difficulties with such a position. Certainly, patient autonomy is a significant value to pursue. Individuals should be actively involved in their own health care. Modern medicine has rightly turned away from a strong paternalistic bent. Yet, paternalism at its core does contain a compelling and conflicting value to autonomy. The Greek lexical roots of autonomy are "auto" and "nomos," which mean self and rule. One ought to make decisions on the basis of what is best for us, but it is assumed that there is already an objective moral order to which we must conform ourselves. The very basis of paternalism is that both the physician and the patient aim to act in a way that is not determined solely by them. God has imbedded within the very fabric of creation certain laws and goods that we cannot violate without losing ourselves. The paternalistic physician, then, acts in the best interest of the patient, but this good is not determined by the physician nor is it determined by the patient. All too often, paternalism is decried as an imposition on the will of the patient. The physician is a god, making unilateral decisions.

While it is true that some physicians do lose sight of the essential aspect of seeking the good of the patient, we should not entirely give up on the central concern of paternalism. To act like a father is really to care like a parent. Physicians are called in their work to essentially care, not cure. To cure means to treat the physical condition, to care is to treat the whole person.

In Catholic ethics, the ethics of care takes precedence. We believe that, fundamentally, life is a gift from God, and we exist as stewards of that gift. We are not, therefore, free to do with ourselves as we wish. We are not autonomous in the sense that our freedom is limited by the will of he who created us in his image and likeness, as Genesis says. Simply put, we belong to God, not to ourselves.

Physician-assisted suicide is a technological application of an ethics of cure. It seeks to solve a problem, not to address the totality of the person. As recent books on communication have pointed out, the male tendency is to seek solutions and to problem solve, while a more feminine approach calls for connection.[36] Medicine, by and large, is dominated by a male mechanical approach. The physician collects signs and symptoms and finds the root of the problem. He or she then applies some solution or another to the diagnosis. Medicine as a profession tends to embrace this approach, whether the physician is male or female.

Quill points to this difficulty in modern medicine. That is one of the reasons why his message resonates so well with the American public. Quill promotes a compassionate medicine, one that cares about the quality of dying. He draws us back to the simple observation that a technologically managed death is often dehumanizing. Yet, Quill's downfall is that his answer to this difficulty is to accept whatever the patient finally desires. To be fair to Quill, he does express some hesitancy about the process of the physician stepping back to allow the patient to choose unilaterally. Yet, in the end, he feels that he has no choice. To confront the moral vacuousness of modern medicine, he offers the emptiness of individual choice, unattached from any framework for choosing correctly. While it seems like a step ahead, in reality it is a non-solution, for it fails to deal with the central problem in physician-assisted suicide: the lack of an objective value system by which both physician and patient are bound, and by which true care is possible. Only when the decisions of both patient and physician are limited to the good of the patient, which is not determined by either but is confronted by both, is care really possible. Otherwise, the patient is a machine, to be fixed or discarded when curing is no longer possible.

Kevorkian is also cure oriented. In place of patient autonomy, however, he concentrates on physician autonomy. In his ethics, the physician is the final arbiter of right and wrong. He does not, however, publicly promote this stand. Instead, he paints a beautiful picture of individual choice. He is simply the assistant, the means by which a person could realize his or her desires. Yet, as he has written, ultimately he desires a world where the physician helps to develop sound policies on death. He evokes a different kind of paternalism, one that is motivated by the eradication of conditions. Indeed, Kevorkian is hardly different from many figures in modern medicine who see the process of technological manipulation as the answer to complex human problems, like population control. He takes the basic premise of cure through technology to its logical end. Many are uncomfortable with his conclusions. The error, however, lies in the premises of his view. Instead, opponents of physician-assisted suicide need to refocus medicine on an ethics of care.

Notes

1. Deuteronomy 30:15–16 (The Jerusalem Bible translation).
2. Thomas Lynch, "Grief, Real and Imagined," *New York Times*, October 30, 1995, A15.
3. J.D. McCue, "The Naturalness of Dying," *JAMA: The Journal of the American Medical Association* 273 (1995): 1039–43.
4. SUPPORT is an acronym for Study to Understand the Prognoses and Procedures for Outcomes and Risks of Treatment. See Alfred F. Connors et al., "A Controlled Trial to Improve Care for Seriously Ill Hospitalized Patients," *JAMA: The Journal of the American Medical Association* 274 (1995): 1591–1600.
5. Joan Temo et al., "Preferences for Cardiopulmonary Resuscitation: Physician-Patient Agreement and Hospital Use," *Journal of General Internal Medicine* 10 (1995): 179–86.
6. Connors et al., "A Controlled Trial," 1596.
7. Connors et al., "A Controlled Trial," 1597.
8. "A Definition of Irreversible Coma: Report of the Ad Hoc Committee of Harvard Medical School to Examine the Definition of Brain Death," *JAMA: The Journal of the American Medical Association* 205 (1968): 337–340.
9. Alexander Capron and Leon Kass, "A Statutory Definition of the Standards for Determining Human Death: An Appraisal and a Proposal," *University of Pennsylvania Law Review* 21 (1972): 87–118.
10. President's Commission for the Study of Ethical Problems in Medicine, Biomedical and Behavioral Research, *Defining Death: A Report on the Medical, Legal, and Ethical Issues in the Determination of Death* (Washington, DC: U.S. Government Printing Office, 1981).
11. Eelco Wijdicks, "Brain Death Worldwide: Accepted Fact, but No Worldwide Consensus," *Neurology* 62 (2006): 20–25.
12. See Pius XII, (24 November 1957), AAS 49: 1031. Also, see John Paul II, "Address to the 18th International Congress of the Transplantation Society," (29 August 2000) http://www.vatican.va/holy_father/john_paul_ii/speeches/2000/jul-sep/documents/hf_jp-ii_spe_20000829_transplants_en.html).
13. John Paul II, "Address to the 18th Congress," § 5.
14. See, for example, Robert Veatch, "The Whole Brain-Oriented Concept of Death: An Outmoded Philosophical Formulation," *Journal of Thanatology* 3 (1975): 13–30, "Brain Death and Slippery Slopes," *Journal of Clinical Ethics* 3 (1992): 181–187, and "The Impending Collapse of the Whole-Brain Definition of Death," *Hasting Center Report* 23, no. 4 (1993): 18–24.
15. Robert Truog, "Is It Time to Abandon Brain Death?" *Hastings Center Report* 27 (Jan./Feb. 1997): 29–37.
16. Martyn Evans and Michael Potts, "A Narrative Case against Brain Death," in *Beyond Brain Death: The Case Against Brain Based Criteria for*

Human Death, ed. Michael Potts, Paul Byrne, and Richard Nilges (Dordrecht: Kluwer Academic Publishers, 2000), 242.

17. Evans and Potts, "Narrative Case against Brain Death," 244.

18. Kenneth Iserson, *Death to Dust: What Happens to Dead Bodies?* (Tuscon: Galen Press, 2001), 19.

19. D. Jones, "Metaphysical Misgivings about 'Brain Death,'" in M. Potts, et al., *Beyond Brain Death*, 98.

20. Multi-Society Task Force, "Medical Aspects of the Persistent Vegetative State," *New England Journal of Medicine* 330 (1994): 1499–1508 (Part 1) and 1572–1579 (Part 2).

21. Multi-Society Task Force, "Medical Aspects," 1574.

22. Pius XII, "The Prolongation of Life," Address, 24 Nov. 1957, *The Pope Speaks* 4: 393–98.

23. Kevin O'Rourke, "Reflections on the Papal Allocution Concerning Care for PVS Patients," in *Artificial Hydration: The New Catholic Debate*, ed. C. Tollefsen (Dordrecht: Springer, 2008), 174.

24. John Paul II, "Address to the Participants in the International Congress on Life Sustaining Treatments and the Vegetative State: Scientific Advances and Ethical Dilemmas," http://www.vatican.va/holy_father/john_paul_ii/speeches /2004/march/documents/hf_jp-ii_spe_20040320_congress-fiamc_en.html.

25. Michael Betzhold, "The Selling of Doctor Death," *New Republic* 216 (26 May 1997): 22.

26. Jack Kevorkian, *Prescription: Medicide. The Goodness of Planned Death* (Buffalo, NY: Prometheus Books, 1991), 202–203.

27. "Kevorkian Encountering Fewer Hurdles in Suicides," *New York Times*, March 5, 1984, A 26.

28. Eduard Verhagen and Pieter J.J. Sauer, "The Groningen Protocol—Euthansia in Severely Ill Newborns," *New England Journal of Medicine* 352 (2005): 959–63.

29. Verhagen and Sauer, "The Groningen Protocol," 961.

30. T-4 stands for Tiergarten 4, the street address in Berlin where it was headquartered. For an extensive explanation of the program, consult Robert Lifton, *The Nazi Doctors*, 65–76.

31. Lifton, *The Nazi Doctors*, 115.

32. "Testimony of August Becker," 21 April 1960 in Heyde Trial. Trial of Werner Heyde, Gerhard Bohne, and Hans Hefelman Generalstaatsanwalt Frankfurt JS 17/59 (GStA) 4 VU 3/61, Strafkammer des Langerichts Limburg/Lahn, in Lifton, The Nazi Doctors, 71, 512, n. 54.

33. Lifton, *The Nazi Doctors*, 123–24.

34. Bas J.N. Schrueder, "The Influence of the German Occupation of 1940–1945 on Psychiatry in the Netherlands," *International Journal of Mental Health* 35, no. 4 (Winter 2006–7): 113–14.

35. Timothy Quill, "Death and Dignity: A Case of Individualized Decision Making," *The New England Journal of Medicine*, Vol. 324 (March 7, 1991): 691-694.

36. See, for example, Deborah Tannen, *You Just Don't Understand: Women and Men in Conversation* (New York: Harper 1991).

Bibliography

"A Definition of Irreversible Coma: Report of the Ad Hoc Committee of Harvard Medical School to Examine the Definition of Brain Death." *JAMA: The Journal of the American Medical Association* 205 (1968): 337–340.

"A New Ethic for Medicine and Society." *California Medicine* 113 no. 3 (September 1970): 67.

Alston, Mary Niven. "The Attitude of the Church Towards Dissection before 1500." *Bulletin of the History of Medicine* XVI (1944): 221–238.

Annas, George. *American Bioethics: Crossing Human Rights and Health Law Boundaries.* Oxford: Oxford University Press, 2004.

Aquinas, Thomas. *Summa Theologiae.* Marcus Lefébure, trans. New York: McGraw Hill, 1975.

Ariès, Philippe. *Western Attitudes Toward Death from the Middle Ages to the Present.* Baltimore: The John Hopkins University Press. 1974.

Augustine. "The City of God" in *A Select Library of the Nicene and Post-Nicene Fathers of the Christian Church. Vol. II. St. Augustine's City of God and Christian Doctrine.* Philip Schaff, ed. Marcus Dods, trans. Grand Rapids. MI: Eerdmans, 1988.

_____. "The Immortality of the Soul." in *Writings of St. Augustine. Vol. 2.* Ludwig Schopp, trans. New York: Cima Publishing. 1947.

Batey, Richard. "The Mid Σαρξ Union of Christ and the Church." *New Testament Studies* 13 (1966–67): 272.

Beers, Mark H. and Robert Berkow, eds. *The Merck Manual of Diagnosis and Therapy.* 16th ed. Rahway. NJ: Merck Research Laboratories,1999.

Bender, L., OP. "Organorum humanorum trensplantatio." *Angelicum* 31 (1954): 139–60.

Benestad, J. Brian. "The Political Vision of Pope John Paul II: Justice through Faith and Culture." *Communio* 8 (1981): 3–19.

Bernays, Edward L. "The Engineering of Consent." *The Annals of the American Academy of Political and Social Science* 250, no. 1(1947): 113–120.

Betzhold, Michael. "The Selling of Doctor Death." *New Republic* 216 (26 May 1997): 22.

Binding, Karl and Alfred Hoche. *Permission to Destroy Life Unworthy of Life: Its Extent and Form.* Leipzeig: Felix Meiner Verlag, 1920 as reprinted in *Issues in Law and Medicine* 8. no. 3 (1992): 231.

Brandeis, Louis and Samuel Warren. "The Right to Privacy." *Harvard Law Review* 4 (1890): 190–96.

Buck v. Bell. 274 U.S. 200 (1927).

Burke, Cormac. *Covenanted Happiness: Love and Commitment in Marriage.* San Francisco: Ignatius, 1990.

Bynum, Caroline Walker. *The Resurrection of the Body in Western Christianity, 200–1336.* New York: Columbia University Press, 1995.

Capron, Alexander and Leon Kass. "A Statutory Definition of the Standards for Determining Human Death: An Appraisal and a Proposal." *University of Pennsylvania Law Review* 21 (1972): 87–118.

Carlino, Andrea. *Books of the Body: Anatomical Ritual and Renaissance Learning.* Chicago: University of Chicago Press, 1999.

Cataldo, Peter J. "Gift as Assistance." *Ethics & Medics* 22. no. 12 (December 1997).

_____. "Reproductive Technologies." *Ethics & Medics* 21. no. 1 (January 1996): 1–3.

_____. "The Newest Reproductive Technologies: Applying Catholic Teaching." pp. 61-94 in *The Gospel of Life and the Vision of Health Care.* Russell B. Smith, ed. Braintree. MA: The Pope John Center, 1996.

Catholic Health Association of America. *Continuing the Commitment: A Pathway to Health Care Reform.* St. Louis: The Catholic Health Association, 2000.

_____. *Setting Relationships Right: A Proposal for Systemic Health Care Reform.* St. Louis: The Catholic Health Association, 1993.

_____. *Catholic Healthcare in the United States.* St. Louis. MO: Catholic Health Association, 2009.

Celsus. "De Medicina. Prooemium" in *De Medicina With an English Translation in Three Volumes, Vol. I.* W.G. Spencer. trans. Cambridge. MA: Harvard University Press, 1960.

Centers for Disease Control. National Center for Health Statistics. "Life Expectancy at Birth. 65 and 85 Years of Age. US. Selected Years 1900-2006." http://205.207.175.93/HDI/ReportFolders/reportFolders.aspx.

Centers for Disease Control. "Assisted Reproductive Technology Survelliance—2000." pp 1-16 in *Morbidity and Mortality Weekly Report* (MMWR) 52 (SS09- August 29, 2003.

CHA Stewardship Task Force. *No Room in the Marketplace.* St. Louis: The Catholic Health Association, 1986.

Chadwick, J. and W.N. Mann. *The Medical Works of Hippocrates.* Oxford: Blackwell, 1950.

Congregation for the Doctrine of the Faith. *Donum vitae (Instruction on the Respect for Human Life in its Origin and on the Dignity of Procreation).* Boston: Pauline Books & Media, 1987.

Congressional Budget Office. *A CBO Study: The Long Term Budget Outlook: 2005.* Washington. DC: The Congress of the United States, 2005.

Connery, John. SJ. "Notes on Moral Theology." *Theological Studies* 15 (1954): 602–06.

Connors, Alfred F., et al. "A Controlled Trial to Improve Care for Seriously Ill Hospitalized Patients." *JAMA: The Journal of the American Medical Association* 274 (1995): 1591–1600.

Cunningham, Fr. Bert CM. "Morality of Organic Transplantation." Washington. DC: Catholic University of America, 1944.

Dannenberg, Andrew L., Deron C. Burton, and Richard J. Jackson. "Economic and Environmental Costs of Obesity: The Impact on Airlines." *American Journal of Preventive Medicine* 27. no. 3 (2004): 264.

DeMarco, Donald. "GIFT as Replacement." *Ethics & Medics* 22, no. 11 (November 1997): 3–4.

_____. *Biotechnology and the Assault on Parenthood.* San Francisco: Ignatius, 1991.

Denzinger, Heinrich and Adolf Schönmetzer. *Enchiridion symbolorum.* Barcinone: Herder, 1973.

Dye, Jane Lawler. *Fertility of American Women: 2006.* Washington. DC: U.S. Census Bureau, 2008.

Edelstein, Ludwig. "Der Geschicte der Sektion in der Antike." pp. 247-301 in *Ancient Medicine: Selected Papers of Ludwig Edelstein.* O. and C.L. Tempkin. trans. Baltimore: Johns Hopkins University Press, 1967.

Eusebius. *The Ecclesiastical History II.* JEL Oulton. trans. Cambridge: Harvard University Press, 1957.

Evans, Martyn and Michael Potts. "A Narrative Case against Brain Death." Pp. 237-48 in *Beyond Brain Death: The Case Against Brain Based Criteria for Human Death.* Michael Potts. Paul Byrne. and Richard Nilges, eds. Dordrecht: Kluwer Academic Publishers, 2000.

Fletcher, Joseph. *Humanhood: Essays in Biomedical Ethics.* Buffalo. NY: Prometheus Books, 1979.

_____. *Situation Ethics: The New Morality.* Philadelphia: Westminster Press, 1966.

Fulgentius. "Mitologicorum libri tres 1:16–17" in *Fabii Planciadis Fulgenti. Opera.* R. Helm, ed. Leipzig: Teubner, 1898

Gaebler, Ralph F. "Is There a Natural Law Right to Privacy?" *American Journal of Jurisprudence* 37 (1992): 319–336.

Galen, *On Anatomical Procedures. The Later Books.* M.C. Lyons and B. Towers. eds. W.L.H. Duckworth, trans. Cambridge: Cambridge University Press, 1962.

Gardella, Peter. *Innocent Ecstasy: How Christianity Gave America an Ethic of Sexual Pleasure.* New York: Oxford University Press, 1985.

Grabowski, John S. "Covenantal Sexuality." *Eglise et Theologie* 27 (1996): 229–252.

_____. *Sex and Virtue: An Introduction to Sexual Ethics.* Washington. DC: Catholic University of America Press, 2003.

Gramatowski, Wiktor, S.J. and Zofia Wilinska Karol. *Wojtylaw swietle publikacji: Karol Wojtyla negli scritti.* Vatican City: Liberia Editrice, 1980.

Gray, Bradford H. *The Profit Motive and Patient Care: A Twentieth Century Fund Report.* Cambridge. MA: Harvard University Press, 1991.

Gustafson, James. "How Does Love Reign?" *The Christian Century* 83 (1966): 654-55.

Guttmacher, A. F. "Biographical Notes on Some Famous Conjoined Twins." *Birth Defects* 3 (1967):10-17.

Haas, John. "Gift? No!" *Ethics & Medics* 18 (1993) 1-3.

_____. "Pastoral Concerns: Procreation and the Marital Act." in *Reproductive Technologies, Marriage and the Church*. Donald McCarthy, ed. Braintree. MA: The Pope John Center, 1988.

Hart, David Bentley. *Atheist Delusions: The Christian Revolution and its Fashionable Enemies*. New Haven: Yale University Press, 2009.

Hauerwas, Stanley. "The Family as a School for Character." *Religious Education* 80 (Spring 1985): 272-85.

Henry of Huntington. *The Chronicle of Henry of Huntington*. Thomas Forester, trans. London: Henry G. Bohn, 1853.

Hilgers, Thomas W. "Answers for Infertility." *Celebrate Life* (May/June 1995): 34.

Hippolytus. "The Apostolic Tradition." in *The Apostolic Tradition of Hippolytus*. B.S. Easton, ed. Cambridge: Cambridge University Press, 1934.

Hollenbach, David. *Claims in Conflict: Retrieving and Renewing the Catholic Human Rights Tradition*. New York: Paulist Press, 1979.

Irving, Dianne Nutwell. "Scientific and Philosophical Expertise: An Evaluation on the Arguments of 'Personhood." *Linacre Quarterly* 60 (February 1993): 18–46.

Iserson, Kenneth. *Death to Dust: What Happens to Dead Bodies?* Tuscon: Galen Press, 2001.

John Paul II. "Address to the 18th International Congress of the Transplantation Society." (29 August 2000). http://www.vatican.va/holy_father/john_paul_ii/speeches/2000/jul-sep/documents/hf_jp-ii_spe_20000829_transplants_en.html).

_____. "Address to the Participants in the International Congress of On Life Sustaining Treatments and the Vegetative State: Scientific Advances and Ethical Dilemmas." http://www.vatican.va/holy_father/john_paul_ii/speeches/2004/march /documents/hf_jp-ii_spe_20040320_congress-fiamc_en.html.

_____. "Many Ethical. Legal and Social Questions Must Be Examined in Greater Depth" (June 20. 1991) *Dolentium Hominum* . Vatican City: Vatican Press, 1992.

_____. *Redemptor hominis*. Encyclical. 4 March 1979. English translation. *AAS* 71 (1979): 257–324.

_____. *Veritatis Splendor*. Encyclical. Boston. MA: Daughters of St. Paul. 1993.

_____. "Amados hermanos." (28 January 1979). English translation in *Origins* 8 (8 February 1979): 534; original Spanish text in *AAS* 71 (1979): 19.

_____. *Centessimus Annus*. Encyclical. (1 May 1991). *AAS* 83 (1991): 793-867.

Jones. D. "Metaphysical Misgivings about 'Brain Death.'" Pp. 91-120 in M. Potts, et. al., *Beyond Brain Death : The Case Against Brain Based Criteria for Human Death*. Michael Potts, Paul Byrne, and Richard Nilges, eds. Dordrecht: Kluwer Academic Publishers. 2000.

Kant, Immanuel. *Critique of Practical Reason.* Lewis White Beck, trans. Upper Saddle River, NJ: Prentice Hall, 1982.

_____. *Groundwork of the Metaphysics of Morals.* H.J. Paton, trans. New York: Harper and Row, 1964.

Kelly, Gerald SJ. "Pope Pius XII and the Principle of Totality." *Theological Studies* 16 (1955). 373–96.

_____. "The Morality of Mutilation: Towards a Revision of the Treatise." *Theological Studies* 17 (1956): 322–344.

_____. *Medico-Moral Problems.* St. Louis. MO: Catholic Hospital Association, 1958.

Kelves, Daniel V. *In the Name of Eugenics: Genetics and the Uses of Human Heredity.* Cambridge. MA: Harvard University Press, 1985.

Kevorkian, Jack. *Prescription: Medicide. The Goodness of Planned Death.* Buffalo. NY: Prometheus Books, 1991.

"Kevorkian Encountering Fewer Hurdles in Suicides." *New York Times.* March 5. 1984. A 26.

Kohler, Hans-Peter, Francesco C. Billari, and José A. Ortega. "Low Fertility in Europe: Causes. Implications and Policy Options." Pp. 48-109 in *The Baby Bust: Who Will Do the Work? Who Will Pay the Taxes?* F. R. Harris, ed. Lanham. MD: Rowman & Littlefield Publishers, 2006.

Kuczmarski, Robert J. and Katherine M. Flegal. "Increasing Prevalence of Overweight among US Adults." *JAMA: Journal of the American Medical Association* 272. no. 3 (1994): 205.

Lassiter, Mark. "Nation's First Baby Boomer Files for Social Security Benefits—Online!" Baltimore: Social Security Administration Press Office, 2007.

Lauritzen, Paul. "What Price Parenthood?" *Hastings Center Report* Vol. 20 (March-April 1990): 38-46.

Lawler, Ronald. *The Christian Personalism of John Paul II.* Chicago: Franciscan Herald Press, 1982.

Lifton, Robert Jay. *The Nazi Doctors: Medical Killing and the Psychology of Genocide.* New York: Basic Books, 1986.

"Letter to Diognetus." in *The Didache. The epistle of Barnabas. The epistles and The martyrdom of St. Polycarp. The fragments of Papias. and The epistle to Diognetus.* Westminster. Md.: Newman Press, 1961.

Linacre, Susan. "Australian Social Trends: 2007." Catalogue 4102.0. Canberra. Australia: Australian Bureau of Statistics, 2007.

Lloyd, G.E.R., ed. *Hippocratic Writings.* "On the Heart." I.M. Lonie, trans. London: Penguin, 1978.

Lynch, Thomas. "Grief. Real and Imagined." *New York Times*, October 30. 1995, A15.

Lysaught, M. Therese. "Is it Killing?" *Human Life Review* 27 (Winter 2001): 48–52.

May, William. "Pastoral Concerns: Procreation and the Marital Act." *Reproductive Technologies, Marriage and the Church.* Donald McCarthy, ed. Braintree. MA: The Pope John Center, 1988.

McCabe, Herbert. "The Validity of Absolutes." *Commonweal* 83 (1966): 439.

McCarthy, Donald. "Response to Catholic Moral Teaching and TOT/GIFT," pp. 140-45 in *Reproductive Technologies, Marriage and the Church.* Donald McCarthy. ed. Braintree. MA: The Pope John Center, 1988.

McCue, J. D. "The Naturalness of Dying." *JAMA: The Journal of the American Medical Association* 273 (1995): 1039–43.

McKusick, V. "Mapping and Sequencing the Human Gene." *New England Journal of Medicine* 320 (1989): 910.

Mill, John Stuart. *Utilitarianism.* Indianapolis: Bobbs Merrill, 1971.

Mosely, Ray, Lee Crandall, Marvin Dewar, David Nye, and Harry Oster. "Ethical Implications of a Complete Human Gene Map for Insurance." *Business and Professional Ethics Journal* 10 (Winter 1991): 73.

Multi-Society Task Force. "Medical Aspects of the Persistent Vegetative State." *New England Journal of Medicine* 330 (1994): 1499–1508 (Part 1) and 1572–1579 (Part 2).

Murphy-O'Connor, Cormac. "A Submission by Archbishop Cormac Murphy-O'Connor. Archbishop of Westminster to the Court of Appeal in the Case of Central Manchester Healthcare Trust V. Mr. And Mrs. A and RE a Child (By her Guardian ad litem. the Official Solicitor)" 14 September 2000. http://www.rcdow.org.uk/cardinal/default.asp?content_ref=45 (accessed November 1. 2009).

Murphy, Walter Murphy. "The Right to Privacy and Legitimate Constitutional Change." Pp. 213-14 in *The Constitutional Bases of Political and Social Change in the United States.* New York: Praeger, 1990.

National Conference of Catholic Bishops. *A Framework for Comprehensive Health Care Reform: Protecting Human Life, Promoting Human Dignity, Pursuing the Common Good.* Washington. DC: U.S. Conference of Catholic Bishops, 1993.

Noonan, John T. Jr.. *Contraception: A History of its Treatment by the Catholic Theologians and Canonists.* Cambridge. MA: Belknap Press of Harvard University, 1965.

O'Brien, Mary Elizabeth. *Spirituality in Nursing: Standing on Holy Ground.* Sudbury. MA: Jones and Bartlett, 1999.

O'Malley, Bishop Sean. *Pastoral letter of November 9. 2001* (Boston: Massachusetts Catholic Conference, 2001.

O'Neill, James J. Jr.. "Conjoined Twins." *Pediatric Surgery.* St. Louis: Mosby, 1998.

O'Rourke, Kevin. "Reflections on the Papal Allocution Concerning Care for PVS Patients." in *Artificial Hydration: The New Catholic Debate.* C. Tollefsen, ed. Dordrecht: Springer, 2008.

Palyi, Melchior. *Compulsory Medical Care and the Welfare State.* Chicago: National Institute of Professional Services, 1949.

Paris, JJ and AC Elias-Jones. "Do We Murder Mary to Save Jodie? An Ethical Analysis of the Separation of the Manchester Conjoined Twins." *Postgraduate Medical Journal* 77 (2001): 593–598.

Park, Katharine. "The Life of the Corpse: Division and Dissection in Late Medieval Europe." *The Journal of the History of Medicine and Allied Sciences* 50 (1995): 111-32.

Persaud, T.V.N. *Early History of Human Anatomy: From Antiquity to the Beginning of the Modern Era.* Springfield. IL: Charles C. Thomas, 1984.

Pinkaers, Servais O.P. *The Sources of Christian Ethics.* Sr. Mary Thomas Noble O.P., trans. Washington. DC: The Catholic University of America Press, 1995.

Pius X. *Tra le Sollecitudini.* Motu Proprio. *Acta Sanctae Sedis* 36 (1903): 329-39.

Pius XI. "Casti Connubii. Encyclical." (31 Dec. 1930) in *Seven Great Encyclicals.* (Glen Rock. NJ: Paulist, 1963.

Pius XII. "Fertility and Sterility." (May 19. 1956) pp. 387-90 in *The Human Body: Papal Teachings.* The Monks of Solesmes, eds. Boston: Daughters of St. Paul, 1960.

_____. "Allocution to a Group of Eye Specialists." (May 14. 1956) pp. 375–76 in *The Human Body: Papal Teachings.* The Monks of Solesmes, eds. Boston: Daughters of St. Paul, 1960.

_____. "Allocution to the First International Congress of Histopathology." (Sept. 13. 1952) p. 204 in *The Human Body: Papal Teachings.* The Monks of Solesmes, eds. Boston: Daughters of St. Paul, 1960.

_____. "The Prolongation of Life." Address. 24 Nov. 1957. *The Pope Speaks* 4: 393–98.

Pokorski, Robert J. "A Test for the Insurance Industry." *Nature* 391 (26 February 1998): 835-8.

President's Commission for the Study of Ethical Problems in Medicine. Biomedical and Behavioral Research. *Defining Death: A Report on the Medical. Legal. and Ethical Issues in the Determination of Death.* Washington. DC: U.S. Government Printing Office, 1981.

Prudentius. "The Book of the Martyr's Crowns (Liber Peristephanon)."*The Fathers of the Church: A New Translation. Vol. 43. Poems of Prudentius.* Roy Deferrari, ed. Sr. M. Clement Eagan, trans. Washington. DC: Catholic University of America Press, 1962.

_____. "Discourse of the Martyr St. Romanus against the Pagans" *The Fathers of the Church: A New Translation. Vol. 43. Poems of Prudentius.* Roy Deferrari, ed. Sr. M. Clement Eagan, trans. Washington. DC: Catholic University of America Press, 1962.

Purves, Libby. "A Question to Break the Heart." *Human Life Review* 27 (Winter 2001): 45–47.

Quill, Timothy. "Death and Dignity: A Case of Individualized Decision Making." *The New England Journal of Medicine.* Vol. 324 (March 7 1991): 691-694.

Quill, Timothy. "Death and Dignity: A Case of Individualized Decision Mak-
     ing." *The New England Journal of Medicine*. Vol. 324 (March 7 1991):
     691-694.
Ramsey, Paul. *The Patient as Person*. New Haven: Yale University Press, 1970.
Richardson, Ruth. *Death, Dissection and the Destitute*. London: Routledge and
     Kagan Paul, 1987.
Schall, James V. *The Church. the State and Society in the Thought of John Paul
     II*. Chicago: Franciscan Herald Press, 1982.
Schrueder, Bas J.N. "The Influence of the German Occupation of 1940–1945 on
     Psychiatry in the Netherlands." *International Journal of Mental Health*
     35. no. 4 (Winter 2006–7): 113–14.
Shnayerson, Michael and Mark Plotkin. *The Killers Within: The Deadly Rise of
     Drug-Resistant Bacteria*. Boston: Little, Brown, 2002.
Singer, Peter. *Animal Liberation: A New Ethics for Our Treatment of Animals*.
     New York: Avon, 1975.
Sixtus V. Cum Pro Nostri Temporali Munere (1589)
Smith, Philip A., O.P. "The Right to Privacy: Roe v. Wade Revisited." *The
     Jurist* 43 (1983): 289–317.
Sofair, André N. and Lauris C. Kaljian. "Eugenic Sterilization and a Qualified
     Nazi Analogy: The United States and Germany, 1930–1945." *Annals of
     Internal Medicine* 132. no. 4 (2000): 312–319.
Sulzbach, Walter. *German Experience with Social Insurance*. New York:
     National Industrial Conference Board, 1947.
Tannen, Deborah. *You Just Don't Understand: Women and Men in
     Conversation*. New York: Harper, 1991.
Temo, Joan. et al.. "Preferences for Cardiopulmonary Resuscitation: Physician-
     Patient Agreement and Hospital Use." *Journal of General Internal
     Medicine* 10 (1995): 179–86.
Tempkin, Owsei and C. Lilian, eds. *Ancient Medicine: Selected Papers of
     Ludwig Edelstein*. Baltimore: Johns Hopkins University Press, 1967.
Tertullian. "Apology." in *Tertullian: Apologetical Works and Minicius Felix:
     Octavius*. . Rudolph Arbesmann, ed. Trans. by Rudolph Arbesmann,
     Sister Emily Joseph Daly, and Edwin A. Quain. Fathers of the Church
     Series. Vol. 10. New York. Fathers of the Church Inc., 1950.
———. "De Anima (On the Soul)." in *The Ante-Nicene Fathers. Vol. III: Latin
     Christianity: Its Founder. Tertullian*. Alexander Roberts and James
     Donaldson. Eds. Grand Rapids. MI: Eerdmans, 1951.
Toledo-Pereya, Luis H. "Galen's Contribution to Surgery." *Journal of the
     History of Medicine and Allied Sciences* 28. no. 4 (1973): 357–375.
Tonti-Filippini, Nicholas. "Donum vitae and Gamete Intrafallopian Tube
     Transfer." *Linacre Quarterly* 57. no. 2 (1990): 68-79.
U.S. Congress. "HR 493: Genetic Information Nondiscrimination Act of 2008"
     http://thomas.loc.gov/cgi-bin/query/D?c110:6:./temp/~c110n04ox8::

_____. "Gaudium et Spes." in *Vatican Council II: The Conciliar and Post-Conciliar Documents: Vol. I.* Austin Flannery, trans. O.P. Boston: Daughters of St. Paul. 1975

Veatch, Robert M., Willard Gaylin, and Councilman Morgan, eds. *The Teaching of Medical Ethics.* Hastings on Hudson: Institute of Society, Ethics and the Life Sciences, 1973.

_____. "Is It Time to Abandon Brain Death?" *Hastings Center Report* 27 (Jan./Feb. 1997): 29–37.

_____. "The Impending Collapse of the Whole-Brain Definition of Death." *Hastings Center Report* 23. no. 4 (1993): 18–24.

_____. "The Whole Brain-Oriented Concept of Death: An Outmoded Philosophical Formulation." *Journal of Thanatology* 3 (1975): 13–30.

_____. "Brain Death and Slippery Slopes." *Journal of Clinical Ethics* 3 (1992): 181–187.

Verhagen, Eduard and Pieter J.J. Sauer. "The Groningen Protocol—Euthansia in Severely Ill Newborns." *New England Journal of Medicine* 352 (2005): 959–63.

Vesalius, Andreas. *De Humani Corporis Fabrica.* Daniel Garrison. and Malcolm Hast. trans. Vesalius Translation Project at Northwestern University. http://vesalius.northwestern.edu/flash.html.

von Staden, Heinrich. "Celsus as Historian?" pp. 251-94 in *Ancient Histories of Medicine: Essays in Medical Doxography and Historiography in Classical Antiquity.* John Scarborough. ed. Leiden: Brill, 1999.

_____. *Herophilus: The Art of Medicine in Early Alexandria.* Cambridge: Cambridge University Press, 1989.

_____. "The Discovery of the Body: Human Dissection and Its Cultural Contexts in Ancient Greece." *The Yale Journal of Biology and Medicine* 65 (1992): 225.

Walsh, James J. *The Popes and Science: The History of the Papal Relations to Science during the Middle Ages and Down to Our Own Time.* New York: Fordham University Press, 1913.

Ward, Lord Justice. et. al., "A (children). Re [2000] EWCA Civ 254 (22 September 2000) Case B1/2000/2969. Sec. II. 11. (Retrieved from www.bailii.org 2 November 2009)

White, Andrew D. *On the History of the Warfare of Science with Theology in Christendom.* New York: Appleton, 1898.

Wijdicks, Eelco. "Brain Death Worldwide: Accepted Fact, but No Worldwide Consensus." *Neurology* 62 (2006): 20–25.

Wilken, Robert. *The Spirit of Early Christianity.* New Haven: Yale University Press, 2003.

Williams, George H. *The Mind of John Paul II: Origins of His Thought and Action.* New York: Seabury, 1981.

_____. "John Paul II's Concepts of Church. State and Society." *Journal of Church and State* 24 (Autumn 1982): 463–96.

Wolicka, Elzbieta. "Participation in Community: Wojtyla's Social Anthropology." Alice Manterys, trans. *Communio* 8 (1981): 108–118.
Woznicki, Andrew. *A Christian Humanism: Karol Wojtyla's Existential Personalism*. New Britain. CT: Mariel, 1980.

Index

Harvey, William, 107
Health Insurance, 88-90
Heavenly Kingdom, 33
Herophilus, 100
Hess, Rudolf, 50
Hilgers, Thomas, 61
Hippocrates, 26, 98-99
Hippolytus, 64
Hitler, Adolf, 50
Hobbes, Thomas, 25
Hoche, Alfred, 50
Hollenbach, David, 87
Humors, 8, 99
Human Genome Project, 86
Humanae vitae, 68
Humani Corporis Fabrica, 106

ICSI, 60
In vitro fertilization, 58-61
Intention, 15
Irving, Dianne, 54

Jehovah's Witness, 40
Jodie and Mary, 112-16
John Paul II, 18, 33,80 132, 136

Kant, Immanuel, 21, 25
Kass, Leon, 129
Kelly, Gerald, 111
Kevorkian, Jack, 136-43
Kidney transplant, 109
Koop, C. Everett, 112

Laborem exercens, 33
Lakeburg twins, 112
Law of Nature, 11-12, 21
Lewis, C.S., 128
Life Expectancy, 90-91
Louis IX, 104
Lumen Gentium, 20, 121
Luther, Martin, 12, 33-34
Lynch, Thomas, 126

Marx, Karl, 12
Masturbation, 59
Material Cooperation, 42
McCormick, Richard, 25
Mectizan, 79
Medicare, 81
Merck, 78-79

Harvard Medical School, 130
Methylation, 55
Michelangelo, 11
Military, 32
Mill, John Stuart, 21, 22, 25
Mondino de Luzzi, 105
Monotheism, 5-8
Moreschi, Alessandro, 108
Morphine, 18
Multi-Society Task Force, 134
Murphy-O'Connor, Cormac, 114
Mutilation, 107-09

NaPro technology, 61
Natural Family Planning, 59-60
Neocortical function, 54-55
Newton, Isaac, 11
Nietszche, Freidrich, 12
Nile River Blindness, 79

Object, 14
Oregon, 138
Origen, 108
Organ transplants, 109
O'Rourke, Kevin, 134
Ovum, 53-55

Pacem in Terris, 74
Parenthood, 68
Persistent Vegetative State, 133-35
Personhood, 48-56
Piercing, 109
Pinckaers, Servais, 25
Pius XII, 108, 134
Polytheism, 5-8, 47
Potato famine, 35
Praeger, Dennis, 24
Preferential Option, 81
Priesthood, 31, 98
Privacy, 86-87
Procreation, 63
Pronuclear Stage Tubal Transfer (PROST), 60
Proportionalism, 15
Prudentius, 102
Puebla, Mexico, 88

Quill, Timothy, 139-43

Ra, 8